To Rose,

with thanks for her encouragement,
the compliments of the author,
and love from Dad.

14 xii 1990

Then A Soldier

THEN A SOLDIER

J.F. McClellan

The Book Guild Ltd.
Sussex, England

The Book Guild Ltd.
25 High Street,
Lewes, Sussex.

First published 1991
© J.F. McClellan 1991
Set in Baskerville
Typesetting by APS,
Salisbury, Wiltshire.
Printed in Great Britain by
Antony Rowe Ltd.,
Chippenham, Wiltshire.
British Library Cataloguing in Publication Data
McClellan, J.F.
    Then A Soldier
    I. Title
    823.914 [F]
                ISBN 0 86332 537 8

AUTHOR'S NOTE

The events and characters in this novel derive from my memories of the year and a half which I spent in Northern Nigeria as a National Serviceman in the mid-fifties. I realize that my knowledge of the country, the Africans and the British Administrators – and indeed of the Army itself – was necessarily superficial, and my memory has no doubt played some tricks in looking back some thirty-five years. I apologize for any jarring inaccuracies or solecisms which may have resulted. My plea in extenuation of such offences is that this IS a work of fiction. Kebira is a fictitious city; and just as things may not have been quite the same in Ruritania as in the other Balkan States, so Kebira may appear to differ in some respects from the other Hausa Emirates. As to particular incidents and the people portrayed in them, the events either did not happen or did not happen precisely in the way described; and the characters, although in some cases drawn from the foibles of some of us who existed in real life, are in no way intended as a representation of any of the real people.

1

Jos came to in a pleasant hotel bedroom, the dominant feature of which was the white mosquito net surrounding the bed. The Venetian blinds on the window were down but the fierce brightness and heat of the mid-morning sun was pressing upon the room. He got up gingerly, still feeling that his head was not quite clear from the effects of the sleeping pills. After he had washed and shaved he walked over to the dining room now feeling for the first time the full glare of the African sun.

As he entered the dining room, he saw Bob Finlay at a table by the window. Bob Finlay was the other newly commissioned Second Lieutenant from Jos's regiment who was making the journey to Africa. He was an earnest young man, constantly eager to improve the shining hour by learning something new, 'getting on' with things or – a form of activity which could sometimes have awkward and painful results – 'just generally widening his experience'. He was serious-minded, self-centred and heavy-going. Jos noted that he had finished his breakfast and seemed to be making notes in a jotter which he always referred to as *The Log Book*. Bob looked up as Jos approached and greeted him excitedly.

'I have just arranged for a guide to take us round Kano this afternoon.'

'Oh Good,' said Jos dully, feeling his head begin to ache already. He was glad when Bob took himself busily off to see if the Hotel had any bumf about the old city on which he could brief himself. Jos enjoyed a leisurely breakfast, tasting for the first time paw-paw a kind of sweet grapefruit grown in Nigeria and soon to become a familiar item of his diet, but that first breakfast was the best. Afterwards he went in to the cool air-conditioned lounge and wrote some letters, occasionally wandering out into the hot white light of day and watching African figures walking with long graceful strides along the little paths in the scrub which separated the airport from the old city.

Lunch was another late and leisurely meal: far too leisurely for Bob who was itching to get off on his sightseeing expedition. He had arranged for the Guide to call at the hotel at three o'clock, and when no-one turned up he got into a state of great vexation. Jos, who was by now feeling drowsy again and was envying all the other hotel guests who seemed to have gone off for a siesta, began to hope that the tour would fall through. But at about quarter to four, a large springy American car swung into the hotel driveway and pulled up at the entrance. A rather fat Lebanese man wearing a crumpled and stained tropical suit got out and announced that this was the car for 'Fiddeley'.

'Finlay,' Bob corrected him irritably, 'and look here you're jolly late.'

The Lebanese ignored this and motioned them into the back seat of the car. He then drove with great style and at frightening speed into the old city. Jos and Bob felt as if they were on a sort of trampoline on the springy back seat. He brought the car screeching to a stop in front of a tall unsmiling Muslim who was standing beside three smart new bicycles. The Lebanese exchanged a few words with the guide and then told Bob that he would meet them again at this spot at six thirty. Then he drove off very fast in a flurry of dust.

Jos and Bob each selected a bicycle and pedalled off after the guide. Jos was not so much attracted by the points of interest which they were no doubt to be shown as in simply being in this ancient, alien city. He was tantalized by the brown mud houses which seemed to be built on a courtyard plan so that they showed blank walls, save for a small door, to the street. Thus only occasionally did they catch glimpses of women and children and dogs and hens in the little courtyards. The men who walked past them with swishing gowns and elaborate turbans looked as if they had stepped out of *The Arabian Nights*. Groups of children ran after them from time to time saying something which sounded to Jos like tourists; he learned later that what they were saying was 'Bature' meaning 'white man' or 'stranger' and that they were pointing at him with the same kind of incredulous glee with which he and other little Scots boys in the thirties had pointed at the then rare sight of a black man.

The chief sights which Bob had arranged to be shown were the reservoir – in the engineering of which he took an informed and enthusiastic interest – and the Mosque. Jos found the string of facts about the reservoir indigestible and altogether too redolent of the dreary "wot we are going on wiv now" lectures in the Army. He found himself struggling with a strange mixture of piety and impiety on entering the Mosque and was surprised that he, a committed, stuff and nonsense type atheist, should experience either feeling. The truth was that his uppermost feeling now was one of lightheaded depression. It was crazy to have cycled about in the mid-afternoon sun on their first day in Africa after the excitement and sleeplessness of their journey out. By the time they returned to the meeting place appointed by the Lebanese even Bob was beginning to wilt. Their depression deepened when he asked them each for a pound for the tour.

'Look here,' Bob protested. 'You're not playing fair.'

'Playing fair?'

'You said we could have the tour for two and six an hour.'

'Ah yes. But what about the hiring of the bicycles? Taxi from the airport and back?'

'Well I think it's daylight robbery.'

'Robbery?' The Lebanese narrowed his eyes to unpleasant slits.

'Oh come on Bob. We may as well pay up.' And Jos handed over one of the one pound notes which still remained from the money he had drawn in London. 'It's the principle of the thing that gets me, I hate to feel I've been done.' Bob protested.

The Lebanese was bemused by Bob's vocabulary. Jos could see him puzzling over 'playing fair', 'daylight robbery', 'being done'. He watched Bob intently until a second pound was somewhat ungraciously thrust into his hand. Then he pocketed both notes and with a shrug of his shoulders motioned them towards the springy back seat of the car. The return journey to the airport hotel was even faster than on the way out, and no-one spoke.

The next morning Jos and Bob said farewell. Bob was flying

9

on to join a Battalion in Western Nigeria. Jos was to go to one stationed in the Northern Region. As he watched Bob get into the little bus which was to take him over to his plane Jos reflected on the casualness with which they had finished this breakfast together and thought of all the other breakfasts at their training depot, at cadet school, all the shared experiences. As he watched the slightly fussy and elderly style of the nineteen year old settling himself into the airport bus, Jos wondered if they would ever meet again.

Jos himself was to travel by landrover to the town of Kebira where his Battalion was stationed; the Second-in-Command of the Battalion had just departed for long home leave, with his wife and family, that morning, and thus a driver and vehicle were to hand at the airport.

At about eleven o'clock, the driver sought out Jos and reported for duty. He was a young Ibo Corporal who announced that his name was Francis. He seemed to be of an excessively cheerful disposition whistling and humming to himself as he stacked the bags and suitcases into the back of the landrover. He ushered Jos courteously into the passenger seat and then springing nimbly into the driver's seat he started the engine and at once drove off at a great pace down the road from the hotel. Any pedestrian or vehicle was greeted with impatient honkings on the horn, administered with the hard pad of his wrist and accompanied by sighs and curses.

'Hey dese people! Dey stupid people too much. Dey go want to die, I tink.' Honk Honk.

Jos was glad when they reached the open road. Though what a road; stretching on and on, fringed on either side by the light scrub of the Northern Nigerian countryside and cutting a long straight streak through it. Francis drove jerkily beating time almost with his foot on the accelerator. The month was April; the end of the hot dry season. The heat was intense. Jos felt his shirt sticking to him and saw the sweat run down Francis's rugged, honest face. Francis must have felt the slight tension created by the heat and the apparently unending aridness of the road. He turned to Jos conversationally.

'Dis be yo first time in Africa sah?' he enquired politely.

'Yes it is.'

'I tink you go like it heah, sah.'

'Well I hope so. I'm sure I will.'

'Dis be fine fine country sah.'

As they were having this conversation Jos noticed that the road was at last departing from its arrow-like probe through the bush and that it was having to curve round some huge boulders or small hills. Suddenly round one of these came an enormous lorry, laden to the top and over with laughing, shouting Africans and all manner of junk and goods and chattels. Across the top of the windscreen was the legend *PREPARE TO MEET THY DOOM, REPENT IN THE NAME OF THE LORD*.

Francis with remarkable skill and judgement swung the landrover leftwards into the extreme edge of the road and just managed to avoid what had seemed an inevitable collision. Jos was badly shaken and found that he was trembling. Francis was chuckling good-humouredly to himself.

'Hey dese people,' he commented indulgently.

'Bloody fools. Maniacs. They might have killed us.'

'Is true,' said Francis, composing his face for a second before relaxing again into a resigned chuckle.

The road resumed its straight and dreary course. The sun beat down fiercely on its reddish yellow surface. Occasionally Jos caught sight of what seemed to be large mixed herds of cattle and goats moving through the scrubby countryside. Once they passed through a tiny shanty settlement with a petrol station prominent at the side of the road, but Francis did not deign to stop, appearing confident in his full tank of petrol and a jerrican stowed in the back of the landrover. Now and then they could see some way from the road a small village of thatch houses, Francis would give a contemptuous jerk of his head in their direction.

'Dey bush people,' he would say.

Once they passed a group of women each of whom carried a lemonade bottle on her head. They scurried in terror to the side of the road as the landrover approached. Jos was aware of a feeling of amused contempt emanating from Francis at the women's discomfiture.

It was late afternoon when they reached the Barracks at

11

Kebira. The road journey had taken about six hours, and Jos felt exhausted. Francis drove up to the Officers' Mess, a delightful large mud construction with thick walls, a thatch roof and cool stone floors. A mess servant in spotless white uniform and red fez appeared and said he would show Jos to his house. They walked along a sandy path fringed with pretty flowering bushes which Jos was to learn later were known as liar bushes. They came to a small round house made of baked mud, with a roof of thatch.

'Dis be yo house sah,' said the mess servant. 'I go fetch yo Boy and tell him to come quick-quick.'

He then withdrew and left Jos to look round his house. Basically it was two rooms: a sitting room and a bedroom, with a bathroom (cold running water only and a dry closet cubicle) added on at the back. The shutters were closed and the place had an unpleasant, stale smell. In the darkest corner of the bedroom was a gloomy-looking bed with dark green mosquito netting. Jos felt uneasy and depressed.

There was a knock at the door and he called 'Come in', expecting his Batman to appear. But, instead, a tall young man with a rather fattish, smug-looking face came in. He began to speak in a genteel Scottish accent.

'Sorry about this old chap. You've caught us with our trousers down. The original Signal from HQ referred to you coming tomorrow, and although the Second-in-Command knew that had been changed and managed to wangle a jeep to take him and all his belongings to Kano on the strength of it no-one saw fit to tell the house member – yours very truly here, so as to get your gidda tidied up and your Boy standing by your bed. Of course it's always the same in this bloody country. Things never work out according to plan. My name's Billy Rogers by the way, and I'm a Cameronian by origin.' He held out his hand with which he shook Jos's limply and a little clammily.

'I'm Jos Maclean.'

'Oh Christ we know who you are. We've been haggling with Brigade for ages to get one of the new subalterns posted to us. We're dreadfully understaffed here. But you'll find that out soon enough for yourself. By the way I'm sorry about this house. The other giddas are a lot nicer. You'll probably get one of them when I go back to dear old Blighty. The Africans say there's a bad Ju-Ju about this house.'

As he said these words a shadow fell across him, and both men turned to the door to see a tall soldier standing there. Billy Rogers laughed.

'Oh it's you Okoko. So you're going to be Mr Maclean's boy are you?'

'Yes sah,' the soldier replied glumly.

'Well see and behave yourself. Come on Jos – short for Joseph is it? – Okoko will unpack and get things ship shape and Bristol fashion here. We'll go and get a snifter or two in the Mess.'

Jos went off reluctantly. He would really have liked to stay and to make Okoko's acquaintance properly, to look round the house and small compound. But Billy Rogers was clearly enjoying himself, and Jos thought it best not to offend him by appearing churlish or ungrateful. The Mess was deserted when they arrived, and Billy made a great noise and general fuss calling for the Bar Boys to open up and to look sharp about it.

'We'll put all this on my bill today, he said, having ordered two pink gins. 'But you're on your own tomorrow lad.'

Billy leant back in the standard, wooden-framed Army lounge chair with which the Mess ante-room was furnished, swirling the pink gin appreciatively round in the glass. He sighed happily and for the next half hour depressed Jos with tales of the inefficiency and peculiarities of their brother officers; the stupidity and unreliability of the Africans; the dullness of the Station; the tribulations of the climate.

'And another thing. There are no bloody women. Thank God I'm on my way out of here.'

As if to belie these last words there was a swish of the bead curtains screening the door, and in came two couples, one of the men plump and imposing, the other slighter, and with a purposeful and business-like air. Both of the women were well-groomed and comely. The two Subalterns got to their feet, and Jos was introduced to Major and Mrs Hamilton and Captain and Mrs Standford-Jones.

Jos tried to remember which of Billy Roger's slanders were

appropriate to which couple while pleasantries were being exchanged. Hamilton, he gathered, was to be his Company Commander and so Jos observed him with particular interest. He saw that beneath the fat and florid signs of good living was a strikingly handsome face animated by a good deal of conscious charm. His wife was a very pretty blonde in her early thirties. She had the archetypal dumb blonde expression of benign puzzlement about all going on around her. Mrs Standford-Jones seemed a similar type: but she was a slim brunette. The two couples appeared to be friendly, and kindly disposed to the newcomer: Jos went back to his gidda to get ready for dinner feeling a good deal more cheerful.

The quick African dusk was already falling, and a light was burning in the house. As he entered his bedroom Jos saw a clean white shirt, slacks and a tie neatly laid out on the bed. Polished mosquito boots stood at the foot of it. Through the doorway to the bathroom he could see Okoko tipping buckets of hot water into the large enamel bath – still looking very glum.

'Yo baff aw ready sah,' he said.

'Thank you Okoko.' Jos began to peel off his clothes. He wondered how well Okoko spoke and understood English and if he ought to make some sort of little formal speech marking the beginning of their relationship. He paused before removing his underpants to say, 'I hope that we will get on well together and that you will like working for me.' Okoko smiled charmingly at this revealing the strongest looking teeth Jos had ever seen. Then his face relapsed into deepest gloom.

'Are you sad about something?' Jos asked as he stepped into the piping hot water.

'Dis house sah. Dis house be bad Ju-Ju too much sah.'

Jos lay back in the water and looked up at the thatch roof. He saw a very large black spider swinging below a large web.

'Well you don't live in the house do you?'

'No sah. But dis be strong Ju-Ju. He go catch me and my wife and my piccin when dat I go work for you heah sah.'

A bright look out for me, reflected Jos. After he had dried and dressed, Okoko gave him a torch which he had thoughtfully borrowed, and Jos set off up the path towards the Mess for dinner. That dinner was typical of the many he was to have over the next year and a half. The company: the single officers – mainly the subalterns, with a sprinkling of senior officers who were waiting for their wives to come out of Africa, and one embittered Captain, the Quartermaster whose wife would not be joining him for this tour of duty. The programme: beer and groundnuts and desultory chat until about eight thirty or nine. Then a long and beautifully cooked and served meal followed by brandy or whisky.

On this his first night Jos had more to drink than was good for him and had to be escorted back to his house, singing and shouting, by Billy Rogers. Billy was pretty tight himself but sober enough to relish seeing the greenhorn home. Okoko happened to be up and outside his little round house – relieving his bladder – as the two young men supporting each other unsteadily came down the path. He regarded them ruefully, and as he climbed back into bed he shook his wife gently and whispered,

'Is true, Tangwe. Dat house be bad Ju-Ju too much. Awready dat my mitre done drink too much.'

Okoko's wife knew scarcely any English but Okoko sometimes chose that tongue to confide to her the various forebodings and puzzlements which he experienced as a manservant to young Army Officers. It was as if these bothersome thoughts could best be expressed in the language of those responsible for them.

2

The early mornings were delightful. Jos grew to love the warm smell of earth in his nostrils as he walked over to the Mess for breakfast. But by eight o'clock the sun had established its tyranny for the day. Its bright hot glare had removed all the freshness and any suggestion of moisture – except for the black stains of sweat discolouring the soldiers's uniforms.

Okoko had a key to the house and would let himself in at about six thirty pulling back the shutters and laying out the fresh, beautifully laundered and starched uniform each day. He was a superb batman, and Jos who had been rather scruffy and badly dressed all his life now found himself the smartest looking officer in the Barracks.

Jos had arrived with rather heavy and shapeless, easily crumpled slacks and shorts bought to War Office specification. Okoko surveyed these grimly the day after Jos's arrival and said he would send for a tailor to come and make 'two three uniforms sah smart-smart'. Jos was alarmed at this suggestion. He had paid good money for the kit he had brought with him, and never having had anything tailor-made for him in his life he viewed with dismay this extravagant idea of Okoko's. The look of reluctance and apprehension on his face must have been clear to Okoko because he said nothing further but, looking very bad-tempered, went off up to the barracks. Presently he reappeared with Billy Rogers.

'You go hask Mr Rogers, sah. He go tell you dis uniform is no goo. Is no use foh heah in Nigeria, sah.'

'He's absolutely right old chap.' The hot potato in Billy's mouth seemed particularly sizzling that morning. 'That khaki drill stuff they sell you at home is no good. We've all been had the same way. We'll get Sunday Mbula up here this afternoon to fix you up.'

Sunday Mbula came at about four o'clock. He was a small very black-skinned man whose own personal wardrobe left much to be desired: a pair of overlong khaki shorts, a green singlet and a pair of very worn gym shoes. His face was badly pock marked. He came on a smart new Raleigh bicycle in the panniers of which were inchtapes and scissors and other tailoring paraphernalia.

'Good afternoon sah. Now we go make you fine fine uniform one time.'

He started whisking the inch tape about Jos's shoulders, waist and limbs.

'Hey but dis be easy sah. You have de perfect measurements. Is not so, Okoko?'

'Is what I go tell my wife.'

'I bring you one suit next tomorrow, sah. Den I go bring you anudder two next next again.'

Jos was so confused and embarrassed about the perfect measurements comment that he forgot to ask the price. But it turned out to be very reasonable, and the shorts, shirts and bushjackets were all made quickly and skilfully. He had arrived on a Thursday and was given until the Monday to settle in. The fitting took place on the Friday, and Jos had his first set of clothes made and delivered by the Sunday.

At half past six on the Monday morning Okoko let himself in with great bustle and excitement, and began pulling the shutters noisily and laying out the shorts and bushjacket made by Sunday Mbula. He had got Jos's boots up to a magnificent shine: he laid beside them a pair of lightweight socks, a pair of thick dark green hose and a pair of soft, light grey officers' puttees which he had managed to borrow from somewhere. Finally he swept up the mosquito netting from the bed and said,

'Better you get up now, sah. Ifn dat you no get up now now you go be late foh you fust day, sah.'

Jos got up feeling slightly sulky at the element of lecturing in Okoko's voice, and went to use the dry closet and to clean his teeth. While he was doing this Okoko quickly heated up some water in a mess tin over a stick fire and brought this in for

17

shaving. After Jos had finished shaving and washing he stepped into the cool crisp shorts and bushjacket. Then he regarded the foot and legdress laid out beside the boots. Socks on first and then boots – no, then hose – then? It must be the boots then. But how did the puttees go on?

'Sah I show you,' said a strange and silky voice. Jos looked up and saw a slim youth of about fourteen or fifteen dressed in white shorts and a long white jacket.

'Who are you and where has Okoko got to?' Jos was surprised at the gruffness of his own voice: but he was put out at having been caught in such obvious puzzlement by this strange boy.

'Okoko go serve in Mess sah, I be his Small Boy sah – you Small Boy.'

Jos was irritated and nervous about all this. Did it mean he would have to pay for an extra servant? Why hadn't Okoko told him it was his turn to serve in the Mess? Today of all days he ought to have been on hand to help with dressing. Then he began to panic. If he didn't get these damn puttees on he really would be late. What a first impression to make.

'Well I don't know about Small Boys – but give us a hand will you?'

The boy motioned for him to sit down on the side of the bed and, kneeling at his feet he began to wind the puttees neatly over the top of the boots and the bottom of the hose. There was something intimate and caressing about the way he did it which made Jos feel uneasy. He found himself looking at the boy's forearms as he wound the puttees round and thinking what beautiful smooth black skin he had.

'What's your name?' he barked out gruffly.

'My name is Ali.' The boy looked up with a gentle smile.

'Well thank you very much, Ali,' Jos said as he stood up and buckled on his Sam Browne. 'But I'll have to see Okoko about this. I can't afford to maintain a whole gang of servants to do his work for him.'

Jos felt boorish as he said this, but the combination of Ali's slightly homosexual air and the depressing atmosphere of the gidda suddenly overcame him. He was glad to get out into the air and on his way up to the Mess.

Billy Rogers and Dave Lawson were alone in the dining room finishing off their coffee and toast.

'By jove you're cutting it a bit fine,' said Billy Rogers with his mouth full. 'Old Hammy is a stickler for punctuality. What's the meaning of it Okoko?' turning to Okoko who had just laid a dish of pawpaw before Jos. 'You mustn't let new master go catch row – eh Okoko?'

'Yes sah,' beamed Okoko looking a bit confused and standing brilliantly to attention in his white tunic and white slacks and red fez.

'Stop shooting the shit, Billy,' said Dave Lawson getting to his feet in his lazy athletic way. 'You can take my bike up to the barracks Jos: that will get you there in time. My platoon are coming down here as we are going to march out to the firing range.'

He swung out of the dining room leaving Billy slightly nettled. He got up too.

'I'm afraid I'll have to go. You'll find Dave's bike round at the kitchen door.'

Jos hurried through his breakfast, picked up his slouch hat and Sam Browne from the coatstand and went round to the Mess kitchen. The bicycle, a high ugly safety model painted dark green, a colour known in the army as drab olive, was leaning against the whitewashed wall. As he seized the handlebars preparatory to mounting it, Jos looked for a moment through the open door into the kitchen. Okoko, the other Mess waiter and Corporal Samuel the cook were all seated at a large table talking loudly – it looked as if they were arguing – in a language which Jos assumed must be Ibo: they were all dressed in spotless white uniforms, starched stiff. In the background was the sound of various cooking noises, presumably for the Quartermaster and the Education Officer and the Medical Officer who began their day later than the regimental officers. Jos could detect the hiss of frying bacon and – the sound which was to become for him the most familiar of all from that kitchen – the scraping of burnt toast. He poked his head round the door and saw a grubby-looking old man dressed in a pair of dirty-looking underpants – the kind known in the army as jungle greens – sweating over a primitive stove. Corporal Samuel spotted Jos and broke off from his heated discussion.

'Goo' mawning sah. I hope you like you' breakfast.'

'Yes thank you Corporal.' Jos's eyes remained fascinated on the old tramp who seemed to be doing the actual cooking. Corporal Samuel evidently felt a word of explanation was called for.

'Yes sah. Dis Small Boy,' and here he nodded curtly in the direction of the old tramp. 'He go help me foh mealtime sah.' As he said this he stepped out into the sunshine and almost blinded Jos with the sparkling whiteness of his chef's hat and tunic.

'Oh I see. He help you for mealtime, Corporal.'

'Yes sah,' exclaimed Corporal Samuel delightedly as at a dull child who had suddenly shown promise of understanding after all.

Jos looked at his watch and decided there wasn't time to probe this particular West African oddity any further. He clambered on to the heavy old bicycle and pedalled off up the bumpy laterite road to the Barracks. He learned later that if you travelled over these roads in a well sprung car at about sixty miles per hour they seemed tolerably comfortable. But on the hard saddle of a heavy old bike doing about eight miles per hour they were really quite painful.

Jos arrived at D company office in rather a sweat and with about two minutes to spare before eight o'clock – 0800 hours as he kept trying to think of it. The soldiers were being bullied about into some sort of formation by the African NCOs for Company Muster Parade. Major Hamilton and the European Sergeant Major, CSM Roberts were standing on the verandah of the company office, the one tapping his swagger stick against his thigh, the other holding his thick Sergeant Major's baton securely in at the elbow at right angles to his body. Major Hamilton regarded Jos coldly.

'Mr Maclean, there is a golden rule in the Army to be where you're wanted five minutes before rather than five minutes after the appointed time.'

It was not quite eight o'clock, but if basic training had taught Jos nothing else it had taught him the unwisdom of speaking back to a superior officer.

'Mr Roberts,' said Major Hamilton turning to the Sergeant-Major. 'Perhaps you would take Muster Parade this morning. Mr Maclean will be in time to do it in the future.'

Roberts permitted himself a brief smirk before offering a great heel-clicking salute, about-turning and left-righting with great swagger out on to the parade ground.

'Will you come into my office please Mr Maclean?'

Jos followed the Company Commander in, feeling a little mutinous – not because of any injustice done to him but because Hamilton had himself broken one of the army codes of conduct in rebuking him in front of his inferior in the army hierarchy.

The company offices consisted of three rooms: one for the Company Commander; one for the Platoon Commanders and the European Sergeant Major; and one for the Company Clerk. He followed Major Hamilton into the grandest of the three rooms: not that it was very grand.

'Mr Maclean,' began Major Hamilton after he had seated himself behind his bare deal table of a desk. 'This Company exists to train soldiers. That is what I care about, and that is what you are going to care about so long as you are under my command.'

Jos struggled with his sense of embarrassment as Major Hamilton appeared to play to an invisible gallery, making his jaw square and hard, his eyes shrewd and penetrating. And why does he keep calling me Mr Maclean all the time – it was all Jos and My dear boy in the Mess at the weekend.

On and on Hamilton went with reference back to his own days as a subaltern in France at the beginning of the Second World War. Now he was praising Roberts and advising Jos to be guided by him – reminiscing about a platoon sergeant who had knocked him, Hamilton, into shape. Jos could see that it was particularly unfortunate that in the scenario forming in Hamilton's mind he, Jos, was being cast as the young prentice hand to Roberts. But there was nothing to do but swallow it all with due expressions of gratitude for the advice, making his escape as soon as he decently could into the Company Clerk's room.

This was the room in which the African Company Sergeant-

Major also had a desk. He was a dignified Hausaman with a neat goatee beard and a beautifully pressed and polished uniform. He got to his feet smartly as soon as Jos entered the room: Jos noticed that the table he had been sitting at was absolutely bare of any paper whatsoever. CSM Musa was, he learned later, all but illiterate and his appointment really an honorific one to a distinguished old warrior – he must have been all of forty five. Jos glanced at the other occupant of the room, the Company Clerk, Lance-Corporal Michael. He seemed a very different customer. He was a light-skinned Ibo in his early twenties. He half slouched to his feet as Jos came into the room and then went on typing what looked like an inventory of equipment. His desk was piled high with battalion and company orders, timetables for training periods, army council orders, forms for clothing, for equipment, for ammunition and so on. CSM Musa roared a command at him in Hausa, and Michael pulled himself erect towering over both Jos and the Sergeant-Major, with a slightly contemptuous smile on his face.

Jos heard himself mumbling 'Carry on please' scarcely able to credit the sound of his voice in the role of the foppish young officer. The incident had however made CSM Musa's day. He had enjoyed greatly the chance to exercise his power over that savvy-savvy boy from the south who sat there all day writing and typing the marks on paper which seemed of such importance to the Company Commander and the European Sergeant-Major.

Like nearly all the other members of the ruling caste to which Jos realized that he now belonged he found himself instinctively liking the respectful traditionalist Hausa such as Musa; and disliking and half-fearing the likes of Michael with their surly competence and thinly concealed irritation with their subservient place in the social and military order. But over the next few weeks and months as he got more and more involved in the running of the Company he came to rely on Michael and to consult him, often in the press of some crisis or other, brushing aside and feeling slightly irritated by Musa's leisurely courtesy.

3

Jos got to know and to dislike heartily Roberts, the European Company Sergeant-Major. It quickly became evident that Roberts was an ignorant and coarse racialist – who seemed to have a quite disproportionate influence over Major Hamilton. It was not long before Roberts took the opportunity of expounding his views on race to Jos.

'Look at these bloody monkeys out there,' he said one morning as the Subaltern and the Sergeant-Major were waiting to go out on Muster parade. 'We dress them up in khaki and boots, but you can't conceal the bloody ape staring out at you can you, sir?'

Jos was ashamed of himself for his lack of courage and presence of mind in responding to remarks of this sort. The effective, rational words which would put Roberts and his racialism in their place never seemed to come in time, at the right time. He tried to reassure himself that he was just waiting for the right opportunity – or sometimes, and not altogether consistently, he reasoned that Roberts was such a hopelessly prejudiced and stupid man that there would be no point in engaging in argument with him.

'I mean take yer old Musa inside the office there, Christ that's a laugh him sitting at a desk. He'd be happier up a tree would old Musa. Still he's one of the best. Not like that savvy little bastard Michael. I'm just waiting for that bastard to put a foot wrong and then I'll ave 'im, I'll 'ave 'im.'

Roberts must have known how ill at ease talk of this sort made Jos, but he must also have sensed that Jos was still too shy and unsure of himself to have a showdown. So Roberts pushed his offensive observations as far as he dared, always managing

to turn the talk to a lighter note or different subject if he saw
that Jos was finally about to come out with some protest. In
this way he had contrived to dig a large moral hole in which
Jos miserably saw himself and knew that he would have to
climb out of if he were to recover his self-respect.

It was while they were on Muster Parade that morning that
Major Hamilton drove up in a flurry of dust in his little sports
car. As Jos walked down the last row of soldiers, inspecting
their belt brasses, he saw Hamilton bound up the steps to the
verandah and burst into the room where the Company Clerk
and the African CSM were sitting. Roberts observed this too,
and, sensing that something was wrong, he hurried through the
remaining stages of the inspection and asked Jos's permission to
dismiss the Company. The two Europeans then marched
smartly back towards the Company Offices. As they did so they
were greeted by a distraught Hamilton followed by a baffled
looking CSM Musa.

'Don't dismiss the Company, Sergeant-Major. Get them
back on parade.'

'Sah!' shouted Roberts saluting; and, turning on his heel, he
roared at the various African Sergeants who were marching
their men off to get them back on parade.

'Oh my God, Jos,' said the Company Commander.

This must be serious, Jos reflected, having worked out that
Major Hamilton made a point of never addressing him as Jos
while there were on duty.

'It's our little dog, Fifi. She didn't come home last night after
we let her out to do her business. Elaine is nearly out of her
mind with worry. You know what they're like these black
savages. They live so near the breadline – I've sacked servants
before now for eating Fifi's food. And now, and now, oh God
we can't help wondering if they may be eating Fifi herself. If
only I could get my hands on whichever one of these black
devils has laid hands on her . . . '

Major Hamilton left unsaid the things he would do in such a
circumstance as he stared out at the parade ground and took
fierce swipes at thin air with his swagger stick.

Jos was aghast: he was still feeling wretched about his lack of
courage in letting Roberts get away with his crudely voiced

sentiments, and now here was the Company Commander behaving just as badly, and in front of the puzzled-looking CSM Musa. Jos remembered the handbooks issued to officers on their way out to West Africa: 'Do not call or refer to an African as a "native" or a "negro": never refer to an African woman as a "negress". These terms may unwittingly give offence.' He hoped that someone near the breadline was indeed tucking into that fat, sleek, bad-tempered Fifi. CSM Roberts came panting up the steps of the verandah.

'Company on parade again sir.'

'Right,' barked Hamilton. 'I want every manjack of them scouring the countryside for my dog; and I want a detailed report of how and where she is found – and she will be found. Is that clear?'

The two Sergeant-Majors got the Company organized for the great search. Hamilton said he would have to go down again to his house 'to be with Elaine.' He clasped Jos warmly on the shoulder as he left the office.

'Jos old chap, I want you to stay here at Company HQ to deal with anything coming in from the orderly room and also to be my point of liaison.' And then he was gone in another flurry of dust. The entire company had by this time gone off also – in search of the dog. Jos strolled into the company clerk's room, Lance-Corporal Michael was busy adding up a row of figures and carried on to the end of it. Suddenly he gave a deep-throated chuckle.

'Dis company sah, she exist foh de training of soldiers.'

Jos never got to like Michael: he was too prickly for that, but gradually he grew to understand him and in many ways to respect him.

Major Hamilton kept phoning at frequent intervals from his house to see if there was any news. He seemed to get increasingly irritated with Jos because there wasn't. The phone rang again, and Jos picked it up wondering how on earth he could phrase the total absence of news this time. But it was the languid fruity voice of the Colonel at the other end.

'That you Maclean – where's the Company Commander?'

'Well he's out sir at the moment. The whole company's on a sort of exercise.'

25

'Jolly good! Jolly good! Look Maclean, when Major Hamilton gets back will you mention to him that I damn nearly ran over that Hunnish little dog of his out on the Jidda road. He really shouldn't let the little brute wander around like that. Half the pye-dogs round here are rabid y'know.'

'Yes sir. You didn't happen to notice which way it was going did you sir?'

'What the hell are you talking about, Maclean? Which way did who go? You feeling all right. Touch of belly palaver? Got to watch yourself in this climate, you know. Now remember to mention to Major Hamilton about the little sausage dog. Mind you,' and here the rich fruity tones dropped to an elaborate stage whisper, 'it's a beastly little dog. All right, Maclean? Jolly good. Jolly good.'

The complacent flow of "jolly goods" was eventually stopped as the Colonel replaced the receiver. Jos decided he had better ring Major Hamilton and give him an edited version of the Colonel's message.

'What the hell have you been gassing away on the phone for?' snapped Major Hamilton. 'Who were you speaking to?'

'The Colonel sir. He's seen Fifi.' There was a pause.

'Have your gone off your chump, Maclean. When I told you to deal with the orderly room and so forth I didn't mean you to get the CO involved in the search. I'll have to apologize to him personally. Awfully decent of him though to take part . . . Elaine, Elaine.'

Jos could hear him cooing to his wife at the other end of the line.

'Bobby has been out looking for Fifi himself and has seen her . . . Where? . . . I say Jos where did the Colonel see her? . . . WHAT? . . . the Jidda road. How terribly decent of him to go out as far as that. Let me see now: Sergeant Kalu's Platoon was to go out that way. Get one of the B Company runners to go off on the road to the rifle range and when he makes contact with Sergeant Kalu to tell him to carry on until he reaches the Jidda road and then to deploy men in both directions until they find the rascal. What a naughty old girl: I expect it was one of those gentlemen pye-dogs that was the attraction – her time must have been starting after all. Well well and to think you got the

Colonel to take a hand in all this. Highly irregular but full marks for initiative. I'll have to get on to the Colonel and thank him straightaway.'

Jos put the phone down uneasily trying to imagine the conversation likely to ensue between the Colonel and Major Hamilton. His only comfort was that the Colonel never seemed to listen to what anyone was saying – and clearly thought that Hamilton had a screw loose anyhow.

Fifi was indeed found on the Jidda road by Sergeant Kalu's Platoon, and in the fullness of time was delivered of a curious looking brood of puppies: the cross between pye-dog and dachshund was not a success aesthetically. And as a reward for his initiative – 'He went right to the top: got the CO on the job' – Jos was eventually presented with the ugliest puppy of all.

4

Jos soon came to understand what Billy Rogers had meant about the unit being under-officered. Although a Second Lieutenant of only a few weeks seniority, Jos found that he was in effect acting as Second-in-Command of a company while having to be platoon commander to each of three over-large training platoons at various critical points where the services – or at any rate the presence – of a commissioned officer were required.

But the most wearisome consequence of the shortage of junior officers was that the chore of duty officer at weekends came round far too frequently. Being weekend duty officer meant that from one o'clock on Saturday afternoon until eight o'clock on Monday morning one of the subalterns was virtually in charge of the barracks, mounting all the guards, doing all the inspections of mealtimes, lines, prisoners and so forth: he had to sleep in the hot, stuffy orderly room and was on call for the emergencies which all too frequently arose.

Nevertheless Jos undertook his first spell as duty officer with a feeling of exultant, if nervous, excitement. He did feel anxious when he thought of the responsibility now on his shoulders, but there kept brimming up a heady sense of power and achievement – that within seven months of having been called up and bullied around the parade ground as a raw recruit he was now – temporarily – in charge of a sizable military establishment. He looked at the telephone, half hoping it would ring and give him the chance to demonstrate his powers of incisive decision-making, leadership and so forth – and at the same time dreading that he would be required to take any action whatsoever.

28

It did not ring, and the hours dragged slowly by. On Saturday evening most of the officers went to the dance at the Kebira Club, and as the landrovers and private cars were disappearing down the road to the Club, Jos's principal feelings were of boredom and envy. He sat at the desk in the orderly room, with a pad of notepaper embossed with the crest of the Royal West African Frontier Force and set about writing to some of the friends and relatives to whom he owed letters. But the letter writing mood was not upon him; and looking at the names and addresses of people back at home in Britain, he found his thoughts wandering to that strange – it now seemed almost surreal – day in London with Bob Finlay on the journey out to Africa. By some trick of the subconscious he had suppressed the memory of it in his first few weeks in Kebira, but now it came flooding back to him in vivid detail.

The day had not begun well. After leaving the overnight-sleeper at King's Cross, he had taken a taxi to Goodge Street where he had to report to the transit depot. This former deep air raid shelter seemed to Jos a fluorescent hell, and after dumping his bags and checking when he had to report back for embarkation he had thankfully climbed the hundred odd steps back into the air.

Then he had wandered slowly southward, experiencing the excitement and insecurity of the young provincial in London, familiar with the names of places from his Monopoly Set among other things – and ignorant of their location and geographic relation to each other. He noted the strange, familiar names: Tottenham Court Road, Charing Cross, Trafalgar Square, Whitehall, Downing Street, Westminster.

He had arranged to meet Bob Finlay at a restaurant near Westminster, and he found it without much difficulty. Bob's father, who came regularly to London on business trips, had recommended it. And there was Bob looking fussily and with an air of reproof at his watch. His face bore the same expression as when, during their basic training together at the Regimental Depot in Scotland, some of the rougher elements in the platoon had committed an act of minor disobedience or failed in some other way to come up to the standards of Bob's public-schoolboy code of the right and decent thing. When he saw Jos a pleasant smile lit up Bob's handsome boyish face. Jos was pleased to see him.

'Hullo, Joe,' Bob greeted Jos cheerfully.

Jos's pleasure abated somewhat. He had never felt that his given name Joseph or any of its diminutives suited him until he came upon the form Jos, when his class were 'doing' *Vanity Fair*. From that time he had always introduced himself as Jos. He could not stop his family addressing him as Joe or even, in the case of one wretched aunt, Joey but he had been fairly successful in getting the outside world to call him Jos. Bob for some reason could not bring himself to say Jos, perhaps regarding it as rather an affected form of the name, and always irritated Jos by calling him Joe.

'When did you get down here?' Bob asked.

'This morning.'

'Good Lord I did better than that, I came a week ago and I've been seeing the sights – taking full advantage of my warrant.'

How bloody like him, thought Jos, the moment of affection now quite gone. They each ordered a "Three Shilling Bargain Business Man's Lunch", and after this had been done, Bob continued with his account of how he had been spending his time in London.

'I've managed to fit in a great deal. Galleries and tourist attractions in the mornings and several shows in the evenings. Dad gave me a jolly nice backhander as a reward for getting my Commission and I think I've really put it to very good use. It has all been very interesting.'

Whenever Bob classified anything as interesting Jos felt waves of boredom lapping round him. It was something about the flat, pedantic way he seemed to be arranging things in his mind. But what he said next made Jos choke and splutter in his soup.

'I was thinking that this afternoon and evening we might explore Soho and perhaps take in that striptease show at the Windmill.'

Jos looked up at Bob in astonishment. Bob looked complacently back. Jos began to understand. Soho, Striptease etc. were also facets of the metropolis just as the Tate Gallery, the

Tower of London and so forth. Bob wanted to be thorough in "doing" London and he was looking for a suitably raffish companion to accompany him on the seamy side. Jos was pleased and on the whole flattered that he had been thought to fill the bill. He had a strong sex-impelled curiosity to see a strip show and whatever other bits of vice were on display, but he would have been too shamefaced to slink around on his own.

'Fine,' he said. 'Good idea.'

They finished their meal quickly and set off northwards again in the direction of Soho.

After wandering about rather aimlessly for a while, noting the strange fare exhibited in the shops of the Chinese Butchers, the Italian Grocers, the Cockney Greengrocers they decided to fill-in the time before the first show at the Windmill by seeing a film. Again Bob surprised Jos by opting for the most risqué film on offer. This was 1955 and the most risqué film was a naturist documentary. Jos struggled with his feelings of furtive embarrassment as they bought the tickets. During the performance Jos experienced momentary feelings of sexual excitement as comely young women revealed their breasts and bottoms in gestures of defiance and liberation; followed quickly by sentiments of irritation and frustration as they coyly averted these portions of their anatomy from view either by dancing off so far into the distance that you couldn't bloody well get a good look at them or by gliding artistically into the semi-cover of a bush or tree or hollow in the landscape. To his horror he noticed that there were some men on the screen about to emerge from a sort of reception centre building which they had entered in the fully clothed state. They seemed however to have the peculiar capacity of presenting their bottoms only to the camera – and that was bad enough – or always to have some piece of furniture or sports apparatus shielding their genitalia from sight.

It became clear from the commentary – none of the frolicsome, happy naturists actually spoke – and from the apparatus being set up that the climax of this wholesome happy life was to be an open air badminton match. And so it turned out to be with – inevitably – two men, backs and bottoms to the camera, playing against two women whose (admittedly ample) bosoms always seemed to be obscured by the bloody net or the men or the rackets; and anyhow the whole thing was shot at far too great a distance to get a really good look. Jos and Bob emerged into the light of day feeling bored and cheated. They had a quick meal at one of the Quality Inns and made with renewed eagerness to see the real thing at the Windmill. There was a queue of men waiting for the next showing. Jos looked at them and wondered how they had the gall to be seen standing there in the street. Bob took his place at the end of the queue and, glancing at his pious face as he joined him, Jos felt almost as if he was filing into Church.

They got rotten seats, too far back for a striptease show. And although these girls were in the flesh and not on the screen and although their prancing about was designed to titillate and not to extol the virtues of a life liberated from clothing, Jos realized that he was feeling the same kind of frustration and fraud as he gazed at the distant young women, their flesh appearing and disappearing amid the ostrich feathers. He was reminded of one of the recruits in basic training who, after thumbing through some pictures of nude women had sighed heavily and said 'This is like fucking eating sweeties with the paper still on.' On a more elevated note Jos remembered, as he craned forward to catch sight of the female bodies, a passage in Lucretius, the key words of which were:

'Tactus enim tactus corporis est sensus'('Touch is the sense which really counts').

Jos felt less grubby for having had this scholarly reflection. But he was also feeling extremely bored and thinking that this was a silly way to be spending his last evening in Britain. He turned to Bob to suggest that they give the rest of the show a miss. But Bob was riveted by the performance: he was leaning forward in his seat and seemed to be trembling with excitement. They waited until the end of the show.

After they came out they walked around silently for a bit. Jos was thinking ruefully that there was not really time to do very much more and yet he was reluctant to head for the transit depot. I'll bet this bugger suggests we ought to get some "shuteye" if we're to be in "good form" for the journey tomorrow. But no: once again Bob startled him by a sudden clearing of his throat and then in the earnest voice of the seeker after truth asking, 'Do you think we ought to visit a prostitute before we turn in tonight? After all it will be almost two years before we are back in civilization again.'

This is a bit much thought Jos. The combination of a Presbyterian home background and intensive army propaganda about the dangers of catching venereal disease made him extremely uneasy about the thought of "visiting a prostitute". And he found himself at once amused and irritated by the straight-laced Bob's ill-expressed identification of prostitution with civilization. They were right in the heart of the prostitute territory now, and just then a tall shapely woman of about thirty accosted them.

'Like a nice time, Ducks?'

'Well now how much would that be?' asked Bob solemnly.

'Thirty bob for a nice young fellow like you.'

'What do you think, Joe?'

'No!' Jos found himself blurting out in a blind panic. He realized he was filled with a mad, unhappy excitement, and some sort of shaming terror made him want to rush away from the woman and the situation.

They walked on, the practical Bob obviously very disconcerted.

'Do you not fancy it then Joe?'

'I'm a bit tired tonight.'

They walked on a little further. Gosh, thought Jos, he'll be thinking I'm not up to it: chickening out. 'Actually I was thinking of rather a younger girl.'

'There's one.'

Bob pointed to a slim fair girl with rather straight legs who was pacing with the unmistakable gait across the road.

'Go on Joe – I'll go back to that other one.'

Jos crossed the road. The girl turned round and again Jos felt the heartstopping excitement and panic. The girl had a sharp plain little face with hard eyes set close together. Jos passed quickly on ignoring her invitations. He looked across the street again and found Bob regarding him with perplexity. Jos crossed over again.

'I've changed my mind Bob. I think I would really prefer to

go back to that other woman.'

'All right,' Bob replied unperturbed. 'That girl will do for me.'

How on earth can he be so matter of fact about it, Jos wondered as he watched Bob go up to the girl, apparently bargain with her and then walk off with her. He went up to the older woman. She seemed to bear him no ill will for his previous abrupt departure and confirmed that her charge would be thirty shillings. They walked off to a house in the adjoining street and climbed some dark stairs to her flat. This turned out to be a small stuffy bedroom. When the woman switched on the light Jos noticed incredulously that it was a red one. He thought longingly of the guilty pleasure of reading *The Red Light* under his desk in third year French. All that seemed so safe and innocent now. He looked at the bed which – not unnaturally – dominated the room: he was sure it was dirty.

'Thirty bob then,' said the woman holding out her hand.

'Yes of course,' Jos mumbled taking a pound note and a ten shilling note from his wallet.

The woman smiled and took off her coat, then still smiling calculatedly at Jos she stepped out of her shoes and began to unzip her skirt and to undo the buttons of her blouse. She slid out of these and then clad in her brassiere, girdle, stockings and pants she sidled up to Jos and said,

'You can take these off for yourself for another ten bob, Jackie.'

Jos had told her his name was Jack – with some vague idea of concealing his identity in case of blackmail or a police raid or the realization of any of the other dark fears in his mind. He was now feeling terrible. The grossness of the transaction between him and the woman appalled him. He looked again at the scruffiness and squalor of the room. He looked for the first time properly at the woman. She had looked quite handsome outside, but now he was repelled by the coarseness and heaviness of her features, by the large pores of her heavily made up skin. Jesus, he thought what am I doing here, how can I get away? He wondered if there was a strong-armed thug somewhere in the building who dealt with clients who welched on their contracts. But I have paid her, he comforted himself.

34

The woman pressed her warm full body against him. Jos stood tense and awkward and felt no flicker of desire. In fact he could feel himself contracting with anxiety and embarrass- ment. The woman stepped back and surveyed Jos coolly.

'Oh Christ, one of these! Well look I haven't all bloody day to waste on you, you know. Do you want it or don't you?'

'I'm sorry,' Jos heard himself squeak.

He looked down miserably noticing that he still had his wallet in his hand. That brought a fresh wave of despondency when he thought of the waste of money. He had just cashed his first cheque that morning on his walk south from Goodge Street: Glyn Mills, Bankers – a cheque book – some difference from the old Trustee Savings Back into which he used to hoard holiday job and prize money and from which he would carefully withdraw the amounts required for coveted books or presents for members of his family. And here he was racing through his first withdrawal of cash via his new cheque book on pornographic films, strip shows and now a prostitute. He sighed sorrowfully. But the woman had also seen the wallet and the crisp new notes which still remained in it. Her attitude softened. She pulled him towards her and asked,

'Is this the first time love?'

To his astonishment Jos felt tears start at the back of his eyes. He didn't know why but the woman's question and the gentle voice in which she asked it made him want to blubber. Perhaps he was thinking of times when he and girls for whom he had "burned" had drawn back from satisfying their desire – partly because of the unthinkable calamity of an illegitimate baby in a respectable Church-going middle class home, but also be- cause of the strong social pressures prevailing in that milieu (particularly upon the girl) to stay "pure" at any rate "intact" before marriage: pressure which in practical terms constrained the boys also. Jos's resulting virginity was the bitter harvest of some tense and stressful frustration, and now he seemed likely to lose it in this dreadful room with this dreadful woman, for whom he did not "burn", indeed for whom he was feeling repugnance.

'Yes,' he squeaked.

'Come on then love,' said the woman softly, unhooking her

35

brassiere so that her large smooth and firm breasts fell forward and pressed into Jos. With expert hands she undressed him and guided him onto the bed and into her.

Looking back on the experience afterwards Jos felt that because of his ignorance and innocence he did not begin to exploit the sensual attractions which Lorraine (that was the improbable name by which she asked to be called) had to offer. But then if he had not been so callow she might not have been so kind. He stayed with her until midnight, giving her an extra five pounds after she had explained that the thirty shillings was the fee for a quick bash only.

It was one o'clock in the morning before Jos found his way back to Goodge Street and descended the hundred odd steps to the dormitory. The beds were in three-tiered bunks and in the bunk below Jos's, Bob was already asleep with a look of utmost piety on his face. Jos got undressed and inserted himself into the middle bunk. He fell asleep almost immediately, and almost immediately – or so it seemed – a loudspeaker was calling on a contingent for the British Army of the Rhine to get up have breakfast and join the bus to the airport. So it went on until six o'clock in the morning when the West African contingent was summoned. By the time Jos had pulled himself together, washed and shaved, Bob was sitting cheerfully before a plate of sausage and egg.

'Well,' he said with a roguish twinkle in his eye. 'How did you get on?'

'Fine. How about you?'

'Oh she wanted too much. So in the end I thought better of it. But it was a very interesting experience.'

Jos ate his breakfast in glum silence, thinking of his now almost empty wallet and convinced that he could feel the first symptoms of syphilis, as dramatically described to the Officer Cadets by the hearty Medical Officer at Eaton Hall, the Officer Training School.

When they got to the airport they were told that the flight would be delayed for five hours because of engine trouble. It was about eight thirty in the morning. Jos reckoned that he must have had about two hours broken sleep at the outside during the night and he was beginning to feel light-headed with tiredness. He tried to get a nap in a chair but he could not get off. And then he remembered that a doctor friend had given him some sleeping pills for the journey the night before in the sleeper train. He took one of these and soon felt the heavy pleasant sensation of drugged sleep overcoming him.

What a jumble of dreams: nightmares really. In one of them he was engaged to Lorraine and had taken her home to meet his Church Elder father whereupon she had embarked on a languorous discarding of her clothes. And then the scene had changed and it was him, Jos, desperately, anxiously rushing from one public lavatory to another trying to find one of those notices in red type about confidential treatment for VD. At last he found one and was searching for paper and pen to write down the address when he felt himself shaken vigorously by the shoulder. It was Bob.

'Hey wake up. We're getting away after all. We shouldn't be too much behind schedule.'

Jos looked at his watch. It was ten o'clock. As a result of his ill-timed sleeping tablet on top of lack of sleep and fatigue, the journey to Africa passed in a drugged stupor. He remembered hazily having dinner in Tripoli, and looking down from time to time on the endless-seeming desert as the plane flew over the Sahara. They landed at Kano. They were in the real Africa, south of the Sahara.

Jos came to with a start. He realized that he had dozed a little in giving way to this flood of reminiscence. And as the last memory of the arrival in Kano came to him, he looked round the orderly room and felt the great heat of the sun-drenched continent about him. It was late now and he stepped out on the verandah of the office for a few moments and said goodnight to the soldier on sentry duty. Then he withdrew behind the office to empty his bladder before crawling beneath the mosquito net which had been erected over his bed in the office. He looked up into the dark green netting before he drifted off into sleep, amazed to think how much he now felt a part of this vast new African world and how far distant and unreal the memories of "home" seemed to be.

5

All his life Jos had belonged to the non-car owning class. As a boy at the school to which he had won a bursary he kept quiet or talked about his uncle's new Jaguar when other boys were discussing the joys of motoring in the family car – or the tedium of having to wash it. Again, as a student, Jos pedalled about on his bicycle while a few of his really well-off contemporaries zoomed about on motor-bikes, in Daddy's car or in a rickety but rakish semi-vintage model of their own. At officer cadet school the lack had been most keenly felt. The handful of cadets who had cars of their own could dash in and out of the nearby town for shopping, meals, dances and girls generally. Jos – and the majority of the cadets – were stuck in their free time wandering round the ground of the historic pile which had been converted for use as their training headquarters. On Saturday evenings these car-less cadets usually ventured out by means of the infrequent and unreliable bus service – supplemented by hitch-hiking and long dreary walking. But never for them the quick dash in on a Wednesday early evening for renewal of the acquaintance of the pretty girl with the warm smile: no, they were stuck with the contemplation for the umpteenth time of the rolling acres belonging to the historic pile and uneasy speculation about what was happening to the girl with the warm smile.

Jos realized that his situation now in Kebira was not dissimilar. It was true that there seemed nowhere very much to go, but insofar as there was, it was invariably an uncomfortably long way off – far too far to walk or to cycle in the heat. There was provision for 'recreational transport' but Jos soon discovered the limitations of this. A senior officer had booked it beforehand or the acting second-in-command's jeep was out of action and he had commandeered the reccy transport truck for the day, and so on.

Jos was thus a ready sucker for the approach made to him one day by CSM Roberts.

'You can't help being sorry for the RSM sir.'

Jos felt he could manage this without too much difficulty. He asked,

'Why Sergeant-Major?'

'Well he's left it too late, hasn't 'e sir?'

'Left what too late?'

'Selling 'is car of course sir. Lovely little job it is too. But he'll 'ave to give it away more or less now that 'e's left it so late.'

Jos's interest quickened but he tried to play it cool.

'Oh yes the RSM is off on long leave in a couple of weeks isn't he?'

'When I think of the offers that man has had for the car, and now of course the traders are just sitting back and waiting for the kill. They know now that 'e's got to sell.'

Jos could contain himself no longer.

'You know I wouldn't mind picking up a car cheaply for my stint here.'

'Well I'd a darned sight sooner see you as a white man got it than these swindlers in the Sabongari.'

Jos felt the familiar unease at hearing the Sergeant-Major's automatic racialism. But Roberts now showed some skill in baiting the hook.

'But I don't see why you should pay a halfpenny more than they would sir. It's the RSM's own fault.'

Jos began to think that perhaps Roberts wasn't such a bad chap after all.

'Do you think I should go and see him about it?'

'Well sir he really would be charmed. I know that what worries him most is the thought of some of them Sunday Bananas buying it up cheap and then flogging it for its true value. I'll speak to him in the Mess tonight – and I'll also warn 'im not to press you more than 'e could the traders.'

Jos was in a great state of excitement all that evening and after breakfast. After Muster Parade he tackled Roberts.

'Oh yes sir I did mention it to the RSM – but he's so fed up about the low price angle that he's thinking of laying the car up for 'is long leave. Bit dodgy doing that in this climate of course but 'e says 'e just can't face selling at the price that's being offered.'

'Well how much is that exactly?' Jos found himself blurting out.

'Oh now sir, you'd better ask the RSM that question yourself. I must be careful not to meddle mustn't I?'

Thus it was that Jos was led to call on the RSM and ask him to name his price for a dreadful old pile of scrap metal which he was going to have to leave behind him in a week's time anyhow. The RSM himself would probably have been content to think of a number – say twenty-five pounds – and settle for that. But as ill luck had it Colour Sergeant Bowes was with the RSM when Jos called.

'Oh now she is a lovely little job, isn't she Ted?'

The RSM grunted a sheepish assent.

'No really sir this is a coach-built job, sir.'

Jos was staring glassy-eyed with pleasure at the little Morris Eight Saloon standing outside the RSM's front door. He sniffed greedily at the aroma of oil and petrol and leather which wafted round it. He scarcely heard Colour-Sergeant Bowes's eulogy.

'Oh she's a real little work-horse sir. Go anywhere won't she Ted? She's as hard as nails sir. Wot is she again Ted? – '48 or '49? Funny thing sir: I know this car like the back of my hand and I always forget whether she's a '48 or '49.'

Colour Sergeant Bowes might have been forgiven this lapse of memory since it was – as Jos discovered when he eventually got the somewhat sketchy looking set of vehicle registration documents – a 1946 model.

'Now sir,' said Colour Sergeant Bowes with a sudden change of tactic 'Wot is the most important thing about a car?'

Jos started nervously from his dreamy contemplation of the little saloon. Shades of similar questions barked out in similar voices during training were evoked.

'Wot is the range of the two inch Mortar?'

'Wot is the *Immediate Action* on the Bren Gun if it stops

firing?'

He found he was experiencing the same panicky uncertainty in response to Colour Sergeant Bowes.

'The engine?' he squeaked hopefully.

'That's right sir,' replied the Colour politely. 'The chassis. Now sir will you look at this chassis. Isn't it a lovely job sir? This car sir, this car is fetching around £250 at home just now. Wot was it you wos thinking of asking as a minimum offer Ted? Was it fifty pounds or sixty pounds?'

Jos's brain whirred with mental arithmetic: eighty pounds for his tropical outfit allowance of which he had so far spent ten pounds on the useless khaki drill bought at his depot in Scotland and seven pounds, ten shillings for the immaculate drill suits made by Sunday Mbula. If he got Sunday Mbula to make him a white mess suit instead of buying trews from Andersons of Edinburgh he reckoned he could go as high as sixty pounds. He was saved by the RSM.

'Forty pounds sir. Are you interested in it for that?'

'Why yes Mr Stormont. That seems very reasonable.'

'Very well sir. I'll get a squad to push it down to your house tomorrow.'

'P-p-push it?' Jos faltered.

Colour Sergeant Bowes leapt into the breach.

'You drive a hard bargain sir and no mistake. Cor! Forty pounds! By golly sir one would have to get up pretty early in the morning to get the better of you sir. Now you see there is a little difficulty wiv the ignition. We'll get some of the motor transport boys – or these African mechanics in the Gari are very good wiv their hands you know sir – and we'll have her going like a bomb in no time.'

The next morning the squad of soldiers came panting and laughing down to Jos's house with the car. When Okoko saw them his face darkened and lengthened. He stood watching them, sighing heavily. Jos who was still elated at the thought of car ownership but anxious at the thought of the largest cheque he had ever written found himself on edge. It was so embarrassing that the car had had to be pushed down and here was Okoko looking so glum and as if poised to say 'I told you so' although he hadn't told him anything yet.

41

'What's wrong Okoko? Don't you like my mato?'

'Oh sah,' wailed Okoko. 'Dis ting go chop yo' money. Dis mato foh RSM sah she be bad mato too much sah. Kai! Hey you bush men,' venting his anger on the recruits 'Why you go stand on dese flowers?'

Jos was surprised that neither the RSM nor Colour Sergeant Bowes had accompanied the recruits, and even more so when days passed without him seeing either of them. At last he espied Colour Sergeant Bowes one day in the NAAFI.

'I was wondering Colour if you could give me some advice about getting a mechanic for the car.'

'The RSM's car sir? Oh yes he's a lucky lad: be back in dear old Blighty by now sir.'

'Yes well you know, about the car. It won't start you know. I was wondering if you could put me on to someone to fix it.'

'Well they say there is a good Yoruba mechanic in the Sabongari sir. Like I said – very clever wiv their hands some of them – oh excuse me sir: there's my missis, looks as if she could do wiv a hand sir. I hope you get fixed up all right sir.'

As Jos watched Colour Sergeant Bowes scuttle off, his heart sank. He thought bitterly of the inert pile of metal by his house, of that handsome cheque for forty pounds, of Okoko's silent glances of reproach at him and at the car. Something must be done. The next day, after his siesta he set off on foot towards the Gari. The Sabongari was a sort of shanty town just behind the barracks. The words mean "New Town" in Hausa; and it was peopled by the various foreign tribes – the Ibo and Yoruba and other smaller groups – in other words those who did not belong to the Hausa and so did not live within the old walls of the city of Kebira.

Jos trudged moodily through the streets shooing a herd of goats out of his way until he came to the shop of the little barber who used to cycle round the officers' quarters ready to cut hair on the verandah.

'Good afternoon sah. You want foh me to come down and cut you' hair sah?'

'No Ochida I was wondering if you knew where the Yoruba mechanic lives.'

'Mechanic foh mato sah?'

'Yes.'

'You get mato sah?'

'Yes.'

'Not dat mato foh RSM sah?'

'Yes.'

'Oh sah. I sorry sah.'

Jos's heart sank further still.

'Yes well you see it does need a little maintenance at the moment. That's why I was wondering about this mechanic. Do you know where he works?'

'Yes sah. Is Festus you mean. We go now-now and see him.'

Festus turned out to be a very little, very black man. His skin was ebony for a start. But it, his hair and his clothes all seemed to be steeped in black oil.

He was bending over the bonnet of an old Buick. He paused and straightened himself when Ochida spoke to him.

'Oh dat mato foh British RSM sah,' he said rubbing his hands on an oil cloth. 'I go come foh you house tomorrow and look at it.'

Tomorrow, next tomorrow, next next again and many others passed before Jos saw Festus again. When he did, it was his feet which he saw protruding from under the car, large parts of which seemed to be strewn around and about. Festus's arms, body and head emerged cheerily.

'Hey dis be fine fine car. You go see. Two maybe tree days time I go fix her.'

Jos was heartened. The car had become a blot – literally – on his landscape: a sudden sinking of the spirits when he thought of it; a wakening up in the morning thinking what is there that is bothering me – oh God yes I remember, the car. Festus was as good as his word: he had become engrossed with the defects of the car and gave unstintingly of his time to repair them. No doubt somebody else was now waiting, wondering if Festus would ever get on with mending his car.

The excitement was almost unbearable when Jos first heard the sound of the engine and saw Festus drive it a few yards up the track to the Mess and then reverse down again. He could have hugged Festus for all the oil and grease on him. The two men laughed together and shook hands. Jos was suddenly

43

aware of a chill constraint over his left shoulder. Okoko was standing, his arms folded and his face long and wooden looking.

'Well cheer up Okoko. The mato is daidai now. See?'

Jos found himself using cheerily and naturally "Daidai" the universal term for "OK" in West Africa. Okoko's glum face did not relent for an instant. But Jos was too happy to notice it. He got into the car and drove off taking Festus back to the Gari.

For a few days all went smoothly – or fairly smoothly. Before leaving him that evening Festus had shown Jos how to clean the spark plugs. Jos found he had to do that rather a lot, and that he used a great deal of oil and that the children who lived around the barracks had given him the new nickname of 'The man with the blue smoke coming out of his tail'. But he had a car. It started. And it got him places.

6

It was shortly after Jos had acquired the car and Festus had got it going that there was a large reception given at the Residency to which most of the European community was invited, including the officers from the battalion. Jos was clutching his invitation card as he came over from lunch at the Mess and started to take his boots off for his afternoon sleep.

'Get my Mess kit ready for this evening, will you Okoko?' he said as he stretched out on the bed.

'Is not Mess Night tonight sah,' commented Okoko as he picked up the boots and discarded leg dress.

'No but I'm going to the Residency.'

'Kai! Babbanbature!' cried Okoko. "Babbanbature" translated literally could mean "big white chief", and sometimes it seemed to Jos that there was an uncanny note of irony in the way that Africans used the term.

The reception was due to start at six thirty, and at about six o'clock Jos stepped into the crisp white Mess kit which Okoko had laid out for him. This Mess kit had indeed been tailored by Sunday Mbula and was always kept in a state of starched spotlessness by Okoko. Okoko surveyed Jos's gleaming figure with satisfaction. Then he place one end of the crimson cummerbund round Jos's stomach and withdrew to the opposite corner of the room.

'Now sah come to me round and round.'

Thus Jos spun himself into the cummerbund almost encompassing Okoko in the last twirl.

Laughing and in thoroughly good humour at the total effect which his valetting had created, Okoko disengaged himself and indulged in a final complacent glance at his handiwork.

45

'You go catch recreational transport tonight sah?' he en-quired chattily.

'No of course not. I'm going in my own car.'

Delicious words to be rolled over and savoured: 'my own car'.

'Oh sah.' Okoko exclaimed in alarm. 'Is big cars foh Resident's House. Is not little cars like yours.'

Jos did not deign to reply, but went out, got into his car and started it up. It chugged heavily up the track to the Mess and then out on to the main road. Okoko stood shaking his head moodily until it had disappeared.

As he parked the car outside the Residency Jos looked uneasily at the rows of gleaming new Peugeots, Volkswagens and Opels, mostly estate cars. He did not feel any more kindly disposed to Okoko for sensing that he had probably been right. However once inside his misgivings quickly subsided. The drink was plentiful, and over in the corner he espied a new face: that of a very pretty girl. Billy Rogers and Dave Lawson – who had both come down in recreational transport – were engaged in conversation with her. Jos found himself in a group of three or four with several other groups between him and the girl: he concentrated on moving slowly towards the new attraction. This involved attaching himself briefly to a group which included the Colonel – who was at his most genial and expansive – and the Resident's wife, a large, horsy woman who was in fact talking about horses as Jos joined the group. She was extolling the virtues of polo and stressing how important it was to keep up membership of the polo club.

'Certainly all your young officers should play, Colonel,' she barked.

'Quite so, quite so,' said the Colonel. 'I think they all do. You don't know of any who don't do you Maclean?'

'I think most of them do,' Jos hedged.

'There you are,' snapped Mrs Joynstone. 'Most of them. That means not all of them. If the Army Officers don't play how is the game to be kept going?'

The Colonel smiled blandly apparently content to interpret this as some sort of tribute to the importance of his men.

'Quite so, quite so,' he mumbled shyly.

46

'Do you play?' Mrs Joynstone suddenly swivelled her attention to Jos.

'Well actually no. I'm not long out of course. And certainly I intend to play.'

'Not long out,' Mrs Joynstone scoffed. 'Why my young niece there,' and here she glanced at the pretty girl towards whom Jos was seeking to advance, 'hasn't been out a week yet, and she's had a few swipes at the ball already.'

Both Jos and the Colonel were startled to hear this since, although Mrs Joynstone's passion for horses and riding was well known, polo was not a game in which the female sex participated – at any rate not in Kebira in 1955. But Jos's interest was quickened by Mrs Joynstone's reference to her niece and he followed her glance, to look at the girl.

'Yes that's the filly there,' said Mrs Joynstone. 'If she can wield a stick within the week I don't see why you can't. Been here at least two months now haven't you?'

Jos could think of one good reason and that was that he had never sat on a horse in his life and had no intention of doing so if he could possibly avoid it. But events were moving fast.

'Why don't you come down tomorrow. I'm sure the Colonel can fix you up with a pony and you can have a shot at swinging a stick?'

'Strike while the iron's hot my boy,' urged the Colonel who was much given to talking in clichés.

'Jane will be practising I know, and you two beginners could keep each other company and not get in the road of the rest of us.'

'Most uncommonly generous of you Mrs Joynstone,' said the Colonel. 'Mr Maclean will be charmed to accept . . . Gather ye rosebuds, Maclean.'

Jos experienced a strange mixture of emotions: extreme nervousness at the thought of having to get up on a horse – elation at the thought of this appointment being made for him to be alone with the girl. He edged over to the next group. The head of the judicial service, always known simply as The Judge, was telling a story about Ju-Ju and the strange and dark forces of the unknown in Africa. Jos was interested to see The Judge unbending in this social gathering: he always seemed

47

such an Olympian figure who would be unlikely to give one the time of day. But here he was looking quite jolly with a large glass of brandy and ginger in his hand.

'I remember on my first tour,' he was saying. 'There was this village in the bush and the whole damned lot of them were living in mortal terror because the witch doctor had been thrown out and in revenge had laid a curse on the village. He had said that evil spirits would come and bring disease and misfortune – and that the villagers would know they were coming when they heard a high pitched wail.'

A pleasant shiver ran up and down the spines of the audience.

'Well,' resumed the Judge, having taken a refreshing sip of brandy and ginger, 'Well . . . .'

Just then the whole room was shaken and startled by a high loud eerie wail. The Judge choked on his brandy and ginger. His audience turned very white, and Turnbull, the local public works department manager who had been imbibing at an inordinate pace cried out in a loud clear voice, which reverberated round the room,

'What in buggeration's name is that?'

That somehow broke the tension and for a few moments there was nervous giggling and chatter. What was so disconcerting was that the wailing did not slacken or change tone in the very slightest: that was what seemed to make it so unnatural and eerie. Some of the men began to edge towards the door with torches and sticks – for already the swift tropical night was descending. The first to regain his composure was the Manager of the local Barclay's Bank.

'It's all right,' he called. 'I know what that is: it's a car horn that's gone into the "on" position – something wrong with its wiring.'

As he heard these words an icy hand clutched at Jos's heart. Oh wise Okoko: if only he had not brought the car to this posh function. The guests were now in the garden – all over the garden.

'I say mind these flower beds you know,' Mrs Joynstone's voice could be heard from time to time above the wail, and the chatter and relieved laughter of her guests, as they blundered into the zinnia and petunia beds.

Each guest had gone to his car and was looking under the bonnet in a knowledgeable way. As Jos approached his little car any shred of hope that it might not be the culprit vanished. The din was unmistakably emanating from the little black bonnet so recently the object of Festus's attentions. Oh sweet Jesus he thought to himself as he looked round at the throng of excited guests now in full stampede over Mrs Joynstone's garden. He lifted the bonnet and gawped ignorantly at the tangle of wires and tubes and oily metal objects which constituted the internal combustion engine. He toyed with the idea of taking out the spark plugs and cleaning them: at least that would give him the appearance of doing something manly and mechanical. He could hear the sound of car bonnets being slammed down as one after another of the guests satisfied himself beyond all doubt that his car was not the source of the noise. He became aware of many eyes looking at him. He looked up and grinned feebly at the encircling hosts.

Firm practical hands – those of one of the lecturers at the technical college – pushed Jos aside and grasped a wire and yanked it out. The silence was impressive. It was broken by Mrs Joynstone asking peevishly, 'How could such a little old car make such a noise?'; and then by the Colonel, no longer benign and, heedless of the ladies present, remarking,

'Look here Maclean, that was your bloody car.'

The Colonel's gift for underlining the obvious was second only to his facility for thinking and talking in clichés. Altogether the car-horn incident cast a damper on the party and it broke up very soon. Jos's final humiliation was that the sounding horn had drained the battery of energy to such an extent that he had to be pushed down the drive to get the car started.

By the time he got up to the mess and his house the bush telegraph had been at work. Several of the children of the mess boys had gathered to admire this phenomenon of "De mato she cry", and stared round-eyed and apprehensive as Jos got out. Okoko was there with a grim I-told-you-so look on his face. Jos went moodily up to the Mess hoping that the others would by now have left the dining room so that he would not have to face any teasing while he was still smarting from the embarrassment of the incident. But alas three of the subalterns were still sitting over their coffee – Billy Rogers, Dave Lawson and Clifford Dainton a Yorkshireman who had recently joined the unit. The tail end of Billy Rogers words as Jos entered the dining room was the sort of thing Jos had hoped to avoid.

'I mean it lets the whole damn unit down . . . .' Billy broke off as he caught sight of Jos.

'Oh there you are Jos: that was a bit of a nonsense at the Residency. I can tell you the old man is in a bit of a lather about it.'

'I thought it was bloody funny,' said Dave Lawson. 'And I was running out of things to say to Miss Cheltenham Ladies College 1955.'

'You might have moved over then and let the rest of us get a look in,' Dainton complained.

He was one of those honest fellows who made no bones about his main interest in life being the pursuit of the opposite sex. Throughout his time in Kebira he had a permanently injured expression on his face presumably because it was not an interest in which he could really indulge in the absence – or at any rate extreme shortage – of suitable quarry. He clearly resented bitterly the fact that his chance of making the pretty girl's acquaintance had been frustrated, first by Dave monopolizing her and secondly by the general shambles resulting from Jos's car horn. It was an added vexation now to hear Dave speaking disparagingly of the girl.

Billy Rogers drained the last drop of coffee from his cup and replaced it firmly in the saucer.

'Well I must say I thought Jane was a perfectly charming girl. And I expect that's the last any of us will see of her during her holiday over here. Mrs J is going potty about the mess which has been made of her garden.'

Here Billy looked pointedly and reproachfully at Jos.

Jos was stung to respond 'Well actually I'm seeing her tomorrow. Mrs J's arranged for me to have polo lessons with her.'

'You're a lucky bugger Jos,' cried Dainton enviously. 'By golly if I could ride a horse I'd be in their pitching too. I can

50

tell you.'

Billy had been stunned by Jos's announcement and had sat staring at him with incredulity. Now however he came to life.

'B-but he can't ride either. And girls don't play polo,' he protested.

Billy had a half share in one of the old ponies kept in the unit stables, and occasionally he would set off, mounted on this animal, for a stately circuit of the barracks feeling no end of a landed gent. He always seemed to sit stiffly upright and somewhat precariously perched. Dave Lawson, who was a splendid horseman, said,

'Well there's nothing to it Jos, but you'd better come with me immediately before lunch tomorrow and I'll show you which end of the beast to look at when you're trying to get on. If you make a mistake there you land up facing the wrong way.'

Jos was relieved and grateful. At this point his soup was brought in and the others withdrew to the ante-room thus relieving him of the sound of Billy's voice expounding on the enormity of trying to play polo before one had mastered the art of riding. Then he stole off down to his gidda avoiding further contact with his fellow officers and let himself in without encountering that other scold, Okoko.

7

It was about one-fifteen when Jos met Dave Lawson behind the squash court. Dave was mounted on a grey polo pony and idly swinging a stick at some long grass. He slipped down when he saw Jos.

'Excellent news,' he said. 'I've managed to get Balthazar from the Mess polo stables for you. Balthazar was the finest polo pony in Northern Nigeria in his prime. He's still damned good but not so fast now of course – and he's become pretty docile with old age. But he plays the ball uncannily – he'll make you hit it.'

Jos looked uncertainly at Balthazar's beautiful, large, treacherous-looking eyes. Why do they call them ponies he wondered. They look very big to me, and what a long way off the ground to be moving never mind leaning over and swiping at a little ball at the same time.

'Come on then,' Dave was saying. 'Stand about here. Put your right hand up on his haunch there. Put your left foot in the stirrup: that's right. Now heave up.'

Jos found himself lying awkwardly parallel to the back of the horse peering through the space between the horse's large pointed ears somewhat as if they were the foresights of a huge rifle. His face was tickled by the rough prickly hair of the mane. He heard Dave sniggering.

'Sit up for God's sake and stop embracing the animal.'

Gingerly Jos levered himself erect. Dave showed him how to hold the reins and where and how to grip with his knees. Jos felt a wave of confidence break over him. He looked about him and was impressed with what a lovely view it was from horse-back level. He now wanted to 'start' the creature. He looked down at the reins and vaguely thought that these were the nearest thing to a dashboard and steering wheel and that the process of locomotion must somehow be connected with them. He gave a vigorous yank on them. Balthazar half-reared and snorted with anger.

'For Christ's sake,' shouted Dave. 'Don't do that. You've just slammed on the brakes. If you want to move touch the horse's sides with your heels.'

After an hour or so of further basic instruction and some experience of walking, trotting and even mild galloping, Dave concluded that with luck Jos might be classified as simply rusty in the general confusion of polo strokes and sticks and balls. Anyhow by now they were both hungry and aware that the Mess staff would be becoming increasingly sulky at the lateness of their lunch. So they went up to the Mess leaving Musa the doki-boy to have Balthazar all groomed and ready by four o'clock.

Jos was again experiencing the curious mixture of anxiety and elation which had come upon him when the idea of the polo lesson had been mooted between the Colonel and Mrs Joynstone. He was apprehensive about how Mrs Joynstone would receive him following the disturbance caused by the car horn and about how he would fare as a horseman, but the prevailing sensation was pleasure at the thought of making the acquaintance of this young, pretty, unattached girl. This pleasure was enhanced by the sight of Billy Rogers' aggrieved face as he surveyed the two horsemen entering the Mess. Jos hurried through his lunch and set off whistling cheerfully to himself down the track to his gidda for a short afternoon sleep.

Okoko began to close the shutters for him to keep out the light and heat. He looked at Jos doubtfully.

'I go wake you foh five o'clock time sah?'

'No Okoko my doki-boy will be calling round at about four o'clock so wake me in half an hour – just before four.'

'You doki-boy sah?'

'Yes.'

'You buy hoss now sah?' Okoko enquired politely as he helped Jos off with his boots and puttees.

'Possibly,' Jos replied grandly, though the idea had not

occurred to him until this moment.

'But I'm just borrowing a pony for a game of polo this afternoon.'

'Kai!' exclaimed Okoko delightedly. 'You get power for polo sah. Hey dis be game for Babbanbature. I go tell dese Boys foh Massa Dainton and Massa Rogers dat you go play polo.'

'Oh well,' said Jos a little uneasily. 'You know I'm just sort of learning.'

But Okoko was paying no attention. He was obviously as pleased at this development as he had been full of misgiving about the car. He went off jauntily pulling the door behind him with elaborate quietness and carefulness so as not to disturb Jos. By now it was about quarter past three, but Jos fell asleep at once so that he had had a refreshing half hour of sleep by the time Okoko came back with the cup of black coffee at quarter to four. He had scarcely time to drink this and to get into his shirt and slacks when he heard the sound of horse's hooves and then Dave's voice bawling at him to get up. Jos stepped outside into the dazzling sunshine and saw Dave mounted on a gleaming black pony.

'I though I'd better ride down alongside you,' he said. 'There's sometimes a bit of traffic on the way, and I can see you don't get stampeded.'

Jos felt a moment of panic when he heard these words but he managed a stiff upper lip grin and said 'Fine.'

The sound of another set of hooves was now heard, and the doki-boy Musa rode up on Balthazar. He was an urchin of about fourteen, with a bad cast in one eye which gave him an unfortunate shifty look. He had a great admiration – as most of the servants and soldiers had – for the tall blond athletic Dave, and he now grinned appreciatively as Dave berated him for some flaw in the grooming of the horse. He understood scarcely a word of English and Dave had been too lazy to learn any Hausa. But they seemed to communicate quite well by tone of voice and gesture. Suddenly Musa slipped gracefully off the horse and bowing to Jos greeted him with the words,

'Sanu mai-Doki!' (Greetings horseman).

'Yawa sanu!' cried Okoko in the background as a sort of 'Hear Hear'.

An uneasy clamminess seemed to ooze into Jos's hands, and he felt his throat dry with nervousness.

Which way do you stand? Which foot in which stirrup? God if I land up on this back to front I will never be able to look Okoko in the eye again. But Dave, who had dismounted, guided him into the right stance, and with a clumsy heave Jos found himself again aloft. Musa took the horse's head and they proceeded in a precarious and wobbly fashion up the track from the gidda. Okoko looked after them with a worried frown.

'He going to play polo? He going to fall off.'

Musa surrendered the reins when they reached the road, and by then Jos had felt some of the confidence he had gained earlier that day begin to return. The two horses walked sedately enough to the racecourse where the polo club had its grounds. The first thing Jos saw when they got inside the grounds was Mrs Joynstone and her niece galloping along a stretch of the racecourse. Dave had dismounted and was reminding Jos how to do so. Jos slithered down the side of the animal and stood again with great relief on terra firma.

'OK Jos you're on your own now. I'm going to see if I can make up a side and have a chukka. You'll be all right: just remember to keep a tight hold with your knees.'

Dave went off to the clubhouse to collect a polo stick and then led his horse over to the adjoining polo field where Jos could see him swinging low over his horse's head and making great hits with his stick. Again Jos felt panic assail him. Oh Christ, he muttered to himself. What am I doing here? Let me get out before that madwoman from the Residency sees me and remembers about the polo. He looked at Balthazar who returned his glance with a supercilious and hostile glare. He looked at the saddle and again thought what a fearsomely long way up it seemed. But these idle wishful thinkings about escape were chased away by the unmistakable sound of Mrs Joynstone's hearty voice.

'Ah the young man with the wailing motor! I've a bone to pick with you about my flower beds. But we'll forget about that for the moment. I can forgive a good polo player anything, so we'll see what we can make of you. I'll just go and get sticks for you and Jane.'

Mrs Joynstone strode on into the clubhouse. Jos looked wildly about him with the desperation of a trapped animal. He glanced up at Jane who was – literally – looking down her nose at him. Nothing for it, he concluded. I've got to go through with it, and I'd better ascend the beast before Mrs J comes out of the clubhouse. Repeating to himself which foot, which stirrup, which hand, which haunch, he positioned himself alongside Balthazar and scrambled jerkily up his side. Jane's fine dark eyebrows were raised in astonishment as his head appeared panting and pretty well cheek by jowl with Balthazar's. Cautiously Jos straightened himself so that he was sitting more or less erect.

'Ah there we are,' Mrs Joynstone came marching back with three polo sticks. 'Catch,' she called throwing one of the sticks to Jane who fielded it deftly. 'Catch,' she called again, this time to Jos who made a feeble flutter of his hands in the direction in which the stick was falling.

'Butter fingers,' Mrs Joynstone snorted. 'No it's all right. Don't get down.' And Mrs Joynstone bent down, retrieved the stick and handed it up to Jos. Get down, thought Jos wistfully: if only I could.

'Now I gather you two haven't actually met yet?' Mrs Joynstone was now saying breezily.

'Well Mr Maclean – Jos isn't it, this is my niece Jane Robbins. Jane – Second Lieutenant Jos Maclean. I hope you'll both be apt pupils.'

After this brief introduction Mrs Joynstone began to make swings with her stick and talk about wrist movements: now she was bending this way and that over her mount and talking about waist movements. Looking back long afterwards on the episode of the polo lesson, Jos realized that Mrs Joynstone, as a superb horsewoman and good ball player, must have been bitterly frustrated by the prevailing convention that only men played polo. She must have itched to take part, and saw the visit of her niece – and now Jos's confession of inability to play – as a welcome opportunity to engage in a little informal practice polo on the side. After demonstrating strokes for five or ten minutes she rode up close beside the two young people, making the pony mince in a tightly controlled turn.

'Right then,' she said suddenly dropping a polo ball at her horse's feet. 'Let's see how it goes.'

She gave the ball a neat strong hit and sent it flying along an inch or two above the ground for some forty yards. It went to Jane's side who galloped after it, but her horse carried on wide of the ball and did not really give her a chance to hit it.

'Right,' called Mrs Joynstone again and sent another ball singing along the ground this time on Jos's side. Balthazar was after it like a shot and followed it closely, positioning himself beautifully for Jos to play a stroke. Cautiously Jos peered over the horse's side and spotted the ball. Cautiously and fearful of losing his balance he poked downwards with his stick, and to his astonishment connected clean and hard with the ball and sent it some thirty yards.

'Jolly good show!' shouted Mrs Joynstone as she galloped past in pursuit. So it went on most of the afternoon. Balthazar by brilliant positioning brought Jos so pat before the ball that he often hit it. Mrs Joynstone was impressed. It was true the young fellow seemed to ride awkwardly but by jove to hit the ball as often as that at his first practice was jolly good going. Jane however, who clearly did not share her aunt's eccentric passion for polo, was having the discomfiture of missing the ball nearly every time – partly because she was a learner but mainly because her pony would not ride into playable positions. Thus she viewed Jos's performance with a somewhat jaundiced eye. She saw very clearly that this was a rabbit of a horseman (and not much of a ball player) who was making a completely false impression because of the skill of his pony. As they were riding back to the clubhouse she became impatient of her aunt's praise of Jos and of Jos's complacent acceptance of it.

'Care for a gallop round the track to finish off?' she asked.

'Oh – er – well . . . ' spluttered Jos who had just calculated that there were about twenty yards between him and the safety of the clubhouse.

'Jolly good idea,' cried Mrs Joynstone. 'These little beggars like a really good run now and again.'

With that, she dug her heels into her pony's flanks and was off round the rails. Jane followed. With a last wistful look back at the clubhouse Jos went after them. To his alarm he felt a

great surge of power and excitement emanating from Balthazar as soon as the rails of the racecourse and the racing track
were clearly before them. Dave Lawson had not mentioned to
Jos that, in addition to being a first class polo pony in his day,
Balthazar had also been a successful racing pony. Balthazar
galloped close into the rails. He went very fast leaning sharply
to the left. Jos had begun sitting awkwardly in a more or less
upright position as for walking or trotting. But he soon found
that he had to bend low over the horse's ears for fear of falling
off. As he clung desperately to the animal he realized that he
was literally scared stiff. He was certain that he was going to be
killed; the only question was whether it would be by being
thrown across the rail or pitched over the horse's head and
trampled to death. Dimly he perceived that he was passing first
Jane and then Mrs Joynstone. Jane felt a spasm of remorse and
pity as she saw the ashen face of terror thundering past her.
Mrs Joynstone thought to herself that the young fellow seemed
mad keen to win and that that wasn't a bad fault in a young
officer. Jos had now concluded that the most likely outcome
was that he would die of fright before any other ill could befall
him. Then all at once he realized that Balthazar was slackening
his pace. Jos pulled gently on the reins and Balthazar slowed
down to a gentle canter and then a walk. Jos looked backwards
and saw that they had completed a lap and that Balthazar
must have concluded that they had passed the winning post.
The two ladies caught up with him and they carried on at
walking pace to the clubhouse.

'You do take things seriously, young man don't you?' Mrs
Joynstone commented.

Jos gave a hysterical giggle which Mrs Joynstone interpreted
as a deprecating laugh.

'I tell you what,' she went on. 'I'm going to put your name
down for the Resident's Silver Cup at the races next Saturday.
Your riding technique is, quite frankly, abysmal – but you've
got the will to win, and that counts for a great deal.'

They had now reached the clubhouse. Dave Lawson was
there and helped Jos somewhat roughly down from his horse.

'Have you gone off your chump?' he asked savagely. 'What
on earth did you race poor old Balthazar like that for? It's

enough to give the poor old chap heart failure.'

'Him heart failure?' Jos exclaimed bitterly.

'Yes just look at his sides heaving. Musa will be furious when he hears about this.'

'Dave: my sides are heaving too. I thought I was going to die of fright out there. This bloody animal bolted when it got on to the race track: I couldn't do a thing about it. And look – I need your help for next Saturday. You arrange the duty roster for bush camp don't you? Please send me out next weekend.'

'Why?'

'Mrs Joynstone has just told me she's going to enter me for the Resident's Silver Cup.'

'And you've agreed?'

'Does anyone ever get a chance to disagree with Mrs Joynstone?'

Jane sauntered over with a tall glass of shandy in her hand looking cool and fresh in her neatly tailored jodhpurs and crisp check blouse. Jos was suddenly aware of his baggy khaki slacks stuffed into his mosquito boots.

'I'm sorry,' she said. 'That was a rotten trick. Are you all right?'

Jos felt himself mesmerized by her lovely dark eyes, by the smoothness of the skin visible at the neck of her blouse. A great flood of happiness came over him.

'Yes,' he replied. 'I feel terrific.'

Jane was taken aback.

'But I mean have you actually done much riding before?'

'Well not too much really. Well to be quite candid I was never on a horse until today.'

Jane looked in alarm at both Jos and Dave. 'Oh dear,' she said. 'Aunt Mabel is determined to enter you on Fireater for the Silver Cup.'

Jos's feeling of well being deserted him. 'Fireater! I don't like the sound of that.'

'It's an absolute swine of a horse,' said Dave matter-of-factly.

'Yes. Aunt Mabel says he's the kind of pony who needs a really determined rider. Oh I must go – Auntie's calling me.'

And with that Jane turned on her heel and walked quickly

back to the clubhouse. Jos looked appreciatively at her departing figure: the slim waist and the trim bottom. But as soon as she had disappeared the feeling of anxiety overcame him.

'Dave, I must get out of this bloody race. Can you get me to bush camp for the weekend?'

Dave straightened himself up from rubbing Balthazar down.

'No can do. It must be a B Company Platoon; and that means Dainton or Grimshaw.'

'Oh Christ! What on earth am I to do?'

'Well,' said Dave thoughtfully. 'There is one way. Next weekend is my day for Duty Officer. I could make way for you if you're absolutely sure.'

'What a sod you are,' said Jos. But there was relief in his voice. 'Will the Adjutant agree to the change?'

'Leave that to me,' Dave assured him.

'All right then,' said Jos. Although weekend duty officer was a tedious chore, it was preferable to careering round the racecourse on a horse called Fireater. Jos felt a weight lift from him. He went into the clubhouse quite cheerfully and there he saw Jane and her aunt sitting on high stools at the bar.

'Ali give this young master a litre of Carlsberg, will you.' Mrs Joynstone called loudly to one of the bar boys. She turned to Jos with a *sotto voce* look on her face, and in a voice that was anything but *sotto* she confided, 'You'll need it to replace some of the sweat.'

Just at this point Dave Lawson, having finished his cosseting of Balthazar and tethered him to the rail which stood in front of the clubhouse, came into the bar. Mrs Joynstone spotted him and at once got down off the bar stool exclaiming

'Hah there's David Lawson: I must see about getting him to play for the Kebira side against the Lagos Touring Team.' Acting as Hon Secretary to the Kebira Polo Club was Mrs Joynstone's more orthodox way of working off her enthusiasm for the game, and in that capacity she now stalked off to address Dave. Jos realized that at last he and Jane were alone. He found himself completely tongue-tied. He smiled in what he hoped was a friendly, admiring and manly way. Jane looked slightly startled causing Jos to think that he must have got the smile wrong. It probably came out as a vacuous leer, he thought.

Jane regarded him with her rather serious gaze and a definite quickening of interest. Gosh he did look so absolutely terrified careering round on that little pony. No wonder if he's never been on a horse before. And how calm he is about the prospect of riding Fireater. She realized she was feeling fond of him and protective.

'Jos,' she said – using his Christian name for the first time. 'I was wondering if you would like to come hacking one afternoon – and perhaps we could finish up with a swim at the residency pool?'

Again Jos felt the flood of happiness engulf him. 'Thank you very much,' he said. 'That would be super.'

I wonder, he thought to himself, what hacking is. But this was partly clarified by Jane's next remark

'You see I do think it would be a good idea to get in as much riding as possible between now and next Saturday.'

'Absolutely.' Jos agreed, feeling slightly deceitful in his knowledge that he would not be a participant in the Resident's Silver Cup. Hacking must be some sort of riding.

'Well should we start tomorrow? Could you come down about four thirty and we could have a short hack until say five thirty and then half an hour's swim?'

'That would be terrific,' said Jos not quite sure if he had any other commitments but determined to get out of them if he had.

As Jos and Dave rode slowly back up to the barracks Jos was smiling to himself at the thought of how Dainton and Rogers would look when they heard that he was to go riding and swimming with the desirable Jane. Dave looked at him questioningly.

'What's up?

'Nothing really,' Jos said smugly. 'Just that I'm to go hacking with Jane tomorrow afternoon followed by a swim at the residency pool.'

Dave shook his head,

'My dear boy,' he said. 'If you can stagger out of bed tomorrow and up to the Mess to sit awkwardly on the edge of a very soft chair you will be doing very well. Personally I doubt if you will be able to sit down again for about a week with all the unaccustomed battering to which you have subjected your bum.'

'Oh I hadn't thought of that,' said Jos.

'Ah well think of it tonight as you lie awake wishing that you had a hot fomentation applied to your sit-upon.'

In fact by the time Jos dismounted to hand over the horse to Musa, he was already feeling stiff and sore; and by the time he had hobbled over to the Mess for dinner he was in no mood to boast of future riding engagements to anyone.

8

Jos could scarcely believe how raw and tender he felt next morning when he got out of bed. He found the business of bending and stretching to put his clothes on extremely uncomfortable, and he tried to avoid Okoko's questioning and sardonic eye as he carefully eased his way into his shorts. When he was ready to walk up to the Mess for breakfast he did so with a fragile and elderly looking gait. As he entered the dining room George, the Quartermaster, formerly Infantry Sergeant Major, raised his large red face from his cornflakes and said

'Cor, look at Gordon Bleeding Richards. You should take the horse out of there now, Jos,' and here he pointed with his spoon between Jos's aching thighs.

'Not feeling so good today, old chap?' enquired Billy Rogers smugly through a mouthful of bacon and eggs.

It was a practice parade for the Brigadier's Inspection that morning, and Jos had to lead his company while the Company Commander and the other Company Commanders watched and criticized with the Colonel. Jos had to abandon any fragile or elderly "saving" of his tender thighs and aching muscles as he engaged in a quick march, slow march, halt, about turn, salute with one's sword, eyes' right and so forth. After the parade the Commanding Officer sent for all the officers and warrant officers and gave them his critical appraisal of the performance of each company. This was an exercise the Colonel much enjoyed. It was the sort of thing he indulged in after almost every activity of the battalion, trotting out the clichés with relish, and occasionally jolting his audience with the shrewdness of some of his comments.

Jos was standing beside Major Hamilton and CSM Roberts

when the Colonel got to D Company in his review of the morning's proceedings.

'Not too bad a show, Hammy: have to watch the dressing of your number one platoon at the eyes' right. The Platoon Sergeant looks as if he's been burning the candle at both ends: he'll have to mind his Ps and Qs. Oh and one last thing: the subaltern acting as Company Commander seems to be suffering from lumbago.'

As Jos and his Company Commander walked back to D Company Major Hamilton enquired acidly, 'What the hell is wrong with you today? You heard what the Colonel said about your personal drill: it pulled the whole company's performance down. And another thing, I hear you made a fool of yourself with that wreck of a car you bought off the RSM.'

Major Hamilton and his wife had both had to miss the reception, being smitten that day with the amoebic dysentery to which the inhabitants of Kebira were from time to time liable and which caused them to stay within running distance of a lavatory or dry closet – the baian gidda, literally the 'behind the house'.

'I'm a bit stiff from riding sir.'

'Well you'd better get yourself in better condition.' Hamilton retorted sourly.

For the rest of the morning Jos was engaged in supervising the kitting out of a new intake of recruits. So far as his battered thighs and buttocks were concerned this was fairly restful. The important thing was to keep an eye on the Regimental Quartermaster Sergeant to make sure he did not short-change the Company in his auctioneer-type patter of 'two pairs shorts, khaki, soldiers for the use of' etc. by the simple device of dishing out only one pair khaki shorts for the use of the particular bewildered bamboozled recruit who was having an abundance of clothing beyond his wildest imaginings piled up beside or upon him. But after the exertions of the morning parade Jos found that even the effort of moving gingerly about among the recruits and the piles of boots and clothing was uncomfortable: he decided that he could not face the prospect of straddling a horse that afternoon. There was a simple way out. All he had to do was to pretend that he had been unable to get one of the

Mess ponies at such short notice: he would go down in his car to the Residency to tell Jane this, taking his swimming things with him in case there was still the chance of the swim.

Festus, having heard about the horn episode, had been much intrigued, and while Jos was on parade had come down to his house, charged up the battery and fiddled happily with the wiring, causing the horn to go into the 'on' position again, the lights to go on and not switch off and then to switch off and refuse to come on. After an hour or two he declared himself satisfied and assured a sceptical Okoko that 'She be fine fine mato again now.' And with that he returned to the lorry – laden with passengers – on the engine of which he had been working when he heard news of 'de mato she cry'.

Accordingly, after his siesta, Jos got into the car and drove down to the Residency. His heart failed him a little as he chugged along the magnificent sweeping driveway down which he had so recently been pushed. But the possibility of going swimming with Jane sustained him. He parked the car a little to the side of the splendid doors of the Residency and went up to ring the bell.

A tall distinguished-looking Hausaman opened the door and told him that the ladies were having tea on the terrace, but that he would announce him. In a moment he returned and ushered Jos through the hallway and out to the terrace at the back of the house. Mrs Joynstone looked up over the fine china teacup from which she was sipping tea with lemon.

'Aha the demon horseman!' she cried. 'Wait a minute: I thought you were going hacking with Jane. You're in the wrong rig for that.'

Jos looked down at his shorts and sandals.

'Well that's what I've come down to tell Jane. I couldn't get the use of a Mess Stable pony this afternoon.'

'Bad luck!' Mrs Joynstone sympathized.

'Oh that is a shame,' said Jane.

'Yes I felt jolly fed up about it,' Jos lied cheerfully.

There was a pause while with varying degrees of sincerity they each contemplated this misfortune. Jos was wondering how he could prompt Jane to suggest that they might just as well now devote the afternoon to swimming. But he reckoned without Mrs Joynstone. With a snap of her fingers she exclaimed.

'I have it. This will be a grand opportunity for you and Fireater to get to know each other.' Whereupon she rang a little hand bell vigorously, and the tall Hausaman appeared again.

'Ahmadu, kawo doki Fireater yanzu,' she commanded.

Ahmadu bowed and withdrew.

Jos could scarcely credit the unfortunate and inexorable turn which events had now taken. Afar off, it seemed to him, he was hearing Mrs Joynstone counselling and advising him.

'Now I don't want you to ride Fireater too hard – just a bit of cantering and trotting – so you two get to know each other. Besides,' and here Mrs Joynstone permitted herself a guffaw, 'You'll probably find it pretty sore riding Fireater in shorts and sandals!'

She chuckled a little at the humour of this as she polished off the last of the biscuits and finished her cup of tea. Then pushing the cup away from her she stood up and said

'We may as well go to meet them. Ahmadu will be bringing Fireater round to the front door.'

Mrs Joynstone led the way with her brisk, slightly mannish stride. Jane followed her, looking very neat and pretty in a blouse and jodhpurs. Jos hobbled on behind. They waited outside the front door for a moment or two. Then round the side of the house came Ahmadu followed by a doki-boy leading a large handsome chestnut horse. Jos's heart quailed as he looked at the height of the saddle above the ground: it quailed still further as he caught a glance of the wicked-looking eyes of the beast. Another doki-boy appeared with Jane's little black pony. Jane went forward and swung nimbly into the saddle. Jos noted that his own stiff sore legs seemed to be moving forward in the direction of Fireater. He found himself standing beside it, with the reins in one hand, looking hopelessly at the animal's haunches. He took a deep breath: one, two, three . . . . Just then a bloodcurdling whine ripped the peace of the afternoon. Fireater, with a massive rearing pulled his head away from Jos's feeble grasp, and kicking a great cloud of dust in the eyes of all those present, bolted off down the driveway.

In a second the entrance area seemed full of Africans all talking and gesticulating excitedly: men, women and children; and also chickens, dogs and cats. Jane's pony had half-reared a little too but she and the doki-boy had managed to contain it and to calm it down. Fireater's doki-boy had rushed off to the Residency stables to get another mount with which to pursue Fireater. Mrs Joynstone was beside herself with vexation, shooing children away from her recently trampled flower beds, and looking anxiously down the driveway whither Fireater had galloped.

Jos, after the first few seconds of relief at the dramatic disappearance of his immediate worry, realized that he had a new and damaging problem on his hands. It was the car horn again. Stealthily he sidled over to it, propped up the bonnet and felt with his hands in the general area in which he had seen the technical college lecturer grope when he had yanked out the offending wire. It must be this one, he concluded, quickly pulled at it and slammed the bonnet shut almost in the same movement. But he deceived no-one. It was obvious what the noise had been, and several of the children were now clapping their hands and jumping up and down with excitement shouting 'De mato she cry.'

Mrs Joynstone glared at Jos savagely and snapped the one word 'Idiot!' before stumping into the house. Jane handed the reins of her pony over to the doki-boy and came over to Jos.

'Don't be too upset,' she said. 'Her huffs never last long – and you didn't really want to ride Fireater in the Silver Cup did you?'

'No,' Jos shuddered emphatically. 'Be sure to see that her huff lasts at least as long as until next Saturday.'

'OK,' Jane grinned. 'I'd better go now and see how she is. Perhaps I'll see you at the cinema show on Sunday night? We might be able to fix something up about a swim then.'

Jos got into his car. To his relief it started without too much difficulty, and he chugged off down the drive. About two hundred yards along the main road he saw Fireater's doki-boy leading him and the horse he had ridden out on in pursuit. Fireater raised his upper lip in a disdainful and malevolent way as the little car went by. Jos was careful to give the horses a wide berth, and he got up to the barracks without further mishap. Okoko was in the little backroom of the gidda in which he did the ironing of the clothes: he was singing cheerily to himself.

'You have nice swim sah?' he asked.

'No.' Jos replied sourly.

'Dat gel foh Babbanbature's House she treat you bad sah?'

'No.'

Okoko shrugged as he saw that the effort to make conversation was yielding no return. He went on with the ironing and sang now very much under his breath. And then he clapped his hand to his brow in an elaborate pantomime of having remembered something.

'Sah I did forget,' he exclaimed. 'Mistah Lawson he come and tell me dat you go be duty hapsa foh next weekend sah. He give dis paper foh you and he say dat you be bery pleased.'

Okoko held out hopefully the battalion orders for the day which fixed the duty officers for the next three weekends. Jos read his name glumly and muttered viciously to himself

'Bugger it!'

Okoko watched him attentively and then cocking his head interrogatively he ventured, 'Sah I no tink you be bery pleased?'

'Okoko,' said Jos. 'You have, as usual, put it in a nutshell.'

With that he went off bad-temperedly up to the mess for a drink before changing for dinner. Okoko unplugged the iron thoughtfully whispering to himself 'Nuts – Nutshell?' He shrugged his shoulders in despair at the peculiarities of the English language. He looked round for Ali the small-boy.

'Ali,' he called peremptorily. 'Why you no heah when dat I want you? Go put dese clothes foh my mitre's bedroom. And dis iron, Ali: it no stay heah. You must make all daidai now. Quick-quick.'

Okoko always made a point of speaking to Ali in English, a language Ali understood only imperfectly. In this way he was able to maintain his position of superiority over Ali. Hausa was Ali's native language and in it he would have had the edge over Okoko, who was an Idoma. Okoko watched Ali reflectively as the Small-Boy hung up the ironed and starched khaki drill for use the following day and laid out the clothes Jos would be wearing for dinner that evening.

'Dese European Hapsas, Ali,' he said. 'Sometimes I tink dey be bushmen proppa.'

9

Jos had one weekend free before the one for which he had – unnecessarily as it now turned out – contrived to be duty officer. On the Sunday he went to the tin-roofed cinema in the Sabongari, ostensibly to see a dated musical comedy but really in the hope of seeing Jane. He had kept hugging to himself her whispered words about seeing him and fixing up arrangements for swimming. He left the Mess immediately after dinner and went on his own to his gidda leaving the other subalterns dawdling over their coffee: he didn't want to arrive at the cinema in a gang with all the rest of the army officers. With this idea in mind he decided to take the narrow footpath which led from his house to the Gari. By the time he set off night had fallen and he needed a torch to pick out the entrance to this narrow track. It was fringed by thick tall grasses, and as Jos walked quickly along it the shadows of the grasses fell before the beam of his torch like black snakes tumbling on top of each other. Jos was never entirely free from the thought that some of these might in fact be snakes, and it was with relief that he at last emerged into the Gari with its strange mixture of shanty type house: some made of wood and corrugated iron, others – like the old city of Kebira – of mud. The path in fact led more or less into the courtyard of one of these mud houses. Jos stepped diffidently round an elderly woman who was stooped over a small wood fire cooking the evening meal for the inhabitants of the house. He pressed on, past the Shebeen from which already the sounds of revelry were coming.

Jos entered the cinema, noting with satisfaction that none of the other officers had arrived yet. He took his seat at the back, next the aisle, from which he could observe people coming in, and take any necessary avoiding or intercepting action. For ten minutes or so no Europeans at all came. The front seats, however, were quickly filling up with Africans. Jos, who in his very recent student days, had been an active campaigner for human rights without discrimination on grounds of creed, colour, etc. regarded the scene developing before him with unease. He tried to still his qualms with the thought that what he was witnessing was simply an economic division which happened to fall on lines of colour. And here indeed was Captain Isa of the native authority police and his wife, sitting prominently and a little self-consciously among the seats which were normally occupied by the Whites. What one never saw was the reverse: the European who was so poor or so indifferent to the status which his white skin gave him that he would seat himself among the laughing, jostling Africans with their different smells of sweat and sharp perfumes.

The Resident's party arrived. The Resident himself sat beside Mrs Isa and engaged her in conversation. Jane was seated between the Resident and his wife. Jos had a good view of the nape of her neck since she had done her hair up in a new style, swept up to the top of her head. It was an admirable nape, and Jos contemplated it with pleasure while he speculated on the best way of contriving the vital few words with her without getting involved with her aunt. He heard the mirthless, loud laugh of Billy Rogers in the lobby, and he slipped out of view by pretending to look for something under his seat. When he poked his head up again he saw, to his annoyance, that Rogers, Dainton and Lawson had filed into the row behind the Resident and that the lecherous Dainton was already leaning forward and talking to Jane.

'Why there's poor Jos all by himself: let's go and sit by him.'

The voice was that of Elaine, Major Hamilton's wife. Jos got up as they approached and ushered them into his row. They sat down on his right hand side, and Elaine began to talk until the film began – and indeed whispered a few distracting comments during the performance itself. Jos cursed this involvement with the Hamiltons: he would have to disengage from them in his attempts to snatch a word with Jane as the audience filed out. As the film plodded its way to its obvious conclusion, Jos began to realize how difficult disengagement from the Hamiltons – from Elaine at any rate – was going to be. He recalled that one of the slanders against her was that she was said to have a weakness for young subalterns: he had rather dismissed this as wishful thinking on Billy Rogers' part, but as she leaned heavily and unnecessarily over to him in order to make some fatuous remark Jos began to credit it. However, he thought, this is not the time or the place to see what comes of that. As the final credits appeared on the screen and the audience rose to its feet to stand to attention for the playing of the national anthem, Jos focussed on the immediate problem. He must delay the exit of the Hamiltons from his row near the back until the Resident's party had progressed up the aisle sufficiently far for the two groups to mingle and exchange pleasantries. Oh God, Mrs Joynstone was moving so slowly for once: don't let her talk to anyone.

'Come on Jos, the show's over – don't you want to let us go?' This archly from Mrs Hamilton.

'Oh I'm sorry: I think I've dropped something down here.' Again Jos made great play with a lost something under his seat.

'Look what the bloody hell are you up to? You were grubbing about on the ground when we came in.' There was nothing arch about this irritable query from Major Hamilton.

'I'm sorry, sir. It's a sort of well, handkerchief.' Jos stalled frantically as he tried to gauge out of the corner of his eye how far the Joynstones had advanced up the aisle. Now for it.

'Ah well can't be helped,' he said suddenly rising up as Mrs Joynstone quickened her pace. He stepped rapidly out into the aisle and beckoned impatiently for Mrs Hamilton to emerge.

'No wait a minute,' said Mrs Hamilton. 'Now that you mention it I had a handkerchief – one of those lace ones Auntie Dolly gave me last Christmas. I must have dropped it.' And Mrs Hamilton began to poke about with her feet and to peer in between the seats.

'No, no – there's nothing there,' said Jos desperately as the Joynstone party drew level and threatened to pass by. To his vexation he saw that Jane was laughing animatedly at some remark of Dainton's.

'I'm positive there's nothing there,' he said as he daringly stepped back into the row and taking Mrs Hamilton by the elbow practically bundled her out into the aisle. He was uneasily aware that Major Hamilton seemed to have gone to ground between the seats, but here he was beside Jane at last. She looked straight through and out the other side of him and passed on. Jos's heart froze with disappointment. And then he realized that a piece of crumpled paper had been pressed firmly into his hand. A wave of hope and relief broke over him – just as well because things were now deteriorating on the Hamilton front.

'But I must have dropped it somewhere,' Mrs Hamilton was wailing as she stood unhappily in the aisle.

'You undoubtedly did my dear,' replied Major Hamilton emerging breathless and red in the face from his search beneath the seats. 'And here it is – Auntie Dolly's lace handkerchief. I'm afraid I didn't see Jos's "sort of handkerchief" which he was so concerned over that he spent most of the evening fussing over it. But here is this actual handkerchief of yours, my dear.'

Major Hamilton delivered this, torn between the pleasure of indulged sarcasm and a general feeling of irritation against Jos. Jos smiled feebly, not caring about either the sarcasm or irritation now that he had Jane's crumpled bit of paper in his hand.

As soon as the Hamiltons had departed Jos hurried out of the cinema and off towards the footpath which led to his gidda. He stepped once more through the courtyard of the mud house where all was now silent and deserted. As soon as he had got far enough down the path to feel safely removed from human contact, he stopped and straightened out the crumpled bit of paper, and shining his torch on it read as follows:

Dear Jos,
Auntie still v. worked up about you playing that joke with your car horn. Been going on about it non-stop. Daren't ask you to swim in our pool. Could I come to yours? Thursday? Leave a note in my pigeon hole at the Club by Wednesday.
J.

Jos felt a shiver of excitement and pleasure as he read this. The excitement was partly due to the telegraphic style of the note with its overtones of urgency and secrecy. Reverently he folded the note up and tucked it into his pocket thinking that Thursday might be a particularly good day at the army pool because there was a hockey match on that afternoon which would attract a large number of the army crowd, either as players or spectators. His torch went out for a second as he fumbled with the note and the button of his shirt pocket. When he managed to find the switch again and to press it, it was to discover a large menacing form standing or rather swaying in front of him. Jos recognized it as that of Corporal Bassey, a wild and troublesome corporal in B Company, given to colossal binges which usually ended up with him being reduced in rank again to a private soldier. He was looking at Jos with an unfocussed glare which seemed full of malevolence. He was mumbling something in Ibo and looked as if he were about to lunge at Jos. The physical symptoms of fear hit Jos forcibly: the feeling of his mouth suddenly dry and a trembling in his jaw. But his head was clear and he felt surprisingly calm. He remembered the lecture on military law at cadet school which had stressed the obligation on officers to avoid drunken other ranks off duty: to take particular pains not to allow oneself to be struck by another rank since this could lead to the other rank's court martial. Jos had always felt that even without this altruistic concern for the career prospects of the other rank he would do his best to avoid being struck. So it proved on this occasion. To turn around and run back up the path would be carrying things too far: would be inconsistent with his dignity as a holder of the Queen's Commission – and besides he remembered that Corporal Bassey was the Battalion sprint champion. But he could step aside and let the Corporal have right of way: that would be prudent and justifiable in the circumstances. He heard his voice saying somewhat squeakily, 'Good evening Corporal.'

But before he could step out of the way, Corporal Bassey lunged at or rather collapsed upon him. He was nearly knocked down with the weight but he managed to stay on his feet, supporting the Corporal's limp-feeling form. He put his arm round Corporal Bassey's back in order to get a grip so as to push him off, and found his hands encounter something sticky and warm. It took only a moment for Jos to realize that it was blood. Gently he lowered the Corporal's body to the ground; he lay face downward revealing a hideous gaping hole in the back of his head from which blood had spurted and flowed down his back. He lay very still and his head began to assume an odd broken looking angle in relation to his body. Jos was convinced that he was dead.

And then he did run. He ran on to his gidda and banged on the door of Okoko's little hut beside it. Okoko came out looking stupid with sleep. But he quickly grasped what Jos was saying and he sent Ali off to the Doctor's gidda and he himself ran up to the orderly office to tell the duty officer. Jos remembered that Major Hamilton was field officer for the week and he decided that he ought to be informed at once. He set off for the Hamilton's house.

He was ushered into the sitting room by Mohammed Yola, the ancient retainer who presided over the Hamilton's household. There he discovered Mrs Hamilton looking crossly at her very shapely legs. She brightened for a moment when she heard Mohammed Yola announce 'Second Lieutenant Maclean, Madam' and turned herself and shapely legs towards Jos.

'I've just discovered a ladder in my stockings,' she said roguishly – and then cried, 'Good Heavens, Jos, whatever's the matter. You look terrible.'

Joss first, irrelevant thought was what on earth is she wearing stockings in this sweltering heat for. His second was to remember that Elaine was renowned for her sensitive disposition. He recalled the "dreadful strain" it had been under on the day of Fifi's disappearance. The bald announcement that he had just bumped into a severely wounded and probably dead soldier was not going to go down well with her or, when he heard of this brutal breaking of news, with her husband.

'I was really just wanting a word with the Company Commander,' he faltered lamely.

'But you've only just seen him!'

With that the door opened and Major Hamilton came into the room.

'What the blazes is wrong now?' he barked out.

'Could I see you alone sir?'

Major Hamilton took in Jos's strained looks and ashen

75

colouring. He turned to his wife,

'Darling, could you leave us for a moment? I expect Jos has come to tell me some beastly, boring piece of shop.'

Elaine went off frowning, looking as if her sensitive constitution might suffer damage also as a consequence of tortured curiosity.

'What is it then?' Major Hamilton asked gruffly. 'I hope it justifies you coming in here at this time of night and frightening my wife half out of her wits.'

'I met Corporal Bassey of B Company on my way back from the cinema, and I think . . . well I think he's been killed.'

'You mean he was lying inert on the road? He's often like that when drunk. Was there any blood?'

'There was blood – a wound in the back of the head. He collapsed on to me. He wasn't lying down when I came upon him.'

'Some drunken brawl I suppose, where was it – outside the Shebeen?'

'No sir. On the little path between my house and the Gari.'

'What a damn silly way for you to go at night. Have you told anyone else yet?'

'Yes sir. My batman is telling the duty officer and the Medical Officer. I thought I should let you know as field officer of the week.'

Major Hamilton looked at Jos for a moment or two curiously.

'All right,' he said. 'We'd better go and see what's happening.'

He went to the door of the sitting room and called along the corridor to the room which the Hamiltons had rather grandly dubbed 'The Nursery' to which Mrs Hamilton had apparently withdrawn.

'Elaine darling,' he called. 'Jos and I have got to go off on a tiresome little chore. I'll be back soon.'

'Oh Timmy,' Elaine cried, emerging from her sanctuary. 'What is all this mystery? Do tell me. Now I'll be worried to death in case you are going to be in danger.'

Major Hamilton managed a derisive and presumably reassuring laugh.

'Not a bit my pet. Just one of the soldiers got himself into a spot of bother.'

Major Hamilton pecked his wife affectionately on the cheek.

Jos and Hamilton then stalked off in silence down the main road, down the turning to Jos's house and then up the footpath towards the Gari. They heard voices ahead of them and soon came upon the medical officer and the duty officer kneeling by the body examining it by the light of a hurricane lamp. Okoko and the Doctor's orderly stiffened to attention as Major Hamilton approached. The duty officer got to his feet and saluted: it was Grimshaw one of the few regular army subalterns – a full Lieutenant – seconded to the Battalion.

'Is he dead?' Hamilton asked.

'As the dodo,' replied Dixon, the Medical Officer. Dixon was a national service captain. Like all the doctor national servicemen he had been given his commission after a short (six week) spell of familiarization with the army's curious square-bashing ways. Dixon had continued to ply his medical trade ever since, mildly amused, sometimes irritated by having to wear a uniform and conform at any rate to some extent to the army's odd rituals. The general service officers – and particularly the other national service ones – regarded the medical officers with a mixture of envy and contempt. Envy because they had been given their commissions on a plate and had not had to endure the physical ordeals of the parade ground or the assault course or the teasing trial of the war office selection board. Contempt because, despite the two or three pips on their shoulders (contrasted with the hard earned one pip of the ordinary national service officer) they looked so scruffy and ill at ease in their uniforms.

Dixon got up slowly from the body and pushed his spectacles back up to the bridge of his nose. They were always falling down and giving him an even less military bearing than the usual run of national service Doctors. Major Hamilton noted with distaste that one of the legs of the spectacles was still held in place by some grubby looking elastoplast: they'd been broken for about eight weeks. Also the man's rig was intolerable even for off duty on a Sunday evening: a soiled cream coloured blouse – you couldn't call it a shirt, a pair of very baggy grey flannels and dirty mosquito boots. My God the fellow had a batman hadn't he?

'I think it must have been one of those machete sort of things they hack at the undergrowth with,' said Dixon now taking off the offending spectacles and breathing on them before polishing them on his shirt (or blouse) and putting them back on. Jos had noticed that Dixon always did this when about to offer the world one of his opinions.

'The footsteps seem to lead away from the Gari. There's no blood until about this area here where he lies – which suggest it was about here that he was struck, but as you can see he must have managed to turn round and he seems to have fallen back up the way he was coming. In fact it looks as if he fell on his assailant. Jos, I couldn't quite make out from your batman how you came into all this: he said something about you being all bloody with shifting the body.'

'Well it was me he fell on to.'

'But that's extraordinary. Didn't you see it happen then? I mean he couldn't have lived more than a few seconds with that wound. It's done terrible damage to his skull.'

Jos suddenly felt a coldness at his heart and the saliva drying in his mouth.

Major Hamilton however was beginning to feel that the medical officer's forensic speculation was somewhat out of order.

'Well we'll soon get to the bottom of all that Dixon,' he said sharply, 'when the police arrive, you just make sure you know what's what on the medical side. You'd better not shift the body until they get here. You've notified the native authority police I take it Grimshaw?'

'Yes sir.'

'Get the bugle sounded to summon the riot squad. Once you've got them at the guardroom throw a cordon round the barracks with them and the guard platoon. Get them to round up for questioning anyone trying to get in or out of the army lines.'

'Sir.' Grimshaw saluted and set off for the guardroom.

Jos looked with surprise and, perhaps for the first time, with something akin to respect at his Company Commander. Perhaps these regular soldiers were incisive and decisive when there really was something to be done instead of exercises to be invented and enacted.

More lights and voices were coming along the track, and soon there appeared Captain Isa of the native authority police and his European Adviser, Mr Carne, a former Provost Marshall in the British Army. They were accompanied by two or three constables.

'I say – steady on.' Dixon greeted them. 'If you chaps come charging along the track like that you'll destroy any clues.'

Major Hamilton rounded on him.

'Dixon, I've already asked you to confine your attention to medical matters. Captain Isa and Mr Carne are experienced police officers and do not require advice from you on how to conduct an investigation.'

Jos held his breath while Dixon cheekily muttered, 'Oh well don't say I didn't warn you.'

'Evenin' Major Hamilton,' said Captain Isa. 'Most distressin' dis kind ting.' His kindly face was puckered with concern.

'Hello, Hammy,' said Mr Carne. 'I hear it's that blackguard Bassey. By Christ he had something like this coming to him if ever any one had.'

The delayed shock seemed to be affecting Jos now. He watched with the feeling of being in a dream as Carne and the medical officer talked together over the position of the body, the footprints, the blood. He felt himself swaying slightly, and then a firm hand at his elbow and Major Hamilton's voice softly in his ear, 'I don't know what this is all about. Just be careful what you say. Don't volunteer any information. And come on down now to the Mess and have something to drink.'

Neither Captain Isa nor Mr Carne seemed to have any objections to the senior officer and Jos withdrawing from the scene, and they walked over to the Mess where the Mess sergeant was on duty by himself. Major Hamilton ordered two large whiskies. Jos felt the neat whisky burn its way down his throat. He looked up from the brown-amber liquid left in the glass to the brown-amber eyes of Major Hamilton boring into him.

'Now you had better tell me what this is all about,' he said.

'These police boys will be asking you some pretty awkward questions very shortly. You had better get it clear in your own mind what you are going to say. How did you come to be using that footpath?'

'It is actually the quickest way from the Gari to my house.'

'Do you usually go that way?'

'No I usually go along the main road and on down via the Mess.'

'But not tonight.'

'No.'

'Do you usually go alone after a cinema show?'

'No.'

'But you did tonight?'

'Yes.'

'Why?'

'Well it's rather a complicated story. I just, well I just wanted to.'

'What were you looking for under the cinema seats?'

'Well nothing really.'

'What were you doing then?'

'The first time I was hiding.'

'Hiding? who from?'

'Well that's rather complicated too sir. I find it difficult to explain. But I assure you it's all very innocent. I hardly knew Corporal Bassey. It's nothing to do with me.'

'Who were you hiding from the second time? Was Bassey in the cinema – that can be checked you know.'

'I don't know if he was in the cinema. I had no interest in him.'

'Did you have a torch with you?'

'Yes sir.'

'What was Bassey doing when you first saw him?'

'I thought he was going to attack me.'

'And what did you do?'

'I said 'Good evening Corporal'.'

'Oh Jos you'll have to do better than that. Look I heard Carne and the medical officer discussing the footprints in relation to the striking of the fatal blow. Apparently yours seem to have come to a halt just at the point the blow was struck –

and there don't seem to be any other recent footprints on the path either coming down from the Gari or leading up from where the house is. In other words the footprints are consistent with you coming upon Bassey from behind, delivering the blow and then struggling with him when he turned round. Is that what happened?'

'Good God no.'

'No I didn't think so. But you'll have to be very careful when Carne starts cross-questioning you. In fact you had better not say anything until we can get a lawyer to look after you. There is a Captain O'Kane at Div HQ whom I think I could get to act for you.'

'But sir this is ridiculous: I just happened to find Bassey. I mean it's nothing to do with me.'

'Was he dead when you found him?'

'No.'

'Was he dead when you left him?'

'I think so.'

'Well then innocent or not, you've got some explaining to do. Didn't you hear or see anyone else?'

'Well I wasn't really paying attention.'

'How do you mean? Why not?'

Jos took a deep breath. Things were now looking so ugly that he decided he had better tell Hamilton about trying to fix a date with Jane. But before he could say anything there was a swish of the bead curtains which hung between the entrance hall and the ante-room, and Captain Isa and Mr Carne came in. The former was sweating with embarrassment. Carne was looking like a bird of prey.

'Maclean, I think we had better take a statement from you,' he said. 'Your account of finding Bassey doesn't seem to tally very well with the medical evidence. Could we just have it again. And I should warn you that this is a formal statement and that you should realize that what you say may be used in evidence against you.'

'I don't quite like the way you put that Carne,' said Major Hamilton. 'But since you have put it like that it would clearly be fairer to Mr Maclean if he were allowed legal advice before answering. It has been a frightful shock to him having this chap collapse on to him – and as his superior officer I am quite clear that he is in no fit state to be interrogated at the moment.'

'But I can't do myself any harm by telling the truth,' said Jos desperately trying to break through the veils of doubt which had begun to enmesh him. 'It's nothing to do with me.'

'Captain Isa,' said Hamilton turning to the fat little African. 'I must request you to order Mr Carne not to take a statement from this young officer while he is in his present distressed condition and is without the benefit of a legal adviser.'

Captain Isa looked even more unhappy and embarrassed than before. The notion of ordering Carne to do anything was obviously excruciating. It was clear that the "adviser" to a large extent ran the show, an arrangement which suited both Carne and Isa. Carne was a natural bully and workaholic. Isa was naturally lazy and pleasure-loving with no great taste for police work, but enjoying the perquisites of office which seemed to flow from his appointment to commissioned rank. Carne saved the situation.

'All right, Hammy,' he said. 'But I must ask you to put Lieutenant Maclean under house arrest.'

'Certainly,' said Hamilton.

With some heel clicking and saluting the police officers departed, and Hamilton and Jos were left alone in the ante-room again.

'Don't look so glum Jos. We'll get all this straightened out. You'd better come back with me tonight: we'll make up a bed for you at my house. Tomorrow we'll get one of the other subalterns to move in to your house with you as chaperon.'

With the growing feeling of being in a nightmare Jos followed Major Hamilton as he led the way back to his house. Elaine was waiting for them, in a fetching dressing gown which indicated the delightful contours of her womanly figure – and in a state of great excitement. Hamilton was at his most masterful with the anxious little woman.

'Just a spot of bother down at Jos's house. I'll explain it all later. Jos will have to stay with us just for tonight.'

Elaine brightened for a second at this news – but only for a second when she noted the jaded, unhappy look on Jos's face. She summoned Mohammed Yola who led Jos to the spare room. There he quickly undressed and slipped – in his under-clothes – under the white mosquito net. He lay on top of the sheets staring up at the thatch roof. How on earth could things have changed so quickly that he found himself under some degree of suspicion for murder? Was it only a couple of hours ago that the extent of his worries had been the fixing of a date with a girl?

10

Sleep would not come. Jos kept going over and over in his mind the incidents which had led to his present plight. As he lay brooding he became aware of a light knocking noise on the shutters. He got up to see what it was, and when he pulled aside the shutters he discovered Okoko's worried face.

'Mitre,' Okoko enquired anxiously. 'Why you no go come fo' yo' own house?'

Jos was immensely pleased to see Okoko. He noted affectionately Okoko's curious pronunciation of master: it always came out as mitre, and caused Jos to think of himself as being in some way invested with the dignity of a Prince of the Church.

'I've been put under house arrest, Okoko: that means I've got to stay with another officer – or another officer has to stay with me.'

'Why dey do dis ting to you, sah?'

'Oh it's just while they find out about what happened to Corporal Bassey, Okoko.'

'Dey tink YOU go kill um?'

'Well I was the last to see him alive. They've got to find out what happened.'

'I find out sah.'

Jos looked at Okoko intently. A source of many minor irritations and misunderstandings between him and his batman had been Okoko's tendency to confuse "find" and "look for". Thus the announcement by Jos that he had lost his fountain pen or his watch was often cheerfully greeted by Okoko with the words 'I find um sah', when what he meant was that he would go and look for the missing objects. What did he mean this time, Jos wondered.

'You mean you know something?'

'I know who go kill um.'

Jos could not now keep down the great surge of relief which these words brought. But he realized that there might be great difficulties still ahead. How could Okoko know? Why hadn't he said anything when the police officers were by the body? Did he have evidence? Would it be strong enough to weigh with Mr Carne?

'How do you know? Who was it?'

'Dat gardener man sah. De one in de gidda next to my own.'

Jos thought for a moment and then identified in his mind the person Okoko meant. He was a tall, elderly Hausaman with a brutal and rather bashed in looking face. He had lately taken a young, plump wife who always smiled warmly at Jos when he passed by the gardener's house. Rumour had it that she smiled a little too warmly at too many soldiers and that Yesufu – the old gardener – was given to beating her up every now and then for her flirtatious ways. Jos remembered that the last time he had gone past their tiny round house Yesufu was looking particularly brutal and grim and the young wife was swollen-faced with weeping.

'Dis ebening, sah, after you go to de cinema: kai! de palaver with Yesufu an his ooman. He go find out dat Corporal Bassey come to his house fo' morning time when he is working in de Hapsas' Mess garden. And he beat her and he beat her. I tink she go die he beat her so much. Den he find out dat dis ebening when he go to see a friend in de old city dat Bassey go come to his house. He go take machet and he go wait fo' Corporal Bassey in de long grass by the path from de Sabongari. Den when de Corporal go come he chop him down one time.'

'And you knew this all the time?'

'Yes, sah, but I no want to say. Dat Yesufu go make big palaver with me if I go tell. He go kill me.'

'But you must tell. The police will see that Yesufu does not harm you. And anyhow I will have to tell now. We shall have to prove it, Okoko. What is it makes you so sure Yesufu is the killer?'

'Because I hear him beat and beat dat ooman of his. I know dat Corporal Bassey want to go come dis ebening fo' his house.

85

Dat's how I know.'

'But you didn't actually see Yesufu set off or hide himself with the machete in the long grass – or come back again?'

'No, sah. I go to bed after the woman stop crying. I go catch sleep. Den you come and say dat you find dead man. When dat I see it is Corporal Bassey I know Yesufu go kill um.'

'Where is Yesufu now?'

'Is in his house asleep with his woman.'

'What about the machete? Was it the one which always stands outside the door of Yesufu's gidda?'

'No sah. I no tink he use dat one. I tink he go take one from the shed in Hapsas' mess garden, and come through from dat side to de path and den go wait-wait fo' Corporal Bassey.'

Jos could see that it might be difficult to prove a case against the old gardener on the basis of Okoko's surmises. But at least this began to make sense of the crime. Here was a motive, means and a likely suspect. It was good of Okoko to have come to see him and to give him this information. He recalled again Yesufu's harsh, baleful face. He could well understand how frightened Okoko must be at the thought of making an enemy of him: indeed he would now be literally risking his life in doing so.

'Thank you, Okoko. I'll be back at my own gidda tomorrow I expect. I think they'll move someone in with me rather than remove me from the scene of the crime. Anyhow my gidda's a bit bigger than most of the others. And then you'll have to help me prove that I didn't kill Corporal Bassey.'

'I go try fo' you, sah. But I catch fear fo' Yesufu. He be bad man proppa sah. He go chop me and all my piccin.'

'Well go home now and get some sleep. We'll try to sort it out in the morning.'

Jos finally fell into a heavy sleep, and had to be shaken by Mohammed Yola when morning came. His shaving kit was in his own gidda; and in his crumpled civilian clothes of the evening before, his face unshaven, he felt ill at ease as he sat at breakfast with the Hamiltons. His heart was a good deal lighter, though, as a consequence of Okoko's disclosure of the previous evening, and he was able to put a relatively brave face on things. Major Hamilton, immaculately turned out in his crisp, fresh uniform, and Elaine, becomingly attired in a summer frock, were each impressed by the stiff (albeit unshaven) upper lip Jos was displaying. Major Hamilton decided to adopt what he considered a benign, jocular role.

'Eat up, my boy,' he said, pushing a mound of buttered toast towards Jos. 'Never let it be said that the condemned man was not offered a hearty breakfast!'

'That's not very nice of you, Timmy,' Elaine chided. She had now been told the reason for Jos's House Arrest, and it had had the effect of stimulating her latent – and normally well controlled – desire for Jos. She regarded his unshaven jaw a little breathlessly, wondering if he could really have struck that huge black soldier, and then, her eye catching his for a second, she felt a rush of protective, almost maternal sentiment at the thought of the poor boy in such danger. She had not enjoyed a breakfast so much for years.

Once they had all finished, Major Hamilton announced briskly that he would walk down to Jos's gidda with him and that he would arrange for a soldier to be posted on guard during the day and for one of the other subalterns to be moved into Jos's house to provide the appropriate custodial presence during the night.

As they were approaching Jos's house they became aware of a loud commotion, anguished shrieks and cries in a high pitched female voice. These, it was soon clear, were issuing from the wildly flailing body of the young wife of Yesufu the gardener. Okoko came running to explain to Jos that she had just heard the news – while bathing her bruised and swollen face at the pump – of her lover's violent death; and was now in a state of desperate and abandoned grief. Major Hamilton surveyed her with distaste, Jos with keen interest and a growing sense of hope: this exhibition fitted in well with Okoko's explanation of the previous evening. He had not yet said anything to Major Hamilton about this, however. Some instinct urged him to wait until he had more in the way of proof and until he did not have to rely on Okoko's unsubstantiated and vulnerable theorizing.

It was ludicrous to find himself confined to his house: he established, before Major Hamilton left, that once the guard had been posted, he could at least walk about the compound, and not literally be shut up indoors. Even so it was a wearisome day. Okoko brought his lunch down from the Mess with an exaggerated show of contempt for and distress over the whole affair: but also with a degree of nervousness as he glanced at the gardener's house, from which rather more subdued sounds of weeping and wailing emerged from time to time. Jos was reminded of the Latin word for wailing – ululatus – that was rather what it sounded like, and he recalled another Latin phrase pectora plangere: to beat one's breasts – that was what the poor woman had been doing in her frenzy earlier in the day.

Okoko gave a start at a particularly desperate cry from the gardener's house and nearly spilled the bowl of soup he was setting down. He gave a fearful glance in the direction from which it came.

'Dat Yesufu,' he said as he set the tureen carefully on one side. 'I heah him sah dis morning. He say to his wife dat ifn she go tell she tink he do it, he go kill her one time. And he say it loud sah so dat I go heah him. He mean he go kill me too ifn dat I speak.'

Jos thought about all this carefully as he ate his lunch. He concluded that he must not reveal Okoko's theory about the murder until he could ensure the immediate arrest of Yesufu: the worst outcome would be if Yesufu were to know he was under suspicion and yet still be at large. The image of Yesufu's brutal face kept coming before his mind's eye.

At about three thirty Mr Carne and an African police sergeant arrived to interrogate Jos. Mr Carne presented this as some routine fact-finding which he was unwilling to defer pending the appearance of Jos's legal representative; and he began in a friendly and reasonable style which clearly did not come naturally to him. Jos could tell from the questions that great weight was being placed on the fact that the only recent footprints on the path had been made by Jos and Corporal Bassey. As Carne fastened more and more on this fact, his line and style of questioning became increasingly aggressive.

'What did you do when you were sure that he was dead?' he asked.

There seemed an unpleasant implication in the way the question was put that Jos had made sure that Bassey was dead, but it was a nuance which Jos did not feel he could or should challenge.

'I ran to wake my boy and get him to inform the duty officer and the medical officer,' he replied.

'Why didn't you go straight to the medical officer yourself? This was a crisis, if you had just come upon a dying man – as you claim – was your first duty not to get medical help as quickly as possible? Was it not extraordinary that in these circumstances you preferred to stand on your dignity and get your batman to deliver your calling card on the medical officer?'

Jos sensed the danger he was in. He remembered Major Hamilton's advice about not answering Carne before he had consulted one of the officers in the division's legal department. But what the hell? He still felt confidence in letting his innocence speak: that his strength was as the strength of ten because his heart was pure.

'Well I knew I would have to alert several people, and I thought it best to get my batman to help me.'

But even as he said this Jos wondered why he had acted exactly as he had done. In a way going to Hamilton as field officer of the week had been a refinement. Getting the medical officer to deal with the body and the duty officer to bring in the police were the essential moves. The truth probably was that he had been so shaken by the discovery of the dying man that he instinctively sought the comfort of the people with whom he had closest contact, his batman and his company commander. But he could see that his actions would be made to look peculiar and suspicious.

'And convenient to replace the machete which you used and which you had taken from outside the gardener's house? It was after you had replaced it that you woke up your Boy wasn't it?

Tell me, how did you clean it up? Did you wash off the blood at the pump and then stick it in the earth a few times to restore it to its horticultural appearance? We have examined it carefully – and you seem to have done a good job in removing the evidence. And no prints on it except the gardener's. But then you wore gloves didn't you? I suppose it was one of the gloves you lost under the cinema seats? Our preliminary questioning of people at the cinema show reveals that before the film started and after it ended you were searching frantically for something under your seat – and that you were very mysterious about whatever it was, and denied having found it – whatever it was. And then the timing is about right. If you ran down the path – and your footprints suggest speed – you would just have had time to get the machete and back up again to attack Bassey with it.'

'Of course I ran,' Jos protested. 'I had just seen a man die and I was running for help.'

'Oh I'll bet you ran then too. You had to clean up the machete before anyone else was alerted or came on the scene didn't you?'

Too late Jos realized he should have tried to stop Carne tricking him into this interrogation. He seemed to be caught more and more in a web of suspicious-looking coincidences.

'But what puzzles us, Jos' – the friendly use of the Christian name was at once disarming and yet put Jos on his guard – 'is motive. What did you have in common with Bassey? What did you have against him? Had he some blackmailing hold over you? Have you been sampling the fleshpots of the Sabongari? We know that Bassey had a girl friend in the Gari who hires out her body to paying guests, and that Bassey acted as pimp and sometimes collected for services rendered or to safeguard secrets unwisely confided in the privacy of the girl's bed. Was that it, Jos? Did you short-change Bassey's lady friend – or did she worm out of you some shameful secret? Why don't you get it off your chest? – If that's what happened, I'm sure we can make this a good deal easier for you, provided you co-operate now.'

'Mr Carne,' said Jos with as much dignity and calmness as he could muster. 'I have told you the truth. I scarcely knew

Corporal Bassey. All I did was to come upon him as he was dying from a wound inflicted by somebody else. I think that in view of the way you are conducting this so-called fact-finding investigation I should follow my company commander's advice and should not say another word until I have consulted a lawyer.'

'I see,' said Carne. 'Your theory is death by the hand of some other person or persons unknown. Well I'm sure you're very wise, Mr Maclean, not to say anything else until you have had the advice of a lawyer on your best line of defence. We'll leave you now – but do think about our little talk and how you might make things easier for yourself. We shall be back, depend on that.'

Jos was considerably shaken by this visit from Carne. He was aware that the policeman had not touched on the line of cross-questioning about which Major Hamilton had warned him – that is, why Jos had chosen such a peculiar route to go to and from the cinema. Jos could envisage how Carne would deal with the explanation that he had been trying to keep apart from the other officers in order to have a word in private with the Resident's niece. He could hear Carne's alternately ingratiating and coldly sarcastic voice – 'But you didn't speak to Miss Robbins at all did you, Maclean? We've had statements from several witnesses to the effect that you and she passed each other by at the end of the film without exchanging a word. And you surely weren't expecting to meet the Resident's niece on that path on the way back? Incidentally why did you go back that way. There was no longer a need to keep apart from your chums then was there?'

As Jos brooded in this way he drew some comfort from the thought that Jane would be sure to speak up for him and confirm that they had been wanting to have a private word at the cinema. And oh yes – the note: that would be evidence to help him. But where the hell was it? He could not recall seeing it since the moment Corporal Bassey fell upon him. Had the police picked it up? Were they putting some damning construction on its meaning? Or had it got trampled into the ground and undergrowth and lost or thrown away? He was roused from these worries by a light tapping on the shutters which were half closed to shut out some of the heat but to let in some daylight. He walked over to the window and discovered Major Hamilton's wife, Elaine hovering furtively by it.

'Quick, Jos, let me in,' she said. 'I have only a few minutes and I don't want anyone to know I'm here, but I just had to see you.'

'Come round to the back door then, Elaine. My boy's house looks right on to the front door.'

He went to make sure the inside bolt was undrawn, and in a moment Elaine was standing in his bedroom. She really is a remarkably gorgeous woman, Jos thought to himself, as she seemed to fill the dark little room with her femininity, her tanned bare legs, her neat but buxom figure, her large blue eyes, her mass of blonde hair.

'Oh Jos,' she said. 'I'm so frightened for you. That odious Carne man has been cross-questioning everyone, all about you and what you were doing in the cinema, and whether Bassey used to visit you and if you'd ever been seen having angry words with him. I've been thinking about you every minute of the day and I just had to come to you.'

With that, to Jos's astonishment and alarm – though in fairness to Elaine – also to his sensual delight, she seized his face between her well manicured hands and pulled it down to hers implanting a long and passionate kiss on his lips. Then her arms were round him and she was clinging fiercely to him, and muttering words to the effect that now that he was in such danger she had had to seize this chance to be alone with him.

'Oh I know it's all hopeless,' she was saying. 'I must be ten years older than you, and there's dear Timmy, and the boys at school in England. But oh Jos when I thought that perhaps they would be taking you away and I would not see you again I just had to come and tell you how I feel.'

Despite the awkwardness of his present situation Jos had begun to respond to the apparent passion of Elaine's embraces. But in his mind he knew that this was the last sort of complication needed. He felt a measure of disloyalty to Jane, with whom after all he was trying to develop a boyfriend/ girlfriend relationship, and he went weak at the knees at the thought of how Major Hamilton would react should he discover his wife's incipient infidelity. Elaine's words about him being taken away and her perhaps not seeing him again served as just the douche of cold water required.

'What do you mean?' he asked in alarm, disengaging from the clinging limbs and apparently insatiable mouth.

'Oh nothing, Jos darling. Just silly little me and my worrying about you. Oh Jos I feel so much better now that I've seen you properly. But I must get back now. It'll be all right. I know it will.'

And with that Elaine slipped out the way she had come, by the backdoor. As she did so, she passed the soldier who had been stationed as guard. He was a large, gawky youth who was startled by the vision of the company commander's wife emerging from the gidda. However he must have reckoned that so long as she wasn't accompanied by the officer under house arrest it was none of his business. So he contented himself with a bashful and clumsy salute and a shuffling of his heels to attention, as Elaine sped swiftly back to her house.

Meanwhile down the path to the front door was coming a great procession with maximum commotion. Billy Rogers had been appointed the live-in custodian to effect Jos's house arrest. He seemed to be coming complete with bag and baggage. His batman, Akpan Iwok, and one or two "Small Boys" were transporting his bed, bedding and various other paraphernalia. Billy was enjoying enormously the role assigned to him. And part of the pleasure would be being able to complain about the monstrous inconvenience suffered. He began on this straightaway after Okoko and Akpan Iwok had manoeuvred the bed and mosquito net canopy into the house and positioned it along the wall opposite to Jos's bed. Akpan had placed the small bedside table and reading lamp at one end of the bed.

'Not there, Akpan. It's bad enough having to abandon my elegant little bachelor pad without discovering that my bed light is illuminating my toes.'

Akpan Iwok was a rather elderly soldier, an Ibo, who had a fussy and old-maidish disposition, closely resembling his master's. As a result they tended to spend much of their time in quarrelsome disputation.

'You no like I go put um foh heah, sah?' Akpan asked in

astonishment. 'How can I know you want to lie for de udder way? Sah I tink is better foh de way I put um.'

'Stop bloody arguing, Akpan. I'm bloody telling you which way I go lie for.'

'But sah . . . .'

'But me no buts, Akpan. Just shut up and do what I tell you.'

With much sighing and huffiness, Akpan remade the bed, repositioned the little table and then ceremoniously placed the reading light on top of it. Only then did he permit the flicker of a smile to cross his face as he pointed at the flex which from that end of the bed could not reach the power socket.

'Well why didn't you say so in the first place?' Billy demanded crossly.

'Sah I try go tell you and you say I not to agroo.'

'Oh well have it your own way. Just get this place ship shape as fast as you can . . . . Ah there you are Jos.' Billy gladly sought the diversion presented by Jos looking into the bedroom to see how his custodian was settling in. Billy's voice changed gear with almost an audible click as he turned his attention to Jos.

'How's it going old chap? Look, if there's anything I can do, you know you can count on me. For a kick off I've made it clear I want to take my chop down here with you in the evenings. I was told I could go up to the Mess for dinner, leaving you with a guard posted at the door, but I wasn't having any of that. I mean what the hell are friends for?'

Jos's heart sank twice over. First at the prospect of being subjected to Billy's undiluted company for so long, and second at Billy's use of the plural in referring to evenings.

'Thanks, Billy,' he said. 'I expect it'll all get sorted out by tomorrow.'

'Of course it will, Jos. That's the spirit. Nil desperandum, even if things do look so black.' Billy beamed encouragingly at Jos. Then he frowned for a moment or two and said, 'I suppose the give away is that you were acting so oddly last night: that's what seems to have put the boys in blue on to you.'

'What are you talking about?' Jos asked, a little rattled.

'Just a moment,' Billy replied putting his fingers to his lips with an exaggerated air of confidentiality. Then he turned to

Akpan Iwok who had just completed the rearrangement of the bedding and was switching on and off the bed light.

'That will be all then, Akpan. See that you're down here tomorrow morning at six thirty with my fresh uniform.'

Akpan Iwok shook his head gloomily as if being set an impossible task, and with a weary sigh he shuffled out of the room, looking particularly elderly and weighed down by the responsibility of having to look after such a martinet.

'And Akpan,' Billy called after the little soldier. 'No wild parties in my gidda tonight. I'll KNOW if you have been besmirching my hearth rug with ladies of ill-repute from the Sabongari. In fact I've a good mind to get you to bring my wireless down: I don't want you engaging in high life dancing to the strains of Radio Monrovia into the small hours.'

In spite of his present worries, Jos could not help smiling at this extravagant notion of Billy's: anything less likely it would have been difficult to imagine. Akpan seemed to be of the same mind, and gave Billy a look of weary resignation as he proceeded stolidly up the path, back to his small round house and his rather shrewish wife.

'You see, Jos,' Billy confided, as soon as they were alone. 'We couldn't help but notice how you seemed a bit keyed up and excited at dinner last night and then slipped off without a word. And then using that funny wee path to the Gari – I wouldn't particularly like to go that way even in broad daylight! Even more peculiar was the way you left the cinema – cutting poor Jane dead in your preoccupation, as far as I could see. We all twigged something must be afoot, but God in Heaven – we had no idea . . . . Blackmail was it?'

Billy stretched himself out luxuriously on top of his bed, as he said this, and then lighting a cigarette inhaled deeply and contentedly.

Jos was now becoming seriously alarmed, and also angry. He guessed who had been putting ideas into Carne's head about him frantically searching for something beneath the cinema seats. He felt sick at the incongruous swamp into which he seemed to be sinking. But he was remarkably clearheaded.

I must get in touch with this lawyer chap, Captain O'Kane, as soon as possible, he thought, and discuss with him how best – from my point of view and that of my frightened batman – to get the Police on to the real culprit. In the meantime I must avoid saying anything or getting into any arguments which might have the effect of adding to the circumstantial "evidence" and suspicion. Surely to God, he thought, proper forensic tests should show that the machete by Yesufu's house was not used for the crime, and surely when the murder weapon is found it will point a trail to the murderer. He regarded Billy coldly.

'Billy,' he said, 'if you really think I killed Corporal Bassey – and I can't believe you do – we may have to live together in this house because the police are insisting on it, but I should be grateful if we did not speak about it.'

Billy was taken aback for a moment, and the look of cosy anticipation – of listening to confidences and of offering kindly comfort – vanished from his face. But then a cunning, crafty look took its place.

'Nuff said, old boy. I quite understand. Mum's the word – I'm with you one hundred per cent on this.'

'Oh Jesus!' Jos exclaimed and abruptly strode into his sitting room, leaving Billy reclining on top of the bed puffing complacently at his cigarette. Jos sat at his desk for a while, various thoughts going through his mind. First that the police were going to take some shifting from the case against him to which they seemed to have committed themselves; second that the finding of the murder weapon might be crucial; third that Okoko and Yesufu's wife were in danger if they did anything to put the police on to Yesufu's track while the old gardener was still at large.

Dinner à deux that evening in Jos's gidda was a strained affair, with Billy now taking the huff because his attempts at conspiratorial camaraderie were coldly received by Jos. And Okoko, who had been missing from the compound until just before he had to serve the meal, seemed particularly jumpy. As Okoko was clearing the dishes away, Billy rose from the table and collecting a large book from his bedside stumped off towards the dry closet.

'If it's all the same to you, Jos, I'm going to have a long sordid read in the baian gidda and expect to find it a good deal more entertaining than your company in your present frame of mind. You can't undo what's been done you know: got to start from where you are now.'

As soon as Billy had withdrawn, Okoko whispered urgently to Jos

'Mitre, sah, dis afternoon I go find dat machet dat Yesufu used. I know wher 'e de. But ifn I go tell den Yesufu go chop me and my piccin.'

Jos thought for a few moments. Then he said, 'When the police come again I will tell them all you have told me. And I will insist that when they take you to find the machete they put a guard on your wife and family.'

Okoko looked doubtful. 'But de police no believe you sah. Dey tink you do it. Dey no guard me and my piccin because YOU hask it.'

Jos had to concede that there was something in this. He wondered if he could persuade Major Hamilton to arrange for soldiers from the company to provide the necessary protection. He resolved that he must ask to see his company commander in the morning, and with that resolution he attempted his second night's sleep under suspicion of murder. He was not helped in this by the presence of Billy Rogers in his bedroom. Having eventually returned from the baian gidda (or BG as it was always familiarly styled) with his bulky "Blood and Thunder" novel, Billy propped himself up in bed with many complaints about the exact positioning of the offending reading lamp. He then read for some time, practically chain smoking, and seeking every now and then to involve Jos by commenting on the story and occasionally reading aloud what he deemed particularly juicy passages. He seemed to have got over his spell of huffiness with Jos.

'Just listen to this,' he said stubbing out his current cigarette and sitting up in bed. 'Her breasts and thighs proudly strained against the gossamer-thin night gown as she dared the intruder to touch her. And even as he ripped the flimsy garment from her, revealing her glorious . . . .'

'For Christ's sake shut up, Billy. I'm trying to get to sleep,

97

and it's bad enough with the light on and you bloody smoking all the time without having to listen to that garbage.'

'Sorry old boy. I thought it might cheer you up. Take your mind off things.'

Eventually Billy switched off the reading light and fell quickly asleep. Soon he was snoring loudly. A good deal later Jos too fell asleep.

Akpan Iwok and Okoko both appeared at six thirty – Okoko just unlocking the door and bringing cups of coffee for the two young officers. Little Akpan was all but submerged in Billy's fresh laundered, pressed and starched uniform, boots, hat, belt, puttees etc. When he eventually emerged and began to spread the uniform out on one of the armchairs in the sitting room, he began a litany of complaints.

'I no 'gree foh dis, sah. Is no goo' foh me to have to carry yoh jacket and KD shorts like dis. Dey go get all scrushed.'

'No such word as "scrushed", Akpan,' said Billy smugly as he got out of bed. 'I really do wish you'd make an effort to speak the Queen's English. Anyhow where's my favourite coffee cup? You know I like my morning coffee in it.'

'Sah, how can I get you yoh uniform and you coffee now now? Small time I go catch more coffee foh you in dat cup and bring it foh yoh hoffice.'

Jos could scarcely wait for Billy to get washed, shaved and dressed and off up to the Mess for breakfast. He had decided that he would write a note to Major Hamilton asking him to come and see him or to send an escort of soldiers to bring him up to the company office. But even as he was planning this, events were overtaking him. He was in fact saved from taking any further action by the rage and grief of Bassey's lover, the young wife of the old gardener. After her day of lamentation she had managed to control herself sufficiently to spend the night docilely with Yesufu. But as soon as he had gone off in the morning to his work in the Officers' Mess garden, she ran heedless of Yesufu or the restraining cries of Okoko's wife to the orderly room, and there she threw herself on the duty officer's protection, and through an interpreter, told him that she was sure her husband had killed Corporal Bassey. The duty officer locked her up in the guardroom for her own safety and phoned the police to tell them of this development.

Mr Carne was reluctant to abandon his theory of Jos's guilt. He had already coined the phrase "Mac the Machete" in explaining to an admiring Captain Isa how the murder had been perpetrated. But, given the violence of the young woman's testimony, he could scarcely avoid looking into her accusation, and questioning Yesufu. And once Okoko heard that Yesufu was with the police, he reported his discovery of the machete. It was lying where Yesufu had hidden it loosely covered with the stony, sandy soil and in very dense undergrowth a few hundred yards from where Bassey had been killed. Okoko had thought to look in that area because he knew the Bush was particularly thick at that point and that in the past Yesufu had hidden one or two articles which he had pilfered from the Officers' Mess there. The machete was identified as of the type kept in the shed of the Officers' Mess garden – to which Yesufu alone had the key and the only finger prints on it were Yesufu's. Although a rough and hurried attempt had been made to get rid of the bloodstains and to conceal them with earth there had not been time to do the job properly since Yesufu's main aim had been to get back quickly to his own house before investigations started following the discovery of the body. The blood group of the traces of blood on the machete were the same as Corporal Bassey's. Faced with this battery of evidence Mr Carne had to revise his theory about the murderer – although his first reaction was to try to implicate Okoko in some sort of a cover up for his master. However once his suspicion finally shifted to Yesufu he did not take long to break him down and to extract a full confession from him. Yesufu was driven away that evening to the prison in the old city.

Okoko was jubilant. His young master was free and safe again. He, Okoko, had got rid of a gloomy and undesirable neighbour. Jos was relieved to emerge from the nightmare which had so suddenly and unexpectedly begun to engulf him. Looking back on the events of the previous two days he found himself impressed with the way Major Hamilton had shown himself much more decisive and considerate when there really was something important to do and to worry about. As soon as it became clear that Jos was no longer a suspect, his Company Commander reverted to type, and started to fulminate about what a damn silly way it had been for Jos to take from the cinema. Jos was glad that he had not after all had to confess about his romance with Jane. His thoughts were free to turn to her note to him and the prospect of seeing her at the army swimming pool on the Thursday. It was like coming out of a black tunnel into the light of day.

11

Jos took some care with the writing of the note of reply to be left in Jane's pigeon hole at the club. He sensed that Jane would expect a telegraphic style of reply to match her own: anything long-winded or sentimental would be out of place. After a while he settled for –

Dear Jane
See you Thursday. I'll wait in the ante-room. Come at three-thirty. Looking forward to it.
Love
Jos.

Wednesday was in fact the first day that Jos stirred out of the barracks. He discovered when he went down to the club that the secret about him having been a murder suspect, if only for two nights, was known to everyone but spoken of in undertones and whispers. He found that he had been invested with a curious double glamour: first, of being someone capable of killing one of the toughest soldiers in Nigeria and, secondly, of being an innocent youth whose stainless character had suffered through accidents which were no fault of his. The fact that the two sides of this glamour were mutually exclusive did not appear to detract from it. He wondered uneasily what Mrs Joynstone would make of it. She did not seem to be at the club, and although Jane was, and although he could perfectly well have whispered his reply to her, she was making such a point of cutting him in public that he saw he must go through with the pigeon hole business. After a feeble game of billiards at which he played even worse than usual, Jos sauntered over to the rack for messages and letters. It was at this point that he realized a weakness in Jane's plan: she did not have a pigeon hole. He decided that he must speak to her, but when he went back to the lounge she and the Resident had gone. With some misgivings he put the note in an envelope and sealed it. He wrote her name on the outside and put it in the Resident's pigeon hole.

That evening he started uneasily from time to time at the thought of Mrs Joynstone opening the envelope and reading the words "Looking forward to it – Love – Jos". He even thought at one point of getting out his bicycle and pedalling down to the club to retrieve the note. But then how would he get in touch with Jane? It was while he was brooding over these anxieties that Billy Rogers leaned over the dining table and said –

'Have you been taking your anti-malaria table, old chap? You're looking a wee bit peely wally.'

'Oh hark at Uncle Bill,' chimed in Dainton. 'The care of his brother officers is his first concern second only to that of his men and of course number one.'

It was curious, Jos reflected, how the boredom of having insufficient to do, the long exposure to each others' – and virtually no others' – company made perfectly pleasant young men churlish and objectionable to each other. But Dainton's next remarks stung him out of this philosophic train of thought.

'The truth is,' Dainton continued, 'he's been overdoing it with that little bint of his up at the Residency. You should share her around Jos my boy if she's proving too hot to hold. They do say these upper-class birds are insatiable: can't get enough of it if you take my point. Tell her she'd be most welcome to take my point if she's proving too demanding.'

Dainton beamed as he concluded, apparently well satisfied with his witticism. Jos's cup of coffee had just been refilled when Dainton began. The next thing he knew was that he had thrown the coffee full in Dainton's face and that it was trickling down his chin and over his white shirt and tie. Dainton went very pale and rose to his feet.

'You'll bloody pay for this.'

'Yes,' said Dave Lawson. 'That is a good idea. Jos should pay for any damage to your clothes, Cliff. Now pack it in all of you. Here's poor old Jos just emerged from suspicion of murder after being in the country for only a few months. No wonder

102

he's looking off colour and that his nerves are in a bad way.'

Jos was grateful to Dave for smoothing things over. He couldn't understand his own action. Everyone knew that Dainton had a coarse tongue, and paid no attention to it. It was also obvious that his sexual frustration was particularly keen at present with Jos apparently about to have an "affair" with the only eligible girl for miles around. Dainton wasn't at all a bad chap and Jos had no wish to make an enemy of him.

'My bloody tie's ruined,' he said grumpily and stalked off. Some of the others got into a rather tense game of poker dice, and Jos went off early to his gidda. There was no lock on the door, and despite repeated requisitions to the Regimental Quartermaster Sergeant, Jos was pretty sure that there never would be. Okoko had drilled him in security as follows:

'Unlock de padlock with dis key sah' (this of an old padlock which Okoko fixed on the outside of the front door). 'Go henter in. Go pull back de bolt on de back door. Go henter out round to de front door and padlock him. Den round de house again to de back door. Go henter in and push de bolt to foh inside.'

The operation was really a simple and obvious enough one but Jos was always fearful that he would somehow contrive to lock himself out altogether, and used to find himself repeating Okoko's instructions as a kind of chant "Go henter in . . . go henter out . . . .' He was glad to get under the shelter of the dark green mosquito net, and fell asleep resolving to apologize to Dainton in the morning, and composing what he would say should Mrs Joynstone turn up at three-thirty in the afternoon instead of Jane.

He was busy next morning helping Corporal Michael with a worrying discrepancy which had shown up in the amount of .22 ammunition held in the company magazine against the ledger entries of ammunition received and fired. Fortunately Major Hamilton was not in the barracks so that they were able to conduct the check in an atmosphere of some calm. But just as they were glumly concluding that there were indeed 1,000 rounds unaccounted for, Company Sergeant Major Roberts looked into the magazine.

'What's all this then?' he asked. 'Poor old Musa's wetting his pants up there in the company office about some missing ammo.'

'Is true sah,' said Corporal Michael. 'A tousand rounds of .22.'

'I expect you or one of your savvy chums have flogged it in the Gari,' Roberts sneered with his usual, uncalled for nastiness when addressing Corporal Michael. Then changing his tone to one of conspiratorial concern he turned to Jos

'But really, sir, this is a bit of a balls up isn't it? Cor if the Major knew he'd flap all the way back from Kaduna under his own wing power. Ammunition and money sir: the two things you must be able to account for in the army.'

Jos was nettled by the way Company Sergeant Major Roberts had been gratuitously rude to Corporal Michael and now seemed to be using the occasion for one of his periodical homilies about the practices and priorities of the army. He did not feel in any way personally inculpated in the loss of the ammunition – at any rate no more so than Roberts who also had a key to the magazine.

'Well we can't do any more today. We'll have to tell the company commander when he gets back and then no doubt there will have to be a Court of Inquiry.'

'Don't you think we should report this at once to the Adjutant sir?'

Jos thought of his afternoon swim being exchanged for an inevitable second count of the ammunition in the stuffy little magazine: he thought of Major Hamilton being greeted on his return by the commanding officer or the adjutant with complaints about the loss.

'I don't think it's serious enough for that,' he said. 'It's only .22 ammunition. I'll tell the company commander informally tonight, Sergeant Major.'

'Sah!' Company Sergeant Major Roberts roared his disapproval, stamping his heels together as the crashing accompaniment to a quivering salute. He about turned and withdrew, marching off in soldierly fashion.

Jos was aware that Corporal Michael had missed nothing of this exchange and was now tidying away the ledger with a half sympathetic, half contemptuous smile. They locked up and walked back over to the company office where Jos had one or two letters and forms to sign on behalf of the company commander before getting on his bicycle and cycling off to lunch at the Mess.

As Jos had calculated, lunch was completed fairly quickly because of the intention of most of the officers to take part in or to watch the mixed hockey match. He hurried off down to his gidda for a brief siesta just like the rest of them giving, he hoped, the impression that he would be at the game.

'Okoko,' he said as he pulled off his boots. 'Wake me at three o'clock please.'

'Tree o'clock sah! Hey I tink you go play foh de mixed hockey game. I go come watch you sah.'

'Well actually no. I'm just going for a swim.'

'But sah all de hapsas go foh de mixed hockey. De Colonel wife she be big big ooman foh hockey number one. She want all de hapsas to play or go clap hands foh her.'

Jos felt a spasm of anxiety. He recalled uneasily that the Colonel's wife had spoken to him at the Naafi the other day saying something about looking forward to how the new recruit showed his paces on the hockey field. And it really was remarkable how everyone had gobbled up his lunch so as to get a bit of afternoon kip before the start of the game.

'Oh well,' he said, assuming a heartiness he now no longer felt. 'She can't want more than eleven on each side, and I gather she's got that.'

Okoko looked extremely glum. 'Yes sah but is substitutes and de clapping foh her with hands sah. She no like if'n dat you no go clap. Hey I never catch so much palaver with any mitre before dis.' And Okoko withdrew muttering gloomily to himself.

Jos drifted off into a pleasant sleep until Okoko wakened him at three.

'You left yoh bicycle at de Mess sah,' he said as he placed the cup on the little bedside table and went over to pull the shutters. 'I go bring um down while you drink yoh coffee so he be all daidai foh you to go to swimming pool.'

'Thank you Okoko, but I'm taking the car.'

'Dat mato sah?' Okoko looked astonished: rather as if Jos had proposed to canter down on a mad bull elephant. Jos felt his usual twitch of annoyance at the low regard in which Okoko obviously held the car. But he contented himself with replying tersely, 'Yes.'

Okoko again withdrew with much shaking of his head and muttering of "Kai!" and "Hey" and "Dat Mato". But Jos paid no heed to him as he spruced himself up to meet Jane. Wrapping his swimming trunks in his towel, he walked up to the Mess and settled down in a chair commanding the view of the driveway up to the mess. He prayed that no hockey players or spectators would interrupt his vigil: the Game was not due to start until four o'clock and it was unlikely that anyone would come near the Mess at this hour. It was immensely peaceful sitting there waiting. Nothing stirred except the slowly revolving fan in the ante-room. He was intensely aware of the shimmer of heat over the stone flagged driveway.

Suddenly she was there, a slim lithe figure walking with curiously long strides up the driveway. She wore slacks and a shirt with a bare midriff and carried her towel under her arm. Jos felt a great wave of relief and joy break over him when he saw her. It was tinged with anxiety lest they should be discovered but he realized that his chief worry must have been that she would not come. He went to greet her grinning with pleasure that she had come. But as he got closer he saw that she had a peevish look on her face, and her opening words were not encouraging.

'What an ass you are,' she said. 'How on earth do you think I got here?'

Jos at once saw how difficult this must have been. Jane did not have a car of her own and would not want to ask for the use of the Resident's for this furtive assignment.

'I'm sorry,' he said lamely.

'I had to walk down to the part of the Gari nearest the Residency and hire a taxi at the crossroads, and I thought it better not to come up here in it so I got out at the officers' married lines and have walked from there. I'm all dry and thirsty. Can we get a drink in the Mess?'

'Well I think it would be better not to get the Bar Boys out just now.'

'No, but I mean can't I get some water?'

'The trouble is the only drinking water is in the kitchen and the Corporal Cook has the key to it.'

'Oh Christ!' Jane exclaimed, glaring very angrily at Jos. He was taken aback by the blasphemy coming from these young, feminine, poshly spoken lips. But his main concern was that the afternoon seemed to be going all wrong. He thought desperately how to retrieve the situation.

'I've got an orange over in my gidda,' he faltered.

To his surprise and relief Jane's peevish expression softened and she kissed him lightly and quickly on the cheek. 'Lead the way then,' she said.

They walked down to his house and he gave her the orange. While she was peeling it and sucking the juice Jos got into the car to try to start it. Okoko who had been having a little sleep in his house came out at the sound of Jos trying to start the car. He blinked with astonishment at the sight of Jane sitting on the verandah. To miss the hockey match was to risk trouble but to miss it and to take the Resident's niece for a run to the swimming pool in "dat mato" seemed foolhardiness on a colossal scale. He shook his head gloomily.

'You want me to go push um sah?' he enquired.

'Well, just a wee push' Jos conceded looking nervously in Jane's direction. He saw her astonished look as Okoko in his off-duty garb of green underpants and soiled-looking singlet strained and grunted to get the car moving. In fact it started fairly easily in gear, and keeping his foot on the accelerator Jos asked Jane to get in. Okoko watched them disappear up the laterite road in a cloud of dust and blue smoke. He continued to shake his head as an indication of his foreboding. He turned to Ali, who had materialized as if by magic when the pushing had to be done, and said

'Ali dis hapsa of mine he go worry me too much. I tink he go make plenty palaver foh himself. Kai when dat big big ooman foh hockey, de Colonel's wife, see he no dere, Kai!'

'Resident's ooman no gree foh him too,' volunteered Ali.

'It go worry me,' said Okoko.

But Jos was not at this moment feeling at all worried himself. Jane had come out of her ill-humour and was now treating the push start of the funny little car as part of the adventure. Jos began to feel the afternoon would go well after all. They were soon at the pool. Jos parked the car carefully at the top of a small rise so that he would be able to let it run down and start it in gear again should this be necessary. They walked over to the swimming pool. To his great relief Jos saw that they had the place to themselves.

'This is a super pool,' said Jane. 'Much bigger than ours. Shall I change in one of these cubicles?'

'Yes. I'll take this one. Help yourself to any of the others.'

As he changed Jos could feel his heart thudding with excitement. He could not believe that this was happening: that for this afternoon at any rate he was to be in the company of a pretty young woman under a hot sun and beside a cool swimming pool. He thought of the others sweating about on the hockey field and mentally pinched himself to check his good fortune.

Jane was already in the pool when he got out. She was wearing a bikini which showed her tall slim figure to great advantage. She was swimming gracefully up and down the pool as Jos splashed in with his ugly belly-flopping dive. They swam for a while and then lay down by the side of the pool sunbathing, talking lazily and contentedly to each other, telling each other about themselves. Jos raised himself on his elbow and looked across at Jane. He found that he could hardly breathe when his eyes lit on the smoothness of her skin, her long shapely legs, her lovely arms and the gentle rise of her pretty breasts under the bikini top. In fact he made an awkward choking sound as he looked at her. She put one hand behind his head and pulled his face close to hers and then she kissed him full on the lips sliding her tongue into his mouth as she did so. Jos pulled her body against his and one of his hands sought the clip which fastened the bikini top. He could never understand how girls were so good at hooking and unhooking brassieres, with their arms and fingers doing the job backwards so to speak when in his limited experience it was always so difficult getting the damned things undone the right way round. He was making heavy weather of it again, but then the top came away and Jane was shyly laying it to one side so that he could see and touch her breasts. Jos gazed at them reverently for a few moments and then bent his head to kiss the pink nipples. He felt in paradise. But only for an instant before the bliss of the afternoon was shattered by a loud screeching of brakes and the coarse sound of the Quartermaster's voice.

'Oh ho Bernard looks as if another mastah has decided a cool afternoon by the pool would be a better bet than the hockey match. That's Mr Maclean's old banger isn't it?'

'Yes sah. Dat be Lieutenant Maclean's mato.'

'Well you park the landrover in the shade after you've taken the beer out and set everything up for me by the side of the pool.'

'Yes sah.'

Jane had managed to get her bikini top back on and Jos had put a respectable distance between them before the Quartermaster came waddling into the area surrounding the pool.

'Hello George,' Jos called in as casual and cheerful a manner as he could muster.

'Cor Blimey,' returned George, his eyes popping at the sight of the two young people and particularly that of the scantily clad Jane. Bernard, the recreational transport driver, who was arranging a little table for the Quartermaster and placing two bottles of beer in the shallow end of the pool for his subsequent refreshment, all but fell into the pool.

'Brought your home comforts I see,' Jos went on, pointing to the beer. George continued to stare at Jane seeming to imply that Jos had brought his home comforts also.

'We were just going actually,' said Jane with great presence of mind, 'hoping to catch the end of the hockey match.' She stood up, revealing as she did so her long slim legs and thighs. 'I'm just going to change.' And with that she slipped into the cubicle where she had left her slacks and blouse. Jos found himself grinning feebly at the Quartermaster.

'Oh dear, oh dear, oh dear,' said George. 'You really have been and gone and done it now, my young fellow.'

'Oh?' queried Jos uneasily.

'Oh Lord love a duck, I wouldn't be in your shoes: not for all the tea in China. The Commanding Officer will blow his top when he discovers that you skived off the hockey, and the Resident's wife will have you up on a rape charge when she finds out about this sunbathing lark.' The Quartermaster shook his head knowingly, and then, spotting that Bernard the driver was taking all this in with interest and relish, he turned to him and said 'Bernard what are you gawping and grinning at? – off you go and wait for me in the landrover.'

'Well it should be all right,' mumbled Jos nervously. 'We'll go up now and mingle with the crowd. No-one will notice that we haven't been there all afternoon.'

'Not a chance,' said George happily, looking at his watch. 'It's just finishing: you'd never get there in time. By the way – the only reason I'm here is that I've been in Kaduna all morning and only got back after the match had finished – all right?'

Jos nodded and hurried off to change. He was beginning to feel a bit alarmed. His unease was not assuaged by Jane saying in her piercing upper class voice as they went back to the car 'What a perfectly horrid little man that is. What a pity he had to come along just as we were getting going.'

Fortunately the car started, and Jos drove as fast as he could in order to deposit Jane at the Residency. They rejoined the road which ran through the barracks and in doing so encountered a stream of people walking from the sports field. Oh hell, thought Jos, some of these are sure to have recognized us and will twig where we have been. As they passed the Officer's Mess they saw the Commanding Officer's car and the Resident's car parked outside.

'Thank God,' Jos muttered. 'Your aunt seems to be at the Mess. We can at least get you back home before she arrives.'

'You're awfully jumpy,' said Jane. 'This whole afternoon's thoroughly spoiled now.'

How peevish she sounds, Jos thought, and she doesn't know the half of it. I've still got to report this blasted ammunition loss to the company commander. They parted somewhat ungraciously at the door of the Residency. For one thing Jos was afraid to switch the car engine off, indeed to take his foot off the accelerator in case the engine stalled. He drove back to the barracks, his thoughts now grimly on the best way of disclosing to Major Hamilton the loss of the ammunition. He decided he might as well get it over before dinner rather than call on the

Hamiltons in the evening. After he had parked the car and knocked at the door he was shown into the sitting room where Mrs Hamilton, returned from watching the hockey match, was sipping a restorative gin and tonic.

'Oh hello Jos,' she said smiling warmly at him, her eyes looking knowingly and intimately into his. 'Timmy is just having his bath. He's been away all day on something terribly hush-hush, and he seems to have had rather a bad day. I hope it's nothing official you've come to see him about. What will you have to drink?'

'Oh nothing thanks Elaine. I'm afraid it is a troublesome thing that's happened in the company. I think he ought to know about it straightaway.'

'Oh couldn't it wait. Timmy already seems very upset about something. How did you like the hockey?'

'Oh well, perhaps I should be getting along then. I suppose it can wait till tomorrow.'

But even as Jos felt a cowardly wave of relief flow over him at the thought of this temporary respite, a loud angry voice came booming from inside the house,

'Elaine love where are you? I can't find my golf cuff-links. You on the verandah . . . ?'

Major Hamilton emerged dressed except for his flapping wrists. He started at the sight of Jos. 'Good Lord, you're here,' he said. 'I wanted to say something to you, but I did not expect you to present yourself here tonight. However since you've come, I may as well get it over with. Sweety, would you mind leaving us alone for a few minutes?'

'Oh Timmy not again. The last time you asked that there was all that horrid business about the dead man.'

'All right, darling, you stay. What I've got to say is not really an official or military matter at all: it is a matter of common courtesy and respect for the feelings of others. You know, darling, the trouble that Priscilla goes to in arranging the Annual Mixed Hockey Game, and you know that all of us in the Unit – soldiers, wives, children, Europeans and Africans alike all feel bound in turn to support the event.'

'Don't I just. I've always hated hockey, and I'm always sure that hard ball is going to hit me.'

111

This was not the reaction Major Hamilton had expected and he was none too pleased by it. However he decided to make the best of it.

'I know darling – but nonetheless you feel bound to turn up for Priscilla's sake.'

Jos was aware that this mild exchange between the company commander and his wife was but a prelude to the rocket about to be delivered against him. The Major now got into action.

'However the first thing I heard on returning to the Unit was that Jos saw fit to go off and enjoy himself at the swimming pool this afternoon: to go off moreover with Mrs Joynstone's niece although Mrs Joynstone has expressed quite clear wishes to the effect that her niece should not be troubled in this way.' Jos could feel a withdrawal of the warm, slightly lustful feeling which normally seemed to radiate in his direction from Elaine. She stepped closer to her husband and the two of them regarded him sternly.

'Now look here, Jos, this just will not do. You are going out of your way to offend all manner of senior people in the unit and in the European community generally. It's not good for you. It's not good for the unit and it's not good for the company. Get a grip of yourself for goodness sake, man.'

'Yes. I'm very sorry sir. It was all a bit unfortunate. I didn't realize that Mrs Redmayne attached such importance to the match.'

'Well I'll say no more about it, and I'll try to head the Colonel off. Come on lets have something to drink. What will it be – a scotch, gin, a beer?'

'A lager thank you sir. There is just one other thing, sir, I feel I ought to mention.'

'Carlsberg or Star? We'll get some up from the fridge for you . . . . Something else is there? Well what is it?' Major Hamilton looked relaxed: the senior executive who had dealt with a tricky little personnel problem and was now ready to help a junior clear up a little local difficulty of some sort. He smiled encouragingly at Jos to begin. Jos took a deep breath.

'There's a thousand rounds of ammunition missing from the company magazine, sir.'

There was obviously a second or two of complete non-comprehension: the encouraging smile remained for that length of time on Major Hamilton's face, somewhat lost and forlorn but hanging on gallantly before disintegrating all over his features and being replaced by a pale sweaty look.

'What did you say?' The words came out slowly in a strangled whisper.

'1,000 rounds, sir, missing from the company magazine.'

'1,000 rounds?'

'Yes, sir.

'Missing?'

'Yes, sir. But, sir – it's only .22.'

'Only .22?'

Both Jos and Mrs Hamilton were beginning to feel uneasy at the way in which Major Hamilton was repeating these fragments of information to himself. His hand had been on a bottle of whisky when Jos made his disclosure. He now poured himself out a very large whisky indeed and swallowed it in two large gulps. He recharged his glass and swallowed this lot in one gulp. Then he spoke.

'Elaine, lovey, your drink needs a top-up. Here we are, some more gin, bit of tonic, ice – what about another slice of lemon? I can't think what's taking that Boy so long to get your beer, Jos.'

Jos and Elaine exchanged worried glances. Gosh I hope the news hasn't driven him completely potty, Jos thought: it isn't all that bad surely.

'When did you discover this?' Hamilton's voice was now cold, hard and unfriendly.

'Mid-day sir.'

'At what time precisely?'

'About 1300 hours sir.'

'What action did you take?'

'Well I didn't exactly take any action, sir. I thought I should inform you first.'

Jos felt the lameness of this reply as he uttered it, and an unpleasant nervousness seemed to settle on his stomach. Perhaps he had been idiotically irresponsible.

'You mean to say you went off enjoying yourself this afternoon knowing that a thousands rounds of ammunition were missing from the company magazine and made no effort to report the loss to any senior officer in the unit?'

'Yes sir.'

There was a long silence while this "Yes sir" congealed in the atmosphere.

'Very well. Will you go now and tell the Adjutant, the duty officer, the field officer of the week and the officer in charge of the riot squad. I shall see the commanding officer myself.'

'But sir, you don't seriously think that anyone planning trouble would have taken the .22 ammunition and left the .303?'

'They might well have done if they happened to have .22 and not .303 rifles.'

'Yes sir.'

' And look here . . . .'

'Yes sir?'

'I must warn you that you have gone too far this time. I shall have to arrange with the Adjutant that you have a continuous spell of duty officer.'

Just at this point the servant arrived with the ice-cold beer. Jos was feeling so depressed that he could scarcely face it. But Major Hamilton motioned the Boy to set it in front of Jos with a grimly hospitable air; and while Jos forced the stuff down Major Hamilton engaged him in polite chit-chat about an officer in Jos's parent regiment who had been at school with him. As soon as the drink was consumed he regarded Jos sternly again and said

'Get off now then and inform the Adjutant and the others. Tomorrow we shall have a fresh count in the Company and depending on the outcome of that arrange for a court of inquiry to be set up.'

The Adjutant and the field officer of the week, on hearing that it was .22 ammunition shrugged their shoulders and hazarded that it would be one of the African NCOs fixing up his friends to get something for the pot, or else perhaps raising some cash by selling it on the blackmarket in the Gari. Jos felt somewhat reassured by their assessment of the situation. The duty officer turned out to be RQMS Blackett, a lugubrious and self-righteous British warrant officer.

'Thieving bastards,' he said. 'You can't be too careful you know. You'd know all about if it you had my job, sir, I can tell you. I've got to look out for every last darning needle. There'll be trouble over this. You mark my words. What do they want to go pinching ammo for eh? I'll be glad when my spell of Duty Officer is over I can tell you.'

The British warrant officers bitterly resented having to take a turn at duty officer, a chore which the Regimental Sergeant Major had agreed they should take on because there were so few commissioned officers in the Unit. And they were expert at finding reasons for dodging it: thus their convivial weekends of housey-housey, beer and ballroom dancing in the Sergeants Mess were not too often disturbed by having to spend the night in the orderly room. But Jos could see a more sinister meaning to the RQMSs remark: he clearly was implying that future Duty Officers were going to be faced with armed insurgents. A poor look out for me then he thought, as he recalled Hamilton's words about a continuous spell of duty officer. He got back to his gidda in a murderous frame of mind, and roared

'Okoko!'

'I coming sah,' called Okoko.

'Where's my bathwater?'

'I go fetch um sah.'

Okoko went out to the soyer stove and began bringing in pails of hot water which he splashed into the bath. Jos was pulling off his clothes and pitching them savagely into an untidy pile in the corner. Okoko ran a little cold water and then came into the sitting room and said with his curious little formal bow

'Baff aw ready sah.'

Jos splashed roughly into the bath. Okoko remained in the sitting room silently and patiently picking up the jumble of clothes, sorting them out, some to be washed, others to be hung up. He called in to Jos who was now slopping about in the bath.

'You like yoh swim with dat European gel sah?'

'Yes.'

'I tink yoh mato it maybe go make palaver again?'

'No. Now look Okoko I'm in no mood to be teased by you

tonight. Where the hell's my towel?'

'Is right dere sah,' said Okoko coming back into the bathroom, 'foh de shelf. Is other palaver sah? With Colonel's wife?'

'There is palaver all over the place Okoko. And I am in a very bad temper and at the moment you are the only person I can safely take it out on. So be careful.'

'Sah?' Okoko was slightly lost.

'You will be pleased to learn Okoko that you will be working your ebony fingers to the bone starching and pressing my uniforms practically non-stop. I am to be Duty Officer not just for this weekend but for many days and nights to come.'

'Dis very bad sah. I no gree foh you to be Duty Hapsa too much.'

'To tell you the truth, I'm not mad keen on the prospect myself, Okoko. But there it is. "A soldier's life is terrible hard, says Alice".'

'Na he be true sah. Is hard.'

After Jos had gone off up to the Mess for dinner Okoko tidied up in the gidda and then withdrew to his little round house. His large fat wife and their three children were on the two beds which occupied almost the entire space. The children had been put to bed for the night, but Okoko's wife was seated on the bed. Okoko sat down beside her, pulling off his gym shoes as he did so.

'Tangwe,' he said, speaking in Idoma. 'That young officer is getting into worse and worse trouble all the time. I told him there was a bad ju-ju about that gidda. I hope that we don't catch any of the bad luck.'

'Everything is all right with us Okoko,' his wife replied comfortably. There was a long pause while she contemplated the three children satisfying herself that they had got off to sleep.

'Tangwe.'

'Yes?'

'I have found out the name of the daughter of the sister of the wife of the Resident. It is Alice.'

12

After Muster Parade the next morning Major Hamilton ordered the recount of the ammunition. The result was of course that Jos had to report that there were still exactly 1,000 rounds of .22 missing. Thereupon Major Hamilton summoned the two Sergeant-Majors, Jos and Lance-Corporal Michael to his room. He regarded Jos solemnly.

'You are quite satisfied that there are 1,000 rounds of .22 unaccounted for, Mr Maclean?'

'Yes, sir.'

'Have you any suggestion as to how this loss could have happened?'

'No, sir.'

'Lance-Corporal Michael have you anything to say? You're sure the ledger is accurate?'

'Yes sah I know it is accurate.'

'CSM Roberts have you anything to say?'

'Well I'm very sorry this should have happened, sir.'

'Thank you Sergeant-Major. Well now . . . .'

'Sah!' CSM Musa interrupted.

'Yes, Sergeant-Major. What is it?' Major Hamilton asked looking puzzled at the intervention because CSM Musa did not usually utter at "Conferences" of this sort, and looking also rather impatient and irritated that the outlining of his crisp plan of action should have been stopped in its tracks in this way.

'Sah, I tink I go find out who do dis ting.'

'Well precisely, Sergeant-Major. That is what we must do.' Major Hamilton smirked slightly as he said this. But then something in CSM Musa's expression made him pause. 'What is it Musa. Do you know who has stolen the ammo?'

'I go find out sah.'

'Yes but how?'

'Let me get all de Platoon Sajis on parade sah. Den I go find out.'

Major Hamilton looked uncertain. But the truth was he had no very clear idea of how he was going to discover the thief although he had been rehearsing an impressive "Appreciation of the situation" according to the best military text books, which he was looking forward to expounding. After a moment or two's thought he shrugged his shoulders. 'Very well Sergeant-Major. Get them on parade now.'

The company orderly was sent off at the double to fetch the Platoon Sergeants. The three men arrived looking puzzled and ill at ease. CSM Musa shouted commands at them which brought them into line on the verandah standing at attention. The senior and most efficient was a light skinned, powerfully built Ibo called Edward Kalu. Sergeant Maiji Katsina was a shifty-eyed, rather incompetent Hausaman who really looked too old and frail to be an effective infantry sergeant but who had some sort of a hold over his men which meant that he was able to drive them hard. Sergeant Yesufu Maiduguri was a tall, very black skinned veteran of the Burma campaign.

CSM Musa spoke to the group very quietly in Hausa. Sergeant Kalu, the Ibo, had to strain a little to follow. He was explaining that the theft had been discovered and that he, CSM Musa, was pretty sure that one of them must have been the thief or at any rate had been party to the theft. The Europeans and Corporal Michael watched the reactions on the faces of the three sergeants. Suddenly CSM Musa changed his technique and took two or three smart paces forward until he was standing only an inch or two in front of Sergeant Kalu. Jos was reminded of the bullying in which the NCOs had engaged during basic training. For a second he was transported back to basic training at the regimental depot in Scotland and could see the vicious, narrow little face of Corporal Maclennan practically touching the spotty, adolescent, frightened one of Private Flett and could hear the rasping voice asking "Are youse sure you blancod yer fucking gaiters Flett?" CSM Musa

118

was conducting his interrogation in Hausa, under a hot sun, but Jos recognized the technique.

'Did you steal the ammunition?'

Sergeant Kalu flashed back an angry glance straight into CSM Musa's eyes and said 'No, sir,' CSM Musa continued to look into Sergeant Kalu's eyes for a few moments and then passed to Sergeant Katsina.

'No, sir,' said Sergeant Katsina. His eyes were evasive, and his lips seemed to be trembling with fear or anger.

CSM Musa looked at him coldly and contemptuously before moving to Sergeant Maiduguri. This time the CSM had to tilt his head backwards and look up to the great height of the sergeant. He looked hard into his eyes for a few seconds and then asked quietly 'What have you done with the ammunition?'

'I don't know anything about the ammunition. I never touched it.' There was a long pause during which CSM Musa kept his eyes fastened on Sergeant Maiduguri's.

Suddenly Sergeant Maiduguri looked away, looked down, and in a changed voice said 'I was in Burma with you CSM Musa. I saved your life once. Why should I take the ammunition?'

'It will go easier with you if you help us to recover it.'

The Europeans could not follow this in detail, but it was becoming obvious from the trapped and miserable look on Sergeant Maiduguri's face that the CSM had found the culprit. He continued to break him down.

'You are a fool Sergeant Maiduguri. How could you hope to get away with this? You hoped there wouldn't be a magazine check before the Kebira Club Indoor shoot and gala day and that after it there would be confusion about the stock of .22?'

The CSM could tell from the look on Sergeant Maiduguri's face as he said this that that was exactly how his mind had been working.

'But what a fool you are. If that was your plan you should have waited until much nearer the time. But you always were too greedy. Now you have lost everything. You had a good job here as a training sergeant: nice houses for your wives. A nice school for your children. Quite soon you would have qualified

119

to retire early with a pension, and I could have got you a job as a night watchman. All that you have lost. But if you tell me what you have done with the ammunition I will try to prevent them from sending you to prison.'

The two men glared at each other. Suddenly Sergeant Maiduguri caved in.

'I sold it to a dealer in the Gari. I will take you to his house. He cannot have sold much of it yet.'

CSM Musa turned to Major Hamilton and explained that he had discovered Sergeant Maiduguri to be the guilty man, and that if the Sergeant could be left at liberty for a little he thought that he would be able to recover most of the ammunition.

'All right but keep an eye on him, Musa. I want to see him in the guardroom before the day is out. Treacherous swine.'

CSM Musa and Sergeant Maiduguri went off together. Jos could see that Hamilton was really upset. He too had been in Burma, and the young Yesufu Maiduguri had been one of the men who had served under him. There was a camaraderie among the officers and men who had seen action together which went beyond divisions of rank and colour. Jos had been quick to notice and to respect this: indeed to envy it. Now one of these bonds had been sundered, and Hamilton was clearly vexed about it. As usual his vexation was expressed indiscreetly and with petulance.

'I'll never trust another of these black bastards again as long as I live,' he confided to the group which included CSM Musa and Corporal Michael. 'Let you down every bloody time. I can remember when Maiduguri came to us. Great raw gangling boy he was. He was one of the ones who really had guts too. Oh bloody hell . . . . Sergeant-Major Roberts, will you take over Sergeant Maiduguri's Platoon today: we can give Corporal Udo Ekim a temporary third stripe tomorrow until we get a replacement from HQ.'

Jos was interested in Hamilton's reaction to all this, but he was above all curious to know how Musa had so quickly hit upon the guilty party. He went into the company office and spoke to Corporal Michael.

'How do you think CSM Musa knew, Michael?'

120

'It have to be one of de Sajis: dey never let de ammo out of dere sight on the range. It could not have been Saji Kalu: he wants to be RSM or a Hapsa. Saji Katsina would have been in de Gari with kudi ebery night if he had sold the ammo – but he has had only small-small kudi and plenty palaver with his wives because dey get nothing to spend. Saji Maiduguri is de one who has been buying presents for his wives and piccin.'

'You mean you suspected Sergeant Maiduguri as well?'

'Yes sah.'

'Well why didn't you say so when we first discovered the loss yesterday?'

Corporal Michael looked at Jos as if he were soft in the head.

'Sah I no want to make de count at all. If I, a young Ibo Corporal, who never was in Burma – hey ifn I go report Saji Maiduguri foh dis ting – sah I no go live very long sah – at all!'

'What about CSM Musa then?'

'Is all right foh him. He be Hausaman proppa. He get power heah more dan de crown on his arm.'

Not for the first time, and by no means for the last, during his service in Africa, Jos felt how little he really knew about what went on in the minds of the Africans. CSM Musa and the wretched Sergeant Maiduguri came back in the late forenoon with about 800 rounds of the ammunition. The end of the episode was a court of inquiry which criticized the company security arrangements for custody of the key to the magazine, and led to Sergeant Maiduguri's dismissal from the Army with loss of pension rights. He was not however prosecuted in the civilian criminal court for theft, and Hamilton and Musa between them managed to get him a job as a doorman-cum-chucker out at the new European club opening in Jidda, a township which had come into existence in the past five years as a result of expansion of tin mining.

Jos personally came off very lightly in the findings of the court of inquiry, but by that time he had already paid for his failure to report the loss of the ammunition immediately by ten days continuous service as duty officer. The Colonel and the Adjutant both clearly felt the sin of omission did not deserve this, but Major Hamilton had committed himself so thoroughly and publicly to a heavy penalty that it would have been too much of a loss of face for him if Jos had been given anything less. The Adjutant tried to do what he could for Jos by drawing easy times for him to turn out the guard. The Colonel felt that it called for one of his fatherly pep talks.

'The old man wants to see you, Jos,' said the Adjutant after he had given him his orders for the first day's duty officer. Jos knocked on the CO's door, opened it on hearing the fruity 'Come in', entered and saluted smartly.

The CO blinked at him benignly, 'Ah yes, Maclean, I wanted to see you. Yes. Quite so. Now the thing is you see: matter of timing. Stitch in time saves nine. Follow my drift? Save the ship with a halfpennyworth of tar applied at the right time. See what I'm getting at? If a thing's worth doin' worth doin' immediately – right? That's the point.' All this was said in a remarkably languid way with the CO sprawling back in his chair and tipping it up so that Jos was fearful it was going to collapse under him. But now he righted the chair and himself, and looking cunningly at Jos asked the question 'Procrastination then – what's that the thief of? – eh?'

'Time, sir.'

'Jolly good, jolly good. Never put off till tomorrow . . . . Are you with me?'

'Yes sir?'

'Jolly good, jolly good.'

The Colonel stared vacantly at his blotter for a moment or two. Jos could see that he was in mental turmoil of some sort, and wondered whether there were any other platitudes about time that he could dredge up. But in fact the Colonel was on to another subject now. He was trying to work in something about the swimming pool hockey-match business which would show that this offence had been taken into account in fixing Jos's punishment but that all was now forgiven. At last, apparently despairing of an appropriate cliché, he sighed and slumped back into his chair again and began speaking as if to himself 'Perfectly understandable to go for a swim on a hot day with a charming gel. Mrs Joynstone's niece a very charmin' gel. But again you see, Jos,' – Jos noted the switch from "Maclean" to "Jos" as a further sign of amiability – and here the Colonel sat up a bit again. 'It's all a matter of timing. A time and a place for everything. No good being in the right place at the wrong time, or the wrong place at the right time. That's how battles are lost and won y'know.'

'Yes sir,' Jos assented.

The Colonel beamed, as if well satisfied at the aptness of his pupil. 'Ah I thought you'd see the point,' he said. 'Well now we mustn't spend all day gassing here must we. Look here why don't you come and have lunch with Mrs Redmayne and me on Sunday, curry lunch, all the trimmings.'

'Thank you sir. I'll still be duty officer of course then.'

'That's all right. All in the course of duty after all. What?'

'Thank you sir.'

Jos saluted, about-turned and withdrew, aware of the general aura of good will and forgiveness, and intrigued as always by the Colonel's capacity for thinking and talking in clichés. As he passed through the Adjutant's room, the Adjutant looked with interest at the slightly bemused and amused look on Jos's face.

'What did he say?' he asked.

'A stitch in time saves a halfpenny worth of tar,' Jos replied, as he saluted and walked smartly from the Office.

A little later the Colonel sauntered into the Adjutant's Office.

'Nice young fellah that really, Tony.'

'Yes sir. It's been an unfortunate business this.'

'Oh I shouldn't worry Tony, I think I managed to straighten him out. Show him how many beans make five: what makes the world go round: what it's all about – that sort of thing y'know. I don't think he'll come a cropper again.'

'No, sir. Good, sir.'

13

Jos began the spell of punishment duty officer on a Monday, and the first few days of it were not too bad. He had his normal duties in the company until lunchtime, and although it was a nuisance to have to remain in uniform all afternoon and evening and to sleep in the orderly office at nights, he had to turn out the guard in the middle of the night only once, and by the Friday evening he was congratulating himself that he was half way through his stint. Okoko was not so philosophical.

'How can I get you fresh-fresh uniform every day and night sah? All day I go wash and starch and press. I have to get yoh bed up to the orderly office ebery day, go make it dere, put up mosquito net, go take it down for morning time. Hey I no gree foh dis work at all sah, at all.'

It was not until the Saturday evening that Jos really felt himself minding the chore keenly: it was particularly galling to be on at the weekend again so soon after the recent self-imposed (and as it turned out unnecessary) stint. The other subalterns left in the Unit landrover for the dance at the Kebira Club.

'I'll give your love to Jane,' said Dainton with an exaggerated leer 'personally.'

'Too bad old chap,' said Billy Rogers. 'We'll try not to get into a drunken brawl and have you arrest us.'

The landrover sped off down the laterite road leaving a wake of dust. Jos got into the clumsy old 15cwt truck which had come to drive him down to his gidda, collect his bed and take it up to the orderly room for the night. Okoko was waiting at the gidda, his face set in a look of hard-done by misery. He and the duty driver loaded the bed on to the back of the truck, and they set off again up the hill to the barracks. It was a particularly hot night. After his bed with its mosquito net canopy had been erected, Jos seated himself at the Adjutant's desk and got out his copy of *War and Peace* and tried to read. But his mind kept wandering from the descriptions of the snowy vastness of the Russian countryside to the hot night outside. He could hear the drums in the old city and also the harsh, jazzy noises of Saturday night high life in the Sabongari: occasional shrieks and yells could be heard amidst the drum-beating and trumpet playing. He could not hear any sound from the direction of the Club: it was too far away, and anyhow the music would be softer, more discreet there. He thought of Jane dancing cheek to cheek with Dainton. Damn! He got up restlessly and paced about the stuffy little office for a few moments. The phone rang. He looked at the instrument with distaste thinking this is bound to be trouble: there could be no other reason for a call to the orderly room on a Saturday evening. He picked up the receiver and said cagily and resignedly into it,

'Duty officer speaking.'

'Hello Jos, it's me, Jane.'

A wave of great relief and joy swept over Jos.

'Hello Jane, where are you?'

'At the Club. I was dancing with Dave Lawson and he told me about your punishment. It's awful. I shall spit in that Hamilton's eye if I see him.'

'No, don't do that,' Jos said nervously.

'Well, shall I come up and see you?'

'What now?'

'Why not?'

'Jane, I can think of nothing nicer, but please, please don't. I'm not quite sure which section of Queen's Regulations I would be in breach of if you were to visit me, but there's bound to be one and I can see myself being duty officer for the rest of my life as a result.'

'I'll never understand the Army. It seems so silly the way you all carry on.'

'Well it is, but I've got to live with it.'

'Oh dear, Auntie's spotted me in the phone box. I'll have to pretend I was phoning the Residency for something. When can I see you?'

'I'm stuck here till Wednesday. I'll come down to the Club on Thursday about five o'clock. Thanks for phoning.'

'Good night then. I wish you were here.'

'Good night – darling,' Jos whispered the last word as he heard the phone being replaced. Now he felt excited and restless but in a brisk cheerful way, and he bustled through to the orderly sergeant and announced that he would take a last look round the African married lines on his way to turn out the guard.

'Is small-small noisy foh Saturday nights sah,' said the orderly sergeant looking distinctly apprehensive.

'Well I should like to see what goes on.'

'Sah, some of the sajis and soldiers dey drink too much sah. Perhaps dey no know hapsa when dat dey see um.'

Jos reflected for a moment and saw the wisdom of the orderly sergeant's advice.

'All right then I'll just go over to the guard.'

Jos took a long time over inspecting the guard, and then went round each of the cells, shining his torch into the sleepy and surprised looking faces of the prisoners. It was eleven o'clock when he got back to the orderly room and undressed for bed. He had just crawled under the mosquito net when he heard a commotion in the next room where the orderly sergeant slept. Jos strained to listen. He recognized the voice of Major Bigwood whose turn it was to be field officer for the week. He seemed to be giving the Sergeant a rocket. Jos scrambled into his clothes, and had got as far as his pants and vest when Major Bigwood strode in. Jos clicked his bare heels together as smartly as possible.

'Sorry to disturb your slumbers Maclean. I'm one of those rare birds: a field officer for the week who believes in taking the duty seriously.' Bigwood was a fattish man of middle height and middle age. He had been in the Pay Corps dealing with finance at Brigade HQ and had transferred recently to Infantry. As his first Infantry posting he had been given command of HQ Company in this training unit. Jos recalled that it was a byword in the unit that he had a fetish about fluff: the

126

discovery of fluff in a barrack room on a tour of inspection seemed to transform him from a mild, dry little man into a raging bully.

'I suppose you have to bring all your bedclothes and so forth up here,' he said looking with distaste at Jos's bed. 'You young fellows nowadays . . . . For all the time why can't you sleep on the desk or on a chair or on the floor?'

For all the time, Jos thought bitterly to himself.

'I've just had to tear a strip off that Sergeant next door for bringing fluff into the orderly office: spread his bedroll right over the desks of the pay corps clerks.'

'Yes sir.'

'You've turned out the guard.'

'Yes sir.'

'Everything OK? Anything to report on the prisoners?'

'The guard were in good order sir. Four prisoners: two from A Company, one from B Company and one from your own Company sir.'

'Well get back to your bed, Maclean. And for God's sake see that the place is thoroughly cleaned out before the Adjutant and the orderly room staff get up here on Monday morning.'

'Yes sir. Goodnight sir.'

Major Bigwood saluted as he left the office and waved his swagger stick in a gesture of farewell. Then he waddled off. Jos crawled once again under the net and slipped between the sheets. He thought of Jane's telephone call, and her parting words "Wish you were here". He shuddered for a moment when he thought of what Major Bigwood's reaction would have been if he had discovered Jane and him in a clinch under the mosquito net. He fell asleep sighing with relief at the narrow escape.

It was irksome the next day, Sunday, to be in uniform when the rest of the barracks was so determinedly off duty and informal. Breakfast at the Mess was particularly galling with George, for instance, wearing a paisley patterned sports shirt, and some of the others planning to go on a picnic. But the morning passed without event; and the Sunday curry lunch at the Colonel's was a leisurely and enjoyable affair, with the Colonel managing to work in a "broad as it's long" over pre-lunch drinks and a "hoist with his own petard" during the meat course. Jos felt entitled to a longish siesta after this, and by evening he was resigned to turning up for dinner in his uniform of long slacks and long sleeved shirt. He treated himself to a brandy after dinner and then strolled up to the orderly office intent on an early bed. He read a few pages of *War and Peace* before closing his eyes and falling into a deep sleep.

It was about two o'clock in the morning when he was dragged up out of delicious pools of sleep to the harsh and dopey half-wakefulness of lying knotted up in his sweat drenched sheets with the telephone ringing loudly in his ear. He struggled awkwardly with the mosquito net and then stepped across to lift the phone. What the hell can this be he wondered apprehensively as he said into the mouthpiece 'Duty officer.'

A high pitched southern voice crackled at the other end.

'Please is dat de Duty Hapsa? I want de Duty Hapsa.'

'Speaking.'

'Yes I want him speaking, please.'

Oh no, Jos thought. Do not let this turn out to be one of those crazy West African experiences when every conceivable misunderstanding occurs: not while I am still half asleep in the middle of the night. He strove to compose himself. It might be important. Was this perhaps the first warning of a riot?

'This is the duty officer speaking.'

'Sah, I am Sergeant-Major Otrukpo coming from Ibadan. I am now arriving in de station sah.'

For a moment Jos was literally speechless with indignation. Then he said icily, 'Why have you wakened me up at two in the morning to tell me this Sergeant-Major?'

'Please sah. I apologize you sah. But I come with all my wives and piccin and my furniture and my wireless, and one wife she get belly sah and de piccin it de come NOW sah.'

This NOW had the effect of jolting Jos into full wakefulness. 'You mean the baby is nearly coming?' he asked, gripping the telephone tightly.

'Yes sah de baby. E de go come now-now.'

'I'll be right down Sergeant-Major. Tell your wife, well, you

128

know, just to hold it.'

'Hold it sah?'

'Oh Christ never mind.'

Jos thumbed through the list of key numbers to find the medical officer's. He derived some small consolation even in this moment of panic from the thought of the smug little doctor being disturbed at this hour.

'This is a bit much,' said Dixon peevishly. 'Someone I haven't treated as a patient. Probably hours before anything happens. Any how these people can usually cope without a medical man.' There was a pause in the stream of grumbles as a new and even more annoying thought occurred to Dixon. 'I hope this isn't some silly prank of yours, Jos?'

It was arranged that Jos would pick up the medical officer on the way down to the station. Jos went next door and shook the orderly sergeant into wakefulness and told him that he had to go out on an emergency, and warned him to attend to the telephone. The orderly sergeant did not look as if he was taking any of this in but Jos decided he could not waste any more time trying to explain things to him. He went on to the verandah to waken the duty driver. Repeated shakings and shoutings seemed to have no effect whatsoever. The duty driver only seemed to curl up tighter and tighter into a coil of unconsciousness with each attempt to dislodge him. Suddenly Jos was aware of the guard, whose turn it was to act as sentry, standing behind him with fixed bayonet.

'Excuse me sah. I go wake him.'

Jos looked uneasily at the glinting bayonet. 'Well be careful,' he said.

The guard bent down over the sleeping form and whispered gently in his ear, 'Adamu, hapsa want you now-now.'

The driver was on his feet and pulling on his boots in a matter of seconds.

Soon they were screaming to a halt outside Dixon's house.

'Piece of bloody nonsense this,' said Dixon grumpily as he emerged. 'The army is just a welfare state for these people.'

What a sour little swine you are Dixon, Jos thought to himself, now beginning to enjoy the events of the night. The moon was nearly full and illumined the countryside so that it looked as he had never seen it before. The enormous expanse of the land, saved from being desert by its tenacious covering of sparse, dark scrub, rolled to the horizon. There the ugly, great boulder-like hills, which seemed somewhat dreary in the daylight, now stood out black and menacing. And the central cluster had a curiously leonine look: the head and shoulders of a lioness. They approached the station. As they did so Sergeant-Major Otrukpo came running towards them, wringing his hands in agitation. Jos noted this with interest, reflecting that he had never actually seen it done in real life.

The Otrukpo family consisted of two wives and five small children, some of them asleep, others gazing from large, round, dark, beautiful eyes. The wife who was having the baby was a slight, apparently very young Yoruba girl: her face was strained with pain but she was more composed and dignified than the Sergeant-Major. Dixon examined her briefly and said he thought there was time to get her up to the medical inspection room in the barracks. They helped her up into the truck, and Dixon got in with her telling the driver to drive as steadily and carefully as he could over the poor road surface.

'I'll send the truck down for you and this lot as soon as we get her up.' Dixon said as he took his leave of Jos.

Jos was glad that the girl was going to the clean, disinfectant-smelling room. On the way to the station, in the moonlight he had been fantasizing about births in primitive conditions, with strong silent men meekly getting lots and lots of hot water, and chain smoking to steady their nerves: the imprint of the Hollywood wild western on his childhood had been deep. But the station at Kebira was disgusting. It was not merely dirty: it had an appalling air of squalor. Even at that time of night, diseased beggars, parading their deformities, dragged themselves past the bench where the family were sitting, crying for money or food. He felt a spasm of shame in recalling his first reaction to the Sergeant-Major's phone call. He thought again of the slight form of the girl which seemed scarcely able to support the huge distension of her belly. He found himself looking reproachfully and with distaste at Sergeant-Major Otrukpo.

The Sergeant-Major was extremely agitated. His only solace

seemed to be in taking out his Pye radio set from a large biscuit tin and gazing at it with admiration. His other wife was a splendidly handsome young woman and she was suckling a very young baby in an absentminded sort of way. Jos felt almost faint when he looked at her breasts and saw how beautiful they were. This being the nineteen fifties, there was a great deal of attention paid to female breasts in the prominence they were given in wired brassieres and corsets, but there was no toplessness, and despite the occasional fumble in kissing girls good night the average unmarried young man had no detailed experience of what a woman's breast was really like: the size, shape, colouring and precise position of nipples were, for example, but imperfectably understood. Trying not to stare too blatantly – though his presence seemed a matter of indifference to Mrs Otrukpo number one – Jos sought to make good the gaps in his anatomical education.

With an effort he forced himself to turn his head away and he found himself looking bitterly at the Sergeant-Major who, for his part, was drooling over his wireless.

At last the truck came back, and Jos shepherded the Otrukpo family into it. The Sergeant-Major and all the children went into the back. The senior wife sat between Jos and the driver in the front. She continued to suckle the baby. It was only as the truck approached the barracks that Jos realized that he had no clear idea of what to do with them all for the rest of the night. The truck stopped outside the medical inspection room, and Sergeant-Major Otrukpo dashed up the steps to see how things had gone. He came back smiling and indeed sobbing with delight.

'Oh sah,' he said. 'He be boy chile proppa dis time.'

Jos looked over his shoulder at the four pairs of eyes in the back and realized that they all belonged to little girls: presumably the baby beside him was female also.

'Congratulations Sergeant-Major – and your young wife, is she all right?'

'My wife?' the Sergeant-Major seemed unprepared for this question. 'Oh yes sah I tink small time she be daidai again.'

Just then there was a loud sucking noise as the baby's mouth was pulled away from one nipple and engaged on the second.

The Sergeant-Major clambered up on to the truck again.

'Where we go now sah?' the duty driver asked.

'Go up to the orderly room,' said Jos thinking ruefully that the present truck load was likely to turn it into a disorderly room. He hoped that the orderly sergeant might be able to suggest some helpful way of dealing with the Otrukpo ménage. It was now four o'clock in the morning. The truck pulled up outside the orderly room, and the orderly sergeant came out to see what was happening. He was half asleep. Seeing Jos sitting in the front seat of the truck, his arm went into an instinctive salute; but as he slowly took in the backcloth of the Otrukpo family his eyes and then his mouth opened wider and wider. His arm remained at the salute for a moment or two before falling with a sluggish thud to his side. He emitted a long drawn out exclamation which sounded like "Allahomdillalai". Jos felt that his simultaneous translation must be improving; because it also sounded exactly like "Cor Blimey". Jos turned round himself to look at the other occupants of the truck – the senior wife suckling her baby, the four children, the table, the little stools, the coia and zana matting, the blackened old pots and pans, the basketful of squawking hens, and presiding blissfully over them all the Sergeant-Major with the biscuit tin under his arm.

'Right Sergeant,' said Jos with a briskness he did not begin to feel. 'What do you suggest we do with them for the rest of the night?'

'Na who sah?' The Sergeant was having difficulty in coming to grips with the problem.

'Them, of course,' Jos snapped, getting down from the truck and pointing back up towards the family and their goods and chattels. His finger happened to point most precisely however at the obtruding breasts of Mrs Otrukpo. The Sergeant's eyes dopily followed its direction and came to rest – together apparently with his mental faculties – on these impressive mamillary projections.

'Well Sergeant?' Jos nagged him back to attention. The Sergeant shook his head to dispel the vision of Mrs Otrukpo's bosom, and his advice when it came was brisk and to the point.

'I tink sah de best ting be ifn dey sleep foh de room next to de

132

duty hoffice. Den in de morning time Saji Major he go to HQ Company and dey give him married quarters sah.'

Jos clutched gratefully at his advice. He told the orderly sergeant to arrange for their bedding down as proposed, and he withdrew himself into the orderly room, into his bed, under the mosquito net, under the sheet and soon into deep sleep.

The awakening was terrible. Major Bigwood appeared to be doing a sort of can-can with rage beside his bed, his nasty little dog yapping at his heels.

'Maclean, what on earth is going on ? The whole orderly office is full of women and children and bedclothes and hens for Christ's sake. It's already seven hundred hours and the place is in absolute shit order. What the hell's happening?'

'Sir.' Jos began wishing that he had at least a pair of pyjamas on. He felt the vulnerability of his position was increased by his nakedness. Just then one of the sergeant-major's hens, having managed to escape from the basket, came wandering in. Major Bigwood's dog gave a furious yelp and chased it round the room. The hen flew clumsily on to the top of a filing cabinet and made some loud squawks. A few of its ruffled feathers floated down, one of them landing on Major Bigwood's shoulders.

'Sir.' Jos pushed his way out of bed and the mosquito net in a desperate attempt to retrieve the situation. Major Bigwood looked with horror at the naked apparition emerging, about-turned and stumped off, too angry and agitated to have anything further to do with the shambles in the orderly office for the time being. The door from the adjoining room opened cautiously and the orderly sergeant poked his head round it.

'I sorry sah. I did forget Major Bigwood no gree foh fluff sah. I get dese people outside now sah. Yoh Boy is heah sah. We get yoh bed down foh yoh house sah.'

Jos was grateful for the sympathy in the orderly sergeant's voice and for his help in getting the Otrukpos disengaged from the orderly office. As he emerged buckling on his Sam Browne he saw Okoko standing wide-eyed with astonishment as the Otrukpo offspring filed out into the early morning sunshine. When Okoko saw him his face broke out into a doubtful grin.

'I tink dese people go worry you foh nighttime sah?'

133

'Okoko once more you have hit the nail bang slap in the middle of the head.'

'I get yoh bed one time sah.' Okoko wasn't familiar with the phrase "to hit the nail on the head" but he had recognized the signs of vexation and suppressed anger in Joss tone. He dug his elbow into Ali's rib and said, 'Hurry with de bed now Ali. Didn't you heah what de hapsa say? What my mitre say? Ifn dat we no get de bed down now now he go hit us with a nail on de head one time. Hey Ali you slow too much.'

14

The Sergeant-Major-in-the-night episode proved to be the worst of Jos's trials during his punishment spell as duty officer. Major Bigwood decided not to make any formal report about the presence of the Otrukpo family in the orderly office: when he began to fulminate informally to the Adjutant he was quickly and deftly given to understand by Captain Stanford-Jones that in his opinion Second Lieutenant Maclean had coped quite well with the Otrukpos and that Major Bigwood had been an officious ass in playing an active role as Field Officer for the week and in particular in going up to the orderly office so early in the morning.

Jos was greatly relieved when the long stint came to an end and he was able to resume a normal existence. Indeed everyone seemed to feel that he had been rather unlucky and, from the Colonel down, was particularly pleasant to him. Although Mrs Joynstone continued to regard him coldly, she did not positively forbid Jane to see him. And they managed to see each other a good deal. The Resident often let Jane have the use of his smart coupé when he was off somewhere in the official car: this was much more comfortable and reliable than Jos's old car.

The last evening of Jane's holiday came. She had the use of the coupé, and they drove out the long narrow red road which led to a banana plantation. They had discovered that they could be fairly secluded if they took the turn off to the manager's house and then pulled into a little copse about half way up.

Jos was in a confused state of mind. He had been flattered and pleased that Jane had singled him out as her beau among the many eligible young men in the district. He was attracted to her, but there were many things about her which grated, and he realized that there were not many sympathetic interests between them – apart from the pressing one of the moment that she was a pretty young woman enjoying the courtship of a presentable young man, and that he was that young man enjoying the courting of that young woman. But now with Jane's returning home the circumstances in which their brief romance had flourished were breaking up. The reality which would then reassert itself was that she would return to a prosperous upper middle class world in the south of England and he would remain to serve his time in the Army before returning to a very different lower middle class world in the north of Scotland. These were not insuperable barriers but was their feeling for each other strong and important enough to warrant taking on the problems of overcoming them? Jos was torn between wanting to keep the affair going and thinking it might be best to draw it to a dignified conclusion. He was in consequence looking solemn and a little sour.

'Aren't you going to kiss me?' Jane asked smiling uncertainly into his discontented-looking face. Jos looked into her eyes and felt the confusion of thoughts and emotions intensified. They kissed for a long time, at first simply deriving pleasurable physical and emotional release from that act of sinking into each other, but, as Jos began to feel sexually stirred by the intimacy, a fresh wave of doubts and uncertainties came over him. Although he had always contrived to give the impression of being an experienced man of the world in sexual matters, the truth was that, apart from the extraordinary episode with the prostitute in Soho, he had never gone further with any girl than necking and petting. Necking was the name given by his school and student friends to the prolonged and abandoned sessions of kissing in which they used to indulge. Petting was an American term he had come across recently which he thought must cover various fumbling attempts to touch and caress a girl's breasts and other intimate parts: this happened much less frequently than necking; was regarded as a sign of great debauchery; and, if the truth be told, was of doubtful enjoyment to either party, given its essentially unsatisfying quality, the drafty, uncomfortable conditions in which it was usually undertaken and the fiendish constraints imposed by the clothing worn by the young women of the period. The thought of sexual intercourse itself terrified him. This was not from lack of a strong sexual drive but because of the powerful mixture of ignorance and fear about the unmentionable subject of sex which prevailed in the environment in which he had been brought up. He knew from the shameful pleasure of masturbation – and indeed from the confused emotions and feelings involved in the experience with "Lorraine" – that sexual intercourse must be capable of producing unspeakable bliss, but between that state and the initial fully clothed encounter with a young woman in a public or semi-public place there seemed to stand grotesque and complicated problems of logistics. Moreover even if these logistical difficulties could be overcome there might lie in wait worries about contracting a debilitating and perhaps fatal disease.

His teenage self had been impressed by the "Clean Living is the only real Safeguard" posters which had warned British citizens of one possible and unwelcome consequence of the triumphal return of the heroes home from the war. And if it was perhaps a somewhat neurotic fear that VD might be contracted as a result of having sexual intercourse with one of the girls from the High School, there was a very real danger, in the absence of any contraceptive precautions, that the unthinkable calamity of an illegitimate baby might happen.

In pre-pill Britain very few of the unmarried young seemed to have the gumption or knowledge to do anything about contraception. There were many sniggering jokes about French Letters but few of those making and apparently enjoying the jokes had any very clear idea of what the articles in question looked like, much less where to procure them or how to use them. The whole thing made for immense and tormenting tension. On the one hand the prospect of an unimaginable ecstasy: on the other obstacles of every sort to snare and frighten those who sought to attain it outside the approved married state. And even then there seemed to Jos to be something ludicrous about the actual mechanics involved. It was enough to rekindle his lost faith in the Deity – on the basis that only a thinking Being could have arranged matters as such a cunning practical joke.

What was particularly confusing and disturbing on this occasion was that Jane did not come from his own environment where the underlying assumption among the young was that sex was altogether too dangerous to indulge in to the full until the state of matrimony had been attained. Although Jane was about four years younger than him Jos had been surprised by the number of ways in which she was clearly much more sophisticated and knew her way about. Perhaps young people in her social set "went further" before marriage. He had never forgotten how taken aback he had been by the way she had inserted her tongue into his mouth at an early stage in their kissing – the day of their first tryst at the swimming pool. Where he came from that was deemed a very abandoned and seductive thing for a woman to do: it was not, Jos reflected ruefully, something which had happened to him before. Thus in addition to his uncertainty about whether this should be a final farewell or not, Jos was unsure what was expected of him (and indeed what he really wanted) in the matter of physical intimacy.

Jane also was confused in her thoughts and emotions. It had been a super holiday with all these young army officers flirting with her, and she had enjoyed having Jos as her boyfriend this past few weeks. It was so romantic now, this farewell in the African night. She wondered if he would tell her that he loved her. She wondered if what she was feeling for him was love. Then would he do more than kiss tonight? She remembered the afternoon at the swimming pool and speculated what might have happened if that dreadful Quartermaster person hadn't turned up. She was excited by the strangeness of the male body, and in a way she wanted Jos to touch her and for each to explore the other. But she was at the same time shocked and frightened by her feelings and already tensing herself to resist him.

Jos had meanwhile decided that they should at least get back to the stage at which George had interrupted proceedings at the swimming pool: that is to say he wanted to hold and caress Jane's breasts. But in this he was faced with an immediate practical problem. Jane was wearing a dress which buttoned down the front, and so in order to get at her breasts he would have to make the very obvious move of undoing these buttons: somehow he felt it would have been easier, more subtle if he could have been doing the necessary unbuttoning and unhooking with his arms round her, and thus discreetly behind her back. He kissed Jane with particular fervour and slid his right hand down so that it was holding her breast through the material of her dress and brassiere. Her eyes were still closed and her lips held his. Carefully and gently he shifted his hand and unbuttoned the front of her dress and slid it round to her naked back to unhook her brassiere. To his relief he managed to accomplish this without much difficulty. He realized that Jane had arched her back slightly in order to help him, and then he moved his hand round again so that he felt the soft warm flesh of her breasts under his hands. Slowly he began to rub them with the palm of his hand and then to stroke her nipples until they stood out hard and erect.

'Oh that's nice Jos,' she sighed. 'I wish we could make love completely.'

'Mmm,' Jos assented, wondering uneasily if this was an invitation to set about doing so – and, if so, how on earth the brake, gear lever and steering wheel could be circumvented, if they were to attempt the enterprise on the front seats: alternatively how they could possibly squeeze into the back seat. But Jane seemed only to have been expressing a general sentiment and went on to ask, 'Will you come and see me when you come back home to England?'

Jos winced as all Scotsmen do when their country's separate identity is ignored or submerged in that of their bigger neighbour and ancient enemy. But it was an instinctive thing, a reflex action, the wince. He had the sense to see that it would be idiotically petty to show umbrage in the present circumstances. Still it was the kind of thing that Jane would always be doing.

'That will be almost a year from now. You will have forgotten me long before then.'

'No I won't Jos. Please come to see me.'

'I'll write to you. If we manage to keep that up for a year I'll

139

come to see you.'

Jos felt as he said these words that that was quite a comfortable compromise and a neat way of dealing with the leave-taking. They kissed and their hands caressed each others' bodies for a little longer. Then Jane very purposefully set about refastening and setting her clothes to rights. Jos kissed her gently as she did so. When she was satisfied that she was again presentable, she said, 'I must go now. All the packing's really done, but Auntie Mabel keeps flapping about the hand-baggage and various little presents she's wrapping up for my parents and young sister. Also she says she thinks I might spend my last evening with her and Uncle Nigel. Oh darling please write. Please come to see me.'

With that Jane started the car and drove quickly back to the Mess. Jos got out, and when he bent down to kiss her he saw that her eyes were wet with tears.

'I will write. I will come,' he said.

She was gone then in a swirl of red dust. Jos stood watching the dust settle, feeling strangely sad and empty.

'Oh Romeo, Romeo wherefore art thou Romeo then – eh?' George the Quartermaster shattered the mood of tender poignancy.

'Nice bit of stuff that,' he indicated with a jerk of his head in the direction of the disappearing car and the Residency. 'Not too hoity toity was she? I had an uncle of hers as commanding officer once y'know. Regular tartar he was. Anyhow she's come in nice and 'andy for you young fellows. You'll 'ave to find something else now she's gone. Ever tried the local produce? They are black but comely as the good book says – and also full of pox. So I wouldn't if I was you.'

So the two officers walked in to the ante-room together, and Jos kept to himself the queer mixture of happiness and sadness which the evening with Jane had brought him. To his surprise he found Major Hamilton in the Mess. Hamilton rarely came over except for drinks before Sunday lunch or on Mess Nights.

'Ah Jos, I've been trying to get in touch with you all afternoon. We're so excited: Fifi's had two bitches and two dogs. She's a plucky little thing. We've reserved one of the dogs for you, and we'll have it over to your gidda just as soon as he's weaned. I told Elaine I'd see you tomorrow morning but she insisted I come and give you the good news straightaway. You see Fifi didn't carry the pups to full term. Four is a lot for a little thing like Fifi. Well I must get off. We'll have your little man across to you as soon as we can.'

'Oh yes sir. Thank you sir.'

Hamilton strode off.

'Oh bloody hell!' exclaimed Jos.

'Come now. Come now. How unkinder than a serpent's tooth is the ingratitude of a junior subaltern.'

'Christ. I don't want a bloody dog, George. Certainly not any relation of that horrible Fifi.'

'Come and have a drink, lad. You look as if you could be doing with one.'

Jos had a drink, and then another, and another. He was discovered about midnight by Okoko puzzling over the formula for unlocking and locking his house, looking feebly at the door and muttering 'Go henter in' as if this was a charm, like open sesame!

'Kai sah. You drink too much. Yoh head go worry you foh morning time.'

'Go henter in.'

'Yes sah. One time sah. We go henter in now.'

After Okoko had put Jos to bed he returned to his little round house and climbed in beside the comfortable plumpness of his wife.

'Tangwe – are you awake?' he asked speaking in Idoma.

'Yes.'

'I just put the young master to bed.'

'Very nice of you Okoko.'

'I think he is very sad because the daughter of the sister of the wife of the Resident is flying away in the metal bird tomorrow.'

'The girl called Alice?'

'That's what worries me Tangwe. First I think she is called Alice but now he keeps talking about Jane and Fifi.'

'Don't worry about it Okoko. A girl can have more than one name.'

141

15

Fifi's pup was handed over to Jos a week or two later. He was a very tiny scrap of dog with a very worried looking little face. Jos and Okoko regarded him uncertainly. Jos wondered whether dog-ownership would be considered good, like horse-ownership or bad, like car-ownership by Okoko. He was therefore relieved to see Okoko's strong white teeth flashing into an approving smile.

'Dis be nice dog, sah. I go teach um about piss.'

'What? – Oh yes you mean house-train him. Yes that's essential, Okoko. I'll leave that to you.'

'And shit.'

'Absolutely.'

The little dog looked even more worried: his face was all frown.

'I think I'll call him 'Ernest', Okoko,' said Jos, inspired by the sight of the anxious and solemn little face.

'Is good name, sah.'

At first Ernest was, of course, too small to accompany Jos about the Barracks, but he grew quickly and was soon a familiar sight, tagging along behind Jos's dark green Army bike or scampering ahead of him on foot. Okoko's house-training had been nasty, brutish and short. He beat the little dog with a cold savagery which turned Jos's stomach, but which proved most effective. It was not long before Ernest would rather have done himself physical injury than soil the floors so lavishly polished by Okoko.

It was in October, after Ernest had started to accompany Jos round the barracks that preparations began for a visit by the General-Officer-Commanding the three West African Brigades: a Major-General. There was to be a parade by the unit to which a wide range of local VIPs would be invited, including the Emir of Kebira, and the Resident. CSM Roberts had been giving the officers sword drill at five o'clock every evening for two weeks. The soldiers lived in a constant state of drill and bullshit. Polished boots, brasses, belts and neatly brushed fezzes were stacked in the Barrack rooms each night at the foot of the wooden boards on which the soldiers slept.

The awesome day came at last. Okoko was helping Jos put on his boots and puttees. Jos realized he himself was experiencing a measure of stage fright.

'Now remember, Okoko,' he said. 'Ernest must be locked up this morning to make sure he doesn't follow me up to the parade ground.'

Okoko paused for a moment in winding the puttee round Jos's ankle, and burst into an explosion of laughter.

'Hey, sah, ifn Ernest go march on parade, eberyone go laugh too much. Hey!'

'Well not quite everyone, Okoko. Not the Colonel, nor the Brigadier, nor the GOC. Nor me. Nor, I assure you, you. So just see that he doesn't get out will you?'

'Yes sah. I go catch Ernest foh heah till dat you go come back.'

When Jos got up to the barracks, the troops were standing at ease in their companies, at the far end of the parade ground, facing the saluting dais and the seats for the civilian VIPs. He walked carefully over to his own company trying not to get dust on his gleaming boots or to crumple or to sweat too much into his beautifully pressed and starched uniform. He had a few final words with CSM Roberts about the detail of the drill, and then walked back to the dais, where the officers were to assemble. The sword he was wearing was rather a long one, and he was obsessed with the fear that he might trip over it. The Parade was to begin at 1100 hours, just as the sun was getting unbearably hot. The spectators began to arrive and settle down in their seats under parasols. Billy Rogers, who had signed on for an extra tour of duty as short service officer instead of taking his national service demobilisation ("The old man says he's not quite ready for me yet in the firm"), and

Grimshaw, the regular army subaltern, were acting as ushers to guide the guests to their places. There was much heel-clicking and saluting as the cars of the Generals and the Resident, with pennants flying, drove up. Jos looked wistfully at the Resident's party and wished that Jane was there.

At last everyone was settled. The RSM roared out the commands which brought the Battalion to attention. The Adjutant (who saw the parade ground once a year and this was it) squeaked in a curiously unconvincing voice 'Fall in the officers!'

One-two, three to attention. One-two, three – right hand clasp the hilt of the sword. One-two, three – loosen sword in scabbard. One-two, three–draw hilt of sword up to be level with chin. One-two, three – bring sword down so that the forearm is parallel with the ground: sword parallel with the body. One-two, three, by the left quick march. Jos was relieved to note that all the other officers were marching in step with him towards the Battalion. He was always nervous of inserting an extra "One-two, three" or forgetting one. Now he must be sure that he was marching on the correct bearing. Where was Company Sergeant-Major Roberts? Ah yes there was D Company, and there was the white mark he had to reach, halt and about turn: better shorten his stride a little. Left, right, left, right, halt – about turn. Standing stiffly to attention in front of the Company, Jos looked straight towards the saluting dais and the spectators. Made it, he thought to himself, relieved. But why was everyone looking at him? And smiling – laughing? Trying not to move a muscle but somehow to find out what was going on, Jos swivelled his eyes first to the left and downwards and then to the right and downwards. Looking up at him, ears cocked to attention was Ernest. Jos's hand tightened on his sword. Oh Okoko, I wonder what you will look like, impaled on the end of this?

The Adjutant was now giving the orders. 'Battalion stand at ease: stand easy.'

Jos looked down at Ernest.

'Go home boy! Home! Good dog. Home boy!'

Ernest wagged his tail, delighted to be taken notice of.

Jos saw the Adjutant and the Colonel in anxious confabulation and each of them looking over in his direction. Then he was startled to hear the Adjutant's voice calling

'Second Lieutenant Maclean, Attention! By the left quick march!'

Jos felt not merely his face but his whole body burning with embarrassment.

'Left Whee-e-el!'

The effect of this command was to point him straight at the Colonel.

'Halt!'

Jos found himself right bang in front of the Colonel. He saluted with his sword. The Colonel's normally amiable and abstracted expression was transformed. His features were working convulsively. He hissed –

'This is the absolute last straw Maclean. This is the sort of behaviour that completely breaks the camel's back.' Jos noted with one part of his agitated mind that even in a crisis the Colonel's tendency to talk in clichés did not abandon him. The Colonel went on. 'This is a military parade, Maclean, not a goddamned circus. Get this animal off parade,' here he pointed at Ernest who had proudly followed Jos across the parade ground, left wheeling with him, and now was settled cosily at his feet – looking up at the Colonel with every appearance of listening attentively and approvingly to what he had to say. 'Put it in the guardroom, and return at once yourself.'

'Sir!' Jos saluted again and marched swiftly over to the guardroom. There he handed Ernest over to the guard commander. Then, his face still aflame with embarrassment, he began the lonely march back on to the parade ground, aware of the stillness of the Battalion, the rustle of amusement among the spectators, hearing his own feet pounding out a solitary left, right, left, right, and seeing out of the corner of his eye the black shadow of his figure against the reddish sand of the parade ground. After that the moves which he and his soldiers had to execute on the parade seemed easy and relaxing – and were all greatly supported by the familiar tunes of the Regimental Band: the fifes and drums.

It had been arranged that once the parade was over, the officers would join the VIPs for pre-lunch drinks at the Mess.

145

Although it was quite some time before Jos and the other subalterns were done with their tasks of ensuring that the parade was properly dismissed and the various companies reassembled in sequence for dinner Parade, or fatigues to dismantle the dais etc., Jos decided he had better not risk incurring further wrath by failing to report for this social occasion: anyhow he felt that he needed a drink. The interview with Okoko would have to wait. He approached the Mess apprehensively. He had never seen the Colonel so worked up about anything before: no doubt he was a bit on edge with the Divisional Commander and the Brigadier both round his neck, not to mention the Emir, the Resident and so forth. Hamilton would probably be pretty decent on this occasion since he had bred the wretched dog and given it to him. Jos undid his Sam Browne and hung it and his hat up on the coat stand.

'Oh Jos,' a cooing voice greeted him, and Elaine Hamilton sidled up beside him, resting her hand on his bare, short sleeved arm. 'What a naughty little fellow that pup of Fifi's is!' she said stroking Jos's arm gently and looking intimately into his eyes.

By a tacit mutual prudence neither Elaine Hamilton nor Jos had ever uttered a word to each other nor of course to anyone else, about the brief, passionate visit which she had paid Jos when there seemed a risk that he might be charged with the murder of Corporal Bassey. Each was always intensely aware of the presence of the other, but on each side it was a limited, uncomplicated sexual attraction, and neither of them would have wanted to incur the messy and hurtful consequences of developing an affair. Jos was therefore a little uneasy to feel the pressure of Elaine's hand on his arm and to detect the smell of gin on her breath. He wondered why she was hanging about outside the ante-room. He assumed she had been visiting the Mess watercloset since there was no other very obvious reason for her to appear on her own in the Mess lobby like this.

'Yes Elaine,' he said looking round warily to see if Major Hamilton was also about to manifest himself: that would be all I need, he thought, to have my company commander suspect me of having an affair with his wife. 'I expect I'm in for it now.'

'Oh no, Jos. Timmy and I were just saying that it shows what a good master you are to that little dog.'

146

'Well that wasn't quite the view the Colonel seemed to be taking.'

'Oh Pooh! Bobby's not being stuffy is he?'

'Well he didn't have me marched across the parade ground to congratulate me on the affection I seemed to have inspired in animals.'

By now they were in the ante-room and Jos excused himself on the grounds that he must go and get a drink and then circulate among the guests. He saw Mrs Sidcup, the rather jolly wife of the Unilever representative at one end of the room and the Generals at the other. He made for the group in which Mrs Sidcup was holding forth, punctuating her remarks with her rather wheezy laugh.

'Oh here's the officer with that dear little dog!' she exclaimed as Jos joined the group. 'How on earth did you train him so well. I've never seen that done before on one of these parades.'

'No, no – it isn't a regular feature in most regiments.'

'And that my dear Dolly,' said George, the Quartermaster, 'is the understatement of the year.' George leaned unsteadily forward as he said this and patted Mrs Sidcup tenderly on her back, the small of her back. George had been entertaining guests and himself assiduously for about three-quarters of an hour.

'Ah Jos,' the Resident had come up upon the group unawares. 'I didn't know you were about to install a Regimental Mascot! You know its a pity the Battalion doesn't have one. It helps to liven up the show a bit . . . . Bobby!' he called over to the Colonel. 'I was just saying to our young friend here that his performance with his dog this morning put me in mind of regiments with mascots. The quick march, left wheel and halt were really first class. You've never thought of instituting something along these lines for the Battalion have you?'

The Colonel was now considerably mellowed as a consequence of several stiff whiskies, and he listened with befuddled interest to the Resident's comments. 'Mascot?' he repeated the word once or twice savouring the sound of it but looking as if he could not quite remember what it meant. 'Good Lord yes!' he exclaimed as memory returned to smooth away the puzzled frown from his face. 'I think you're right, Nigel. We ought to have a mascot.' He beamed happily for a few moments, warming to the idea. 'What should it be I wonder?'

George who seemed to have suffered some sort of reverse in his rather elephantine attempts at flirtation with Mrs Sidcup: been given the message that her bottom was definitely not for pinching, was now sunk in a bitter alcoholic haze. He was half-attending to this chatter about a regimental mascot and found himself sourly commenting, only half *sotto voce*,

'Why not the bush cow? That should be our mascot. Lunch and dinner every bleeding day: roast bush cow. Stewed bush cow. Stuff the bloody bush cow. Tough, stringy, ineligible bloody bush cow. All that remains is for us to have the perishing animal come on parade as well.' He contemplated gloomily the dregs of the pink gin in his glass.

The Colonel's hearing was acute, even if his other faculties were impaired by the volume of pre-lunch drinks with which he had been restoring his morale. He paid no attention to George's dietary complaints but he seized on the idea of the bush cow as the regimental mascot.

'Bush cow!' he exclaimed. 'Now there's an idea! Why, of course that's the very thing. We are in the heart of bush cow country here: see the blighters everywhere you go. Look here. Never leave undone. Strike while the iron's hot. I'm going to take the Brigadier's temperature on that straightaway.' And with that the Colonel wove his way purposefully towards the Brigadier.

He was back in two or three minutes with a distinctly crestfallen look on his face.

'I flew that kite about the bush cow over the Brigadier. Didn't rise to it at all. Said something about it being the fiercest beast in West Africa: said it was really a kind of buffalo. Did you know that Maclean?'

'Er – well as a matter of fact I did sir.'

'Well what beats me is why it was ever suggested that we should keep one here as a mascot.' The Colonel blinked in a hurt, confused sort of way. The Resident was looking uneasily at the Colonel and at the Quartermaster, each of whom was showing signs of greater intoxication than was at all seemly at a pre-lunch drinks party – particularly one which they were hosting. He exhibited all the signs of the experienced diplomat wanting to get away from trouble before it happened.

'Bobby!' he said enthusiastically. 'Wonderful party! I'm going to have to round up my gang and be getting off home now. Thank you ever so much for . . . .'

'Incredible, that's what I meant to say.' The Resident's skilful disengaging speech was interrupted by George who was vaguely aware that he had used the wrong word in describing the bush cow as ineligible.

'Yes,' said George well satisfied to have solved this mystery. 'Incredible bloody bush cow: that's what it is.'

'Actually old man,' intervened Billy Rogers, flushed with self-importance from his duties as an usher and also from the amount of gin-and-tonic which he had felt it necessary to consume in discharging them. 'Actually,' and here he put a patronizing arm across the Quartermaster's shoulders. 'You were quite right. Bush cow is ineligible – for anything! And also incredible. But I think the word you were groping for, George, was inedible.'

George's small, bloodshot, drink-befuddled eyes looked blankly and suspiciously at Billy. They contained a "beware poofter" element as he disengaged from Billy's patronizing embrace.

'Wonderful parade, Bobby. Marvellous show. And delightful drinks party . . . .' The Resident stood not upon the order of his going any longer.

And in fact once the Resident's party had gone the other guests began to thin out quite rapidly. The Major-General and the Brigadier were lunching at the Colonel's House, and the single officers soon had the Mess to themselves.

'Bit of a nonsense that dog of yours going on Parade, Jos.' Billy Rogers commented aggrievedly, nibbling at the cherry in a glass of Pimms which had turned out to be surplus to requirements in a lavish order he had commissioned on behalf of a group of guests. He seemed to be moving from the euphoria of a few drinks too many to the gloom of feeling hung-over.

'Aye,' Dainton laughed raucously. 'The old man seemed

149

pretty steamed up about it when he was giving you a rollicking on the parade ground, Jos. Made you put the poor little bugger in jankers I see. As a matter of fact I suspect the episode has affected his brain. What was all that about him wanting to get a bush cow as a pet? The Brigadier thinks he's gone off his rocker.'

'Not as a pet. The Resident suggested it might be a good idea if we had a regimental mascot, and the CO was so pissed he went blundering off to the Brigadier and asked him what he thought about having a live specimen as a mascot.'

'That's the bit I heard,' said Dainton. 'The Brigadier did not mince his words: lot of scathing stuff about it being the fiercest animal in West Africa. I hope the poor old CO is making out better at lunch. Come on let's go and eat.'

'First of all I want to see Okoko,' said Jos and stalked off grimly to his gidda.

Okoko was sitting listlessly on the back doorstep, gazing glumly at the ground.

He hoisted himself to his feet as Jos approached and turned a face of mute suffering towards him.

'Kai sah I do you bad sah. I sorry too much.'

Jos was shaken by the look of pain in Okoko's eyes. But there was considerable momentum to his anger and it drove him on to say, 'Yes. I'll say you do me bad. You've made a complete fool of me. Damn you. The simplest thing I ask and you bloody well let me down.'

It was like taking a whip to a dying man. Okoko's head slumped forward and he groaned, 'Is true sah. Is true.'

'Well how did it happen, Okoko?'

'I go catch Ernest like you say me sah. I go put um foh house and lock um in. Den I go wash yoh clothes sah. I see yoh KD Bush shirt he no dere sah. So I say "Hey Ali. Go to my mitre's house. Go fetch his KD Bush shirt one time." I give um key, and he go sah. Den I see Ernest go fast fast too much foh parade ground, and I come here sah to be sad.'

'Jesus! I always knew trouble would result from all these damn hangers on like Ali. You're supposed to be my batman and do the work and not to act like a head butler or something.'

150

'Is true sah. I do you bad.'

'Well you'd better go up to the Guardroom now and get Ernest out of jail. And you'd better get my long slacks and evening kit bulled up again. I wouldn't be surprised if I get an extra duty officer spell out of this.'

'Hay sah I sorry too much.'

Jos inspite of himself could not but feel mollified by the look of extreme contrition, sympathy and indeed suffering on Okoko' face. Suddenly it burst in to a dazzling grin.

'Ernest in de guardroom you say? Kai! He go before the CO. Left, right, left, right. Halt! Private Ernest I go give you tree days confined to barracks!' Okoko doubled with laughter at the thought. The hard lines returned to Jos's face as he watched Okoko giggle off towards the guardroom. They set deeper still when he discovered that he had indeed been given an extra spell of weekend duty officer.

16

After lunch on Saturday the ugly little 15cwt truck called at Jos's gidda to transport his bed and night attire up to the orderly room. Okoko went up with the truck in order to make up the bed and generally make things as comfortable as possible. Jos followed on, on his bicycle, with Ernest padding at his heels. When he got up to the orderly room he attempted to have his usual siesta. But it was a brief and uneasy affair: the electric fan was on but it could not compete with the heat burning through the corrugated iron roof. The fanless thatched roof of his own gidda was much cooler.

At five o'clock Okoko brought him a cup of coffee; and after drinking it he set off to inspect the serving of the evening meal to the recruits in his own company. A soldier who belonged to the Tiv tribe was the company cook. He had the deep facial scars of his tribe which made his face appear somewhat sinister in repose and conflicted with his normal jovial and animated style. His name was Corporal Agba. He came bustling forward as Jos approached.

'Ho! Ho! Good ebening sah. Fine fine chop dis ebening sah. Dese boys,' indicating the assembled soldiery, 'get full bell too much with dis good chop.'

'I'm glad to hear it, Corporal Agba,' Jos replied warily, thinking what a bullshitter Agba was.

'I begin now sah?' Corporal Agba queried politely, pulling up a little stool for himself and setting it before the two large cauldrons, one of yams, the other of soupy gravy. Jos nodded for him to begin and selected a piece of yam for himself, salted it and began to munch it. Corporal Agba flourished his ladle and began serving the soldiers as they filed past. Closely examined, the corporal was a disgraceful sight in his grubby green vest and his stained white trousers. The immediate impression he created however was one of dazzling hygiene: this was due to a vast chef's hat gleaming white on the top of his gleaming black face. As he had approached the kitchen, Jos had seen Corporal Agba cleave his way through the platoon of patiently queueing recruits in order to don this headpiece: he clearly appreciated its presentational effect.

Seated comfortably on his little stool Corporal Agba sloshed the viands on to the passing soldiers' plates. After a while he turned conversationally to Jos and asked, 'Yo' dog fine sah? He be good dog I tink sah: cost you plenty of money sah?'

Jos stiffened. The West African flair for taking the mickey out of the European could sometimes amount to genius – but it was usually done more subtly than this.

'He's OK. He's a good enough little dog. Didn't actually cost me any kudi.'

'Ho! Ho! "Kudi"! Oh sah you speak Hausa pass all dose udder hapsas.' Corporal Agba poured out this flattery, detecting the note of suspicion in Jos's voice and realizing that he had perhaps sailed too close to the wind in referring to the dog so soon after the shambles of the Divisional Commander's Parade. Nervously suiting his actions to his words, the Corporal poured out lavish helpings of gravy on to the dishes of the recruits who happened to be passing at the time. Jos continued to regard him warily. He suspected that his attempts to speak Hausa were a subject of jest among the Africans. Corporal Agba sensed that he might have put his foot in it again. His skin did not permit him to blush, but he perspired even more freely than he had been doing as a result of his cooking activities. He took his anxiety out on the recruit who now stood before him.

'Oh you stupid boy. What fo' you go put yoh plate fo' dere? You tink I fit go waste time fo' you? I go put you fo' guardroom ifn dat you do dat anudder time.'

'Good yams,' said Jos to ease the situation.

'You chop yams sah!' exclaimed Corporal Agba, as if he had just noticed this amazing phenomenon. He beamed at Jos for a moment or two in apparently speechless and incredulous admiration.

'Oh sah you gree fo Africa too much now. When dat you come go fo' home, dey tink dat you be Africa man proppa. When dat yo' mudder and yo' brudder see you come, dey say "Hey who be dat man dere? Who be dat *black* man?" ' – this an insincere tribute to Jos's painfully acquired suntan – 'Dat no be our dear brudder who go Army. Kai!' Corporal Agba was quite carried away by the little scene he was enacting. The fortunate recruits who happened to be served while he was portraying the magnitude of the mudder's and brudder's presumed astonishment had brimming ladles slammed down on their plates. The unfortunate ones who were passing as he was seeking to convey the seed of doubt about Jos's personal identity had droplets of gravy dribbled hesitantly on to tiny bits of yam. Jos began to feel embarrassed and to think that the welfare of the troops would best be served by his withdrawal from the scene. In any case he intended to have a look now at the African married lines. So he whistled to Ernest and cycled off.

The married lines were the rows of small mud and thatch houses where the permanent staff at the training depot – mainly noncommissioned officers – lived with their wives and children. Every now and then the CO became obsessed with the need to "smarten them up a bit", to "get a grip on the hygiene angle". He was going through one of these phases at the moment: indeed he had given a talk in the education officer's room to officers and warrant officers, class I, under various headings which he had scratched up on the blackboard *The Health Hazard, The Fire Hazard* etc., gesticulating wildly at the blackboard and at his audience with a long pointer, thereby creating in the minds of some of those present doubt as to whether they would survive the pointer hazard without the loss of at least one of their eyes.

As Jos turned down the path leading to the married lines he saw afar off glinting in the sun the fire buckets, empty, as usual, and, coming towards him the "Headwoman of the Married Quarters" to protest – as usual – that she had just checked them a few moments previously and could not understand what had happened. She was a charming lady, very black skinned and rather voluptuous, except for her thin and bandy-looking legs which appeared coyly at the foot of her long khaki skirt. This skirt and a red sash which had been converted into a massive but rather fetching brassiere were the bait by which the Unit prevailed upon one of the NCOs wives to "Take responsibility for the condition of the Married Lines". Mrs Bagarmi was ideally suited for the job. She bore the periodic rockets and fussings from the RSM and the Colonel with dignified equanimity, and had a knack of silencing the latter – stopping him in mid-rocket – by smiling at him thus revealing gums innocent of all but two fierce-looking canine teeth. Jos for his part always made a point of avoiding that smile if he possibly could. Therefore despite the current concern of the Colonel with the fire hazard, Jos contented himself with remonstrating very mildly about the emptiness of the fire buckets.

'I 'gree sah. I 'gree!' Mrs Bagarmi exploded emphatically. This was another of her disconcerting pieces of lifemanshp: to outdo one in the fervour with which she espoused the criticism one was seeking to make. 'Dem bad people, dey come take water I tink.' Here she gave a jerk of her chin in the general direction of the Sahara Desert. Then she looked intently and anxiously at Jos.

'You get power again, sah?'

Jos looked at her apprehensively, wondering what tactic she was about to employ in order to change the subject from fire buckets and to put him on the defensive.

'Hey dat doki,' Mrs Bagarmi continued. 'He be bad doki too much sah. Kai!' And here she shook her head with worried misgiving.

So that was it. After his experiences with polo and polo ponies, Jos had stayed clear of horses for a while. But shortly after Jane had gone home he had taken a half share in the docile old pony which Billy Rogers rented. In fact Billy hardly ever sought to exercise his right to ride the pony, and Jos had found his part share of White Cloud a useful supplement to the means of getting about the countryside. The previous Sunday he had been coming back from a visit to the Assistant District Officer with whom he had taken to playing an occasional game of chess. As he was making his stately progress back he had detected unwonted signs of liveliness in the elderly horse and he had – foolishly – decided to encourage it into a gallop just, as it happened, as they were passing the African married lines. Unfortunately the horse had put his foot in a hollow or his old legs had momentarily given way beneath him. The result was that Jos had somersaulted over the horse's head and landed up on the threshold of B Company Latrine Corporal's house.

All week he had had to endure the sight of anxious black faces, asking how was mastah and – the more daring ones – how was dat bad doki dat trew mastah. Mrs Bagarmi now threw all caution to the winds and went in for an orgy of insincere ham-acting.

'Dat yo' doki he be bad doki pass all dose udder dokis fo' udder hapsas.' She was rolling her eyes, wagging her finger and shaking her head. Jos muttered something about the horse not really being so vicious and intractable and was about to make his getaway leaving Mrs Bagarmi in possession of the field and the still empty fire buckets when they were both startled by a sudden outburst of squawking, barking and shrieking. Jos looked round just in time to see Ernest disappear into the womens' bath house in pursuit of a scrawny fowl. The screams redoubled with aquatic overtones.

'Here hold this,' Jos said to Mrs Bagarmi, leaning his bicycle over to her. He made for the door of the bathhouse. He did not like the and-this-is-the-man-who-speaks-to-me-about-fire buckets look in her eye but he felt that there was no time to be lost. Judging from the screams at least one of the bathers was having hysterics. The door of the bathhouse stood wide open: in fact it had been off its hinges for several months. Jos stood awkwardly in the doorway.

'Ernest . . . Ernest . . . ERNEST . . . wheeee . . . wheeee . . . wheeee . . . good dog . . . good boy . . . come on Ernest . . . .'

A horde of children began to gather round laughing and clapping their hands and calling excitedly to Jos.

'Heel boy heel boy . . . HEEL!' he thundered sternly. Not a sign of him. Christ, thought Jos, what do I do now? Why on earth are the women so panicky about a little dog like Ernest? Two of the children, whom he recognized as Mrs Bagarmi's, seemed on the point of doing themselves physical injury with giggling. But his shouting and whistling were going otherwise unrewarded. Nothing for it, Jos concluded, but to go in and grab the little brute. He ventured in whereupon there was a crescendo of noise which made the previous uproar sound like the Glasgow Orpheus Choir during the pianissimo parts of the Eriskay Lovelilt.

For a second or two there was a wild flashing of gleaming black and brown bodies, and then silence and nothing to be seen except nine pairs of eyes, largely whites of eyes gazing over the top of the trough-like sink which ran down the middle of the bathhouse. Jos assumed that Ernest also must be over on that side. Oh God he realized uneasily: it was the thought of me following Ernest which they must have been so agitated about! How on earth do I get out of here with any semblance of dignity or authority? Indeed how do I get out of here without having to face a charge of attempted mass rape. If only I could communicate, he mused. If only he had stuck into his Hausa classes he might be able to calm the women down, assure them of his honourable intentions. The only phrase he could think of was "Bring me my bathwater straightaway".

That was clearly not much help: indeed perhaps open to misconstruction in the circumstances. What about "Bring me my dog straightaway". But what was the word for "dog"? And anyhow how could the phrase be adjusted to subtract bathwater and add the unknown word for dog. And for Christ's sake a fat lot of good that would do!

While Jos was wrestling with these problems of linguistics and communication, Mrs Bagarmi sauntered in. She addressed Jos in reproachful tones.

'Sah, dey say dey no want you to henter here.'

'No, no . . . I quite realize . . . good heavens . . . .'

'Dey say dat ifn you go dere,' and here Mrs Bagarmi gave another of her vigorous chin jerks to indicate the other side of the trough 'dey no get cloth at all sah, AT ALL.'

'Well yes of course . . . all I want . . . .'

Mrs Bagarmi fixed him with her sceptical worldly eye as if to say that she knew what the all was that men usually wanted.

'Sah,' she said with a heavy and irritating sigh, 'I tink dey make plenty palaver ifn you go dere,' again pointing with her chin in the direction of the sink. 'I tink de best ting is I go catch Henrest.'

Meekly Jos agreed, thinking gloomily that her corruption of Ernest to Henrest might be all too grimly appropriate . . . . He was reassured on this point however by renewed squawking as Mrs Bagarmi strolled round to the other side of the sink. Presently she strolled back with the hen gripped by its legs in one hand and a wet and deeply embarrassed looking Ernest grasped by the collar in the other.

'I tink it better we go now sah.' The odd sceptical glint was in her eye again. Jos squirmed under it uneasily. She clearly thinks I'm a sex maniac he thought.

And thus they emerged from the shade of the bathhouse to the cruel light of day, a foursome reading from right to left – the hen, Mrs Bagarmi, Ernest and Jos. Outside there seemed to have foregathered the entire complement of "married families" – in serried ranks and breathless with anticipation. The women and children gaped with totally unconcealed curiosity. One or two of the more sophisticated NCOs struck a just-happened-to-be-passing-by-on-my-Saturday-constitutional pose: but it was not well done. Mrs Bagarmi alone maintained her equipoise. She looked boldly about her and bawled at an urchin of about ten 'Hey you boy I tink I done tell you go catch water foh dem fire buckets.'

Jos recognized this as the *coup de grace* for him. The boy showed no glimmering of understanding until Mrs Bagarmi addressed him in Hausa. It was clear that the English version had been directed at Jos and meant 'I be one up on you again sah and dat'll teach you to go mention dem ole fire bucket anudder time.'

He never did.

17

It was shortly after the dog-on-parade incident that another, and much more disturbing canine event occurred. This was primarily the fault of Betty Stanford-Jones, the Adjutant's wife. Betty was an impulsive and warmhearted young woman who greatly tried the patience of her quiet, efficient and hardworking husband, Tony.

Captain Anthony B Stanford-Jones, was of a different stamp from the other regular officers in the unit. They for the most part saw their secondment to a colonial regiment as very much a case of having been put out to grass by their parent regiment, and as an opportunity to savour the life style of the upper classes, with servants, drinks before dinner, pony in the stables etc., in advance of the next posting, which might well be to civvy street and a desperate search for a job. But Tony Stanford-Jones was an ambitious career officer who had volunteered for the secondment in order to be appointed as an Adjutant at a relatively early age. And he regarded the posting as a very useful widening of his experience generally. He was at once besotted by the (considerable) physical charm of Betty and exasperated almost beyond endurance by her frequent acts of foolishness – many of which seemed to cause him a measure of professional embarrassment.

The dog population at the barracks consisted of the Hamilton's dachshund, Fifi, the mongrels resulting from her union with the pye-dog, of which Ernest was one, a bad-tempered little cairn terrier belonging to Major Bigwood and a smooth-haired fox terrier, the property of Colour-Sergeant Bowes. But around the barracks, the old city and the Sabongari, there were various tall, tawny-coloured dogs, always referred to as pye-dogs, half-wild and tending to move around in packs, but half-tame in their propensity to regard a particular house as their source of scraps.

One of these dogs, a rather handsome specimen, took to following Mrs Stanford-Jones about. At first it was very timid and always kept a respectful, fearful distance. But once Betty became aware that the dog had taken to following her – and to lying outside her house when she was in it – she became immensely flattered. There was no doubt that they made an attractive picture; the tall, slim, tanned young woman and the tall, tawny animal loping along behind her. The upshot was that Betty determined to "make a proper pet" of it. So instead of getting the boys to leave out the occasional scraps for the pye-dog, she took to coaxing the animal to come and eat from her hands. It was a short step from that to having the dog come into the house, lying in front of the (forever unlit) fireplace and so forth. Tony viewed all this with considerable unease but he knew that Betty was bored half to death while he was busy at the orderly office – and being the Adjutant he tended to work long and irregular hours – and he had not the heart to thwart her. The dog became more and more amenable, and developed affection for Tony also, sometimes following him up to the Barracks – for instance on the days when Betty went with the other wives on a "girls' Shopping Expedition" to Kaduna. On these occasions the dog would follow Tony into the mess while the Adjutant had the quick beer which he sometimes treated himself to on his way back to the married quarters, and because of that a large proportion of the European population of Kebira became implicated in the unfortunate events which were to follow.

The dog slept in a kennel which Betty had got the house servants to make, on the verandah of their house. She often took it for a little walk in the cool hour before breakfast, before the sun got properly up. She had given it the name Rupert and the beast was beginning to answer to her calls very readily. About two months after the adoption of Rupert she went out early one morning and tiptoed up to the kennel, calling archly "Who's a sleepy boy then? Who's going to come a walk with mummy? Come on Rupert you can't lie there all day." And so on. Smiling her smile of mock reproof she looked into the kennel. And then she recoiled in shock. Because what confronted her was a hideous twisted snarl, and the head in which the bared fangs were exposed was twitching convulsively. As the dog's eyes sought to focus on Betty it rushed at her and, fortunately, past her, with a tormented, howling bark. Tony had been awakened by the noise, and was swiftly out on the verandah to protect and comfort Betty. By the time he got there poor Rupert was racing round the compound in a private agony, not at that moment a danger to anyone. Ali Dikwa, Tony's Batman, now appeared, and, taking one look at Rupert hissed out the words 'Mahaukachin Kare'! Tony's Hausa was not good, but he had made his own diagnosis.

'Rabies?' he asked Ali.

'Yes, sah. He must go die.'

Betty screamed and wept and pled with her husband for poor Rupert's life, a second opinion and so on. But Tony's overriding concern now was to have the dog put down before it ran amok and started biting soldiers, civilians – men, women and children. He was not a particularly good shot himself, but he remembered that Ali Dikwa was a marksman. He led Betty gently into the house and, giving her some brandy, persuaded her to lie down on the bed from which they had just risen. Then he wrote a note to the armoury sergeant instructing him to supply Private Ali Dikwa with a .303 rifle and ten rounds of ammunition; and he told Ali Dikwa to speed off with the note to the armoury on his, Tony's bicycle.

The dog meanwhile seemed to be having convulsions in one corner of the compound; and Tony and his cook and Small Boy shooed and shouted away the group of spectators which was rapidly beginning to form. In about fifteen minutes Ali Dikwa was back, and by the time he presented himself with the rifle and the rounds of ammunition, Tony had had a chance to think about the wider implications of the affair. He had no reason to think that Rupert had bitten anyone, but he had an uneasy feeling that drastic measures tended to be taken in such cases on the grounds that the rabies virus was extremely infectious. Therefore if, as seemed almost certain, the dog was rabid, he feared that an enormous programme of injections

161

would probably have to be undertaken in order to safeguard those who had patted and fondled the dog over the past few weeks. The expense, the inconvenience and the distress were going to be considerable; and all this was not going to look good as an entry in his Curriculum Vitae. On the other hand if there was any chance that the dog was just having some sort of fit, all the disturbance – and its potentially awkward career consequences – could be avoided. Clearly he could not take the risk of not having the dog put down, but it occurred to him that there might be advantage in having it done in such a way that it would be possible to test whether the dog had in fact been rabid. Tony was an ambitious little fellow.

He and Ali Dikwa advanced out from the verandah into the compound. Ali Dikwa loading the rifle as they went.

'It's OK to shoot from here, Ali.' Tony said. 'There are no houses or paths behind where the dog is. And, Ali, don't aim for the head: we may want to have the brain examined.'

Ali Dikwa regarded Tony for an instant as if he thought that it was the Adjutant's brain which required examination. But then he pressed the rifle butt snugly into his shoulder, and breathing calmly and steadily he trained the sights of the rifle on the convulsive dog, and with the smooth confidence of the marksman, he gently squeezed the trigger and shot poor Rupert through the heart.

Jos was just buckling on his Sam Browne before going up to the Mess for breakfast when he heard the shot. 'Oh Christ!' he muttered, frantically trying to remember the drill for assembling the riot squad: being officer commanding the riot squad was one of the least welcome of the chores he had recently had imposed upon him. It's a bugle call, he remembered, but he could not recall how to activate the bugler; and, he reflected bitterly, I'll bet none of the buggers in the squad recognizes it. He dashed out of the gidda and ran up towards the Mess. But before he got anywhere near the Mess he encountered several excited children – members of the Mess servants' families. Jos recognized the Mess sergeant's elder daughter and asked her what all the commotion was about. The girl explained breathlessly 'Dat kare foh Mrs Adjutant he de go mad and done die.'

Just then Sergeant Ali Kontagora, the Mess sergeant him-

162

self, appeared and confirmed that this was the case. Jos heaved an enormous sigh of relief and went on up for breakfast.

In the course of the morning the news of Rupert's madness and Ali Dikwa's marksmanship spread all over the barracks. The Adjutant was sorely tried by it all. For one thing his wife Betty was in a distressed and hysterical state, blaming him, blaming Ali Dikwa, blaming herself, Africa, the army and so on. He did not like to leave her but he knew he should be in the thick of things: arranging – or circumventing – the preventive measures which the medical officer would now be bound to consider. He got the cook's wife, a rather jolly Ibo woman who ran her own stall in the market in the Sabongari, to sit with Betty while he cycled up to his Office.

Tony's first move once he had dealt with a few urgent papers on his desk, was to knock on the Colonel's door – which led off from the orderly office – and to ask the Colonel if he thought his wife would be available and willing to go over and comfort Betty. The Colonel had of course heard of the affair by now and was showing signs of being thoroughly put out by it. But he agreed readily enough to the Adjutant's request.

'Of course, Tony. Friend in need, friend indeed,' he said getting up from his desk and positioning himself where he could most easily see out of the window. Tony had noticed that this was a favourite position whenever the Colonel seemed to feel at all bothered by events in the office. Tony wasn't sure whether the Colonel saw the window as a means of escape or as a source of inspiration. Either possibility would accord with the way the Colonel tended to look wildly up and down the parade ground when the problem was a particularly tricky one. 'Yes, Tony. I'll ask Priscilla to go over to Betty straightaway, complete with a shoulder to cry on. But y'know it was a damn silly business taking one of those dingo things into your house like that. Always knew no good would come of it.'

Tony recalled bitterly the affectionate fuss which the Colonel had made of Rupert at the drinks party which he and Betty had given last weekend. But he kept his counsel. Just then Dixon the Medical Officer knocked at the door, gave his awkward, self conscious salute and walked in.

'Ah there you are, Bert,' said the Colonel. 'Now what's to be done about this mad dog? – mad dogs and Englishmen – eh?'

'Well from all accounts the dog seems to have been mad all right, sir, and I gather that it has been put down. The question is what is to be done about the human beings who have been in contact with it?'

'But no-one was bitten by the poor brute,' protested the Colonel.

'No, sir. But the infection is in the saliva of the animal. Anyone who has patted it or brushed against it with their bare skin – particularly if they have, as soldiers and children often have, grazes or cuts.'

'Good Lord!' the Colonel exclaimed, looking uneasily down at his bony knees, and then with alarm at his plump forearms and hands, the knuckles of which were quite badly scratched. The scratches were the result of no more soldierly activity than a playfully amorous – but as it turned out singularly ill-judged – piece of horseplay on the night of his third wedding anniversary.

Throughout most of his time as a professional soldier the Colonel had been a bachelor, but three years previously he had married while in Britain on home leave, the widow of a Harley Street Specialist. Although he had delayed into his early forties before entering the wedded state, once in it the Colonel had proved himself a most ardent and devoted husband. On the occasion of the third wedding anniversary he had been quite carried away by the champagne with which he had plied himself and Priscilla, and as a result had attempted too enthusiastically and too soon to unzip his wife's dress. She had promptly zipped it up again, catching the skin on his knuckles in the zip, and sent him with a flea in his ear to spend the night in the spare room. The Colonel morosely recalled the episode and looked gloomily at the marks of the scratches on his fingers: unmistakable entrance points for rabid infection.

'What's to be done then?' he asked.

'Sir,' Tony broke in. 'I wonder if we need to take any drastic measures yet. I have the head of the animal in my office,' and here he nodded towards the connecting door. 'I suggest the best thing in the first instance is to send the head to the laboratory at the military hospital in Kaduna for analysis to see if the animal really had rabies.'

The Colonel glanced uneasily at the connecting door to the adjutant's office, but before he had a chance to opine, Dixon cut in – with relish, 'Out of the question,' he said. 'By all means let us get the lab boys to do their stuff. But it will have to be Lagos, you know: military hospital Kaduna is not equipped for that sort of thing. No doubt there will have to be all sorts of bumf and precautions involved in transporting the suspected source of infection that far. And we certainly can't afford to hang around waiting for all that to take place. No,' and Dixon's zest increased as he went on, 'We'll have to draw up a list of all military and civilian personnel who have been in contact with the dog, and have them immunised.'

'What? – you mean Africans too?' the Colonel queried, letting his candid racism show.

'Certainly, sir,' replied Dixon dryly. 'We are talking of human contact.'

'Might as well do the horses and household pets as well,' said the Colonel sourly and illogically.

'No sir,' Dixon replied, enjoying the exchange more by the minute. 'We can destroy those if they begin to show symptoms.'

Tony was becoming more and more worried by all this. Any hopes he might have had that the immunisation programme could be delayed or confined to anyone actually bitten by the dog had been dashed by Dixon's determined enthusiasm to mount an immediate and comprehensive programme of injections. And now he could just imagine the reaction of the Colonel and horsy Majors if their ponies had to be put down. Moreover he was picqued that his idea of preserving the head for analysis had been given such short shrift by the medical officer.

'What exactly will be involved?' he asked.

'Oh you know Tony,' the Colonel intervened. 'It'll be a jag in the arm like typhoid or tetanus, the usual thing. Bit of a bore, but we'll just have to grin and bear it.'

The Colonel seemed to be having a momentary return to good humour in explaining things to the Adjutant. He went on, turning jovially to Dixon 'Or will it be a jag in the bottom? Eh? Is that what we'll have to grin and BARE? Eh? What?'

With this sally the Colonel felt himself almost restored to his usual breezy spirits. He surveyed the fussy little doctor and the anxious looking adjutant with the utmost complacency.

'Well actually, no, sir,' said Dixon, savouring every moment. 'It will not just be a jag in the arm. The antidote can have a pretty powerful effect on the muscles, and it has been found that the best place to inject is the stomach.'

The Colonel's jocular murmuring of 'grin and bare it' under his breath was stopped in its tracks.

'And I'm afraid I will have to give fifteen injections to each patient. I plan to do one a day for a fortnight and a day.'

'Good Heavens!' exclaimed the Colonel, moving back to his desk and sitting down heavily. 'I had no idea .... Good Lord ... fifteen ... in the stomach ....'

Tony looked miserably out of the window, mentally seeing his annual report plummet down from "Fit for promotion to field rank" to a comment on the lines of "Has tried hard, but somehow seems to create work and trouble".

'Well then,' said Dixon briskly. 'Perhaps I could borrow the Orderly Room Quartermaster Sergeant or someone to draw up the list. Clearly all officers, their wives, children, Mess servants ... ' and he moved towards the orderly office in order to draw up his plan of operation. The Adjutant followed him looking more anxious by the minute. The Colonel sat where he was, drumming his fingers on the desk and muttering to himself 'Good Lord ... fifteen ... in the stomach ... ' in a bemused sort of way.

It was that evening in the mess that the single officers heard what was in store for them. Clifford Dainton came stumping in with the news as the others were sitting over their pre-dinner drinks. Dainton's face was glittering white with indignation.

'Have your heard the latest bleeding idiocy?' he asked, and without waiting for a reply, continued, 'Because that stupid bitch Betty double-barrelled bloody Jones took that damn pye-dog into her house we've all got to get fifteen jags apiece in our bellies.'

'Good Gwacious!' cried Langley, the latest of the young National Servicemen to be appointed to the unit, spluttering in his gin and tonic and sitting up in alarm.

'Look here old man,' said Billy Rogers turning to address Dainton sternly. 'This is an Officers' Mess. You really must learn not to use other ranks' vocabulary in referring to fellow officers' wives.' Since getting his second pip, after deciding to stay on an extra year, Billy appeared to have appointed himself an arbiter of good taste and etiquette in the Mess.

'Oh bugger off!' snapped Dainton. 'Trust you to be bothered by bloody good form when we're all about to be turned into pincushions.'

'Well they don't leave the needles in you know, Clifford,' observed Dave Lawson mildly.

'No but it's bloody diabolical. That stupid woman. And I expect the MO's over-reacting as usual.'

Jos listened to all this with interest. During his time in the Army he had been frightened on several occasions by having to attempt acts of physical bravery, skill or endurance; and often he had been humiliated by the poor showing he had made. But whereas many of the "hard men" in basic training and at cadet school had wilted (sometimes literally fainted) at the sight of the needles with which they were periodically injected, he had always regarded such occasions as something of a relief from the constant chasing and bullying of the parade ground, the rifle range or the assault course. The pin prick of pain, even the dull, feverish throbbing of the antidote 'taking" were, on his scale of suffering, perfectly tolerable. Dainton would perhaps display the heart of a lion in quelling a riot: but he was obviously terrified by the prospect of fifteen injections in the stomach.

But after listening to Bert Dixon's little lecture (joyfully delivered) on the symptoms, course and fatal consequences of the disease rabies, they were all so much more terrified of the disease than its prevention that they queued up almost eagerly each day for the needle in the stomach. There was something about the needle going into the stomach which set the teeth on edge, but the prick itself was not particularly painful, nor did there seem to be too much in the way of feverish after-effect. That was just as well because otherwise virtually the entire unit would have been *hors de combat* for a fortnight. Dixon had a thoroughly enjoyable time, relishing in particular an acid

167

exchange of telegrams with Brigade and Divisional HQ about supplies of serum. Jos came upon him one day, in the second week of the immunisation programme, scribbling with great gusto the draft of a telegram in which he was emphasizing that "he could not be responsible for the lives of those in his medical charge if another batch of serum was not delivered within three days."

Dixon buzzed for a messenger to take this over to the orderly room for immediate despatch, and leaned back luxuriously in his chair. He looked terrible in fact, having been working practically non-stop for about nine days. But he had an aura of the deepest satisfaction.

'That'll put a bomb under them,' he said. 'Red Tape. Honestly! You wouldn't believe it.'

'What about the head?' asked Jos to change the subject and avoid another flow of Bert's righteous indignation against army bumf, bureaucracy etc.

'What head?' asked Bert looking quite blank.

'The dog's head. Have they done the tests yet?'

'Oh that! No, not a word. Mind you old Tony made an awful botch of severing it, and there was the usual cock-up and delay before it finally got to the lab in Lagos.'

Jos saw that he had not really managed to divert Bert from his obsessive stream of complaints, and, confirming the time of the next set of injections for the soldiers in his Company who were on the contact list, he slipped off.

It was the day after the last contact had had his last injection that the telegram from Lagos reached the Adjutant's desk. It's all a bit academic now Tony thought wearily as he slit open the envelope. Probably be all on the one hand this and on the other hand the precise opposite. But what he read there made him sit bolt upright, and inhale and then exhale slowly a long deep breath. The telegram stated baldly 'No repeat no evidence of rabies in canine brain specimen received for analysis.'

Tony placed the telegram face down on his desk and looked cautiously round the room. For ease of communication he and the Orderly Room Quartermaster Sergeant shared this room, and indeed there was no door between their desks and those of the soldiers who did the clerical and typing duties of the unit. It

168

was an open-plan office arrangement ahead of its time. The Orderly Room Quartermaster Sergeant was out, and apart from the soldier who had delivered the telegram no-one else was looking in Tony's direction. He nodded curtly to the soldier who had brought the telegram.

'Thank you. that will be all.'

The soldier saluted, about turned and marched off.

Tony lit a cigarette and thoughtfully inhaled. Various possible courses of action occurred to him. Drop that little bastard Dixon in the shit for over-reacting was the first and most tempting one. But no: that would not do. He would be just as besmirched as Dixon in any attribution of blame for the immediate action they took. Anyhow the whole point was they could not have taken the risk of doing nothing. Gradually he became more and more convinced that the worst outcome from his point of view would be to have to inform all those martyrs who were now beginning to boast about their narrow (painful and bravely borne) escape from rabies that the whole thing had been a false alarm. And oh Christ what would he say to Betty then about the murder of Rupert? But how could he suppress the information in this damned telegram? God, he thought, I wish I'd told Ali Dikwa to blow its brains out. He stared glumly at the telegram. That's funny, he thought, it hasn't gone the usual round of copies to Brigade HQ, Kaduna, Uncle Tom Cobbly and all: not even copied to MO Kebira. He felt a flicker of hope. He looked at the signature "J.D. MacCrae Lt. Col RAMC" I know him, he thought: he chaired that daft seminar on *Disease – The Most Deadly Enemy* at the Aldershot Course just before I came out here. Tony lifted the phone and asked for Divisional HQ Lagos. After a long time and various wrong connections he managed to get Colonel MacCrae. He began by buttering the Colonel up over *Disease – The Most Deadly Enemy*.

'No sir. Just looking at this telegram and your name caught my eye sir. Never forgotten that seminar, and I thought I must just take this chance to say how much I admired the way you put it all across and handled it.'

The Colonel was clearly a vain man and was delighted to listen to this. His reaction encouraged Tony to go on in this

169

fashion, ladling on the most outrageous flattery. Then when he could almost hear the Colonel purring at the other end of the line Tony said as if as an afterthought, 'By the way – about the telegram. The thing is your man here (young Dixon, not long out, national service Officer of course) felt he had to go through with the inoculation programme. And we of course respected his professional judgement and gave him one hundred per cent support. Men, women, children the lot. Only thing to do according to Dixon and we wouldn't have dreamt of querying the medical view on a thing of this nature. But inevitably of course a massive injection programme of this sort has caused a bit of a stooshy. Quite unfairly your man has become a bit of a public enemy number one – even among some quite senior officers. It really is ridiculous. My CO and I have done everything we could to show our solidarity with the RAMC on this. However I was just thinking that it might be bad from the morale point of view if we came right out now and told everyone that the whole thing had been completely unnecessary. I was wondering if it might be better, morale-wise, if we reported rather in the sense that the test could not be conclusive but of course, given the symptoms, no option but to assume that the dog must have been rabid.'

'"Suppressio Veri", you mean?' queried Colonel MacCrae.

'Well, shall we say putting the Nelsonian eye to the microscope?'

'Ha! I like that, Stanford-Jones. You're a diplomatic fellow. Yes I see no reason why we shouldn't regard the margin of doubt as being a bit wider than perhaps the telegram suggests on a first reading. I certainly don't want any nonsense from general service officers about medics over-reacting. Who saw the telegram? – Oh just you really. All right. I can't send another telegram of course. But you can interpret the one I have sent as you have suggested. I'll not challenge it.'

'Thank you sir. I'm sure that's best,' said Tony.

And so the rabid dog verdict was fudged. In answer to all queries – and there weren't very many: most people preferring to assume that their heroic sufferings had not been in vain, but had saved them from a dreadful fate – Tony muttered confidentially on the lines of "almost certainly rabid, but you know what these boffins are: won't give you a straightforward black and white reply."

Fortunately Dixon who might have probed this waffle had no interest in doing so. He did not want his Herculean programme to be seen as an officious and totally unnecessary over-reaction. And he had never put much faith in the brain analysis idea anyhow since it had originated with the Adjutant and not with him.

The one person with whom Tony had not merely to fudge and mask the truth but to stand it on its head in the form of an outright lie was his wife. From time to time in the days after the "putting down" of Rupert she would sob a little and say "Tony I wonder if poor Rupee was just having a little fit. I wish we could have got a proper Vet to look at him." Although the despatch of the dog's brain to Lagos was common knowledge in the barracks, Tony had not actually disclosed the details of the severed head to Betty, mumbling instead something about "laboratory tests to double-check exactly what the trouble was". The day after the discussion with Colonel MacCrae he put his arm round Betty's shoulder as they were sitting with their after-dinner brandies.

'Just had the results of the post-mortem on poor old Rupert, darling,' he said in a sad soft voice. "'Fraid it was rabies: I'm now quite satisfied there is no question of it being anything else. Of course it's all couched in medical gobbledegook. But, knowing how you feel, I wanted to get to the bottom of it. So I phoned up Colonel MacCrae in Lagos himself – he's the chap who ran that last course I was on at Aldershot: one of the best medical brains in the Army. We had quite a long talk, and after I told him how I interpreted the laboratory's report he told me I'd got it spot on. I'm so sorry darling. But you do see Rupert would have died a terrible death, and he had to be put out of his misery for his own sake and that of the whole unit – the women, the children . . . .' Tony gulped down the rest of his brandy before folding Betty in his arms and letting her have a final sobbing of her heart out for poor Rupert.

18

The arrival of Captain Digby Stevens made a big difference to the routine of Jos's life. Captain Stevens was appointed as second-in-command of the company and was thus able to attend to the administrative duties which Jos had had to try to combine with his duties as a training officer and platoon commander. Jos was now able to spend more time on the training of the recruits.

Captain Stevens was a plump, unhealthy looking man in his late thirties. He found life in the Kebira Mess unbearably dull, and pined for the arrival of his wife in a way which the single officers found tiresome.

'How can you chaps bear to sit here night after night doing damn all except playing darts and drinking beer? Haven't any of you sampled nightlife in the Sabongari? Why not come up with me and explore it a bit? George – an old soldier like you: surely you've been?'

'They're all riddled with pox. I wouldn't touch them.'

'I'm not talking about fornication, George. But what about a bit of drinking and dancing? Don't they do this high life dancing here? Very erotic to watch so I'm told. Or stripping – I'll bet there are strip shows to go to.'

'Oh well you can keep all that sort of thing as far as I'm concerned,' said George sourly. 'Just get you worked up to no avail that kind of thing.'

'Well what about you young ones then? God we'd never have won the war if we'd all been as spineless as you lot. It doesn't really matter for me. My wife will be here in a week or two's time and I'll be restored to a life of connubial bliss. But you young fellows, letting the best years of your lives slip by sitting on your bottoms every night. I can't understand it.'

Jos was thinking how the sparkle had gone out of life now that Jane had gone home. It was dull in the Mess in the evenings: indeed he had taken to going back to his gidda quite early and was getting through the long books he had brought out with him. *War and Peace* had long since been completed. *Vanity Fair* had been re-read, and he was currently in the middle of *Middlemarch*. But perhaps Stevens had a point. There was a unique opportunity to discover what night life in an African shanty town was like, and they were all ignoring it. They WERE spineless. He opened his mouth to speak, but it was Dainton who got in first.

'I quite fancy it, Digby. These pussy-footed bastards have never been willing to sample the local talent. The Gari's out of bounds after dark you know: except for the cinema nights.'

'Out of bounds!' Stevens guffawed. 'What is this? – a Prep School? I repeat, we'd never have won the war with the feeble kind of spirit you chaps display.'

'I'd quite like to come too,' Jos heard himself saying.

'Ah that's more like it. Any more for the skylark?'

'Well I think you're bloody fools. Don't blame me when you come back riddled with pox. And the CO won't like it.'

'My dear George. I wouldn't be jumping for joy myself if there should be such an unfortunate outcome of our little expedition. But I assure you there is to be no question of pox, as you so graphically put it. I shall regard these young officers as being in my charge: under my wise old wing. We are merely going on a voyage of exploration.'

'God help them then, Digby. That's all I can say.' And George buried his head with gloomy foreboding in his tankard of beer.

Jos and Dainton soon found themselves on the familiar dusty road to the Sabongari with an animated Captain Stevens beside them. There was a full moon so that they did not need their torches. Jos noted again how the countryside seemed transformed, alien in the moonlight. The strangeness was accentuated by the muffled noise of the drums coming from the old city and the muffled beat and sounds of music from the shanty town. And on this occasion the feeling of strangeness

173

and difference was partly because of the vague expectation that the evening would somehow involve an encounter with the opposite sex.

There were no pavements in the Sabongari. The streets were fairly broad, and the whole town was built in a series of more or less rectangular blocks, all formed round one large rectangle, the market place. At the street corners one was liable to walk into a herd of sheep-like goats which were kept by various townsmen. But there were few other pedestrians. The houses were built round inner courtyards and, like the houses in the old city, presented a blind, windowless aspect to the streets. The noise of music increased as they walked down the street, but it was difficult to tell from which houses it came, which alleyway to take to arrive at the source. Anyhow they became less and less sure how the arrival of three white men, uninvited, into someone else's party would be received.

'We should have brought one of the African NCOs to guide us,' Captain Stevens observed after they had wandered about aimlessly for a while.

'Oh yes. The Colonel would have loved that,' said Dainton.

'I can't understand why you chaps are so timid and law-abiding. There's no point in wandering about like this not knowing where to go. Are there none of the African Sergeants who could be asked to show us around?'

'Well we can hardly try to dig them up at this time of night,' said Dainton. 'We shall just have to regard this as a recce, gathering information so that we are better equipped to "appreciate the situation" before our final attack.' Dainton could never resist an opportunity to attempt one of his elephantine mockeries of military jargon and thought processes. And Digby Stevens was after all a regular soldier even if a rather idle and scruffy one.

'Yes,' said Jos. 'This is hopeless. Let's get back to the Mess and try again another night. I could probably get CSM Musa to give us a contact.'

But even as Jos was saying this a tall robed figure stepped out of one of the alleyways and said in the good English of the educated Northerner, 'Good evening, sirs. Have you come to enjoy a bit of relaxation in the Sabongari?'

'That is exactly what we are hoping to do,' Stevens replied.

'You are from the barracks I think. We do not see many Europeans from the barracks these days. Would you like to come and drink some beer?'

With that and a gracious movement of his white robe, the softly spoken Northerner ushered them into the dark alleyway. Captain Stevens bounded in like a hound who had just caught scent of his prey. Jos and Dainton followed more gingerly, tensing their backs for the knife which they half expected to be stuck into them. The alleyway led into a little courtyard in which there were one or two wooden tables at which some men were drinking. They found themselves seated at one of these in the company of the tall stranger.

The stranger spread his hands out on the table, and Jos noted that he wore an expensive looking gold watch beneath his robe.

'Now, sirs,' he said. 'Let us drink to your enjoyment of the Sabongari.' With that he clapped his hands and a ragged-looking boy appeared who was ordered to bring in some beer. It turned out to be rather flat, rather warm Star Beer; and at first as Jos and Dainton sipped it they found themselves thinking that they would have been better off drinking their usual ice-cold Carlsberg in the Mess. Jos noted that their host himself seemed to be drinking some sort of fruit juice. There was no sign of any women or dancing. Their host had an unpleasant, villainous unctuousness about him which made both Jos and Dainton feel ill at ease. But Captain Stevens seemed to be enjoying his company. They were discussing how it came to be that he, Ibrahim Sokoto, a Hausaman came to live in the Sabongari rather than in the old city.

'Yes, sirs: it is more convenient for me to live here in the Gari because of my business interests. I hire out sewing machines and bicycles. I have this little place for refreshments – and one or two other interests.'

The conversation went on in this way. Captain Stevens asked to be allowed to buy a round of drinks, and some more warm, flat Star Beer was served – at, Jos noticed, an extortionate price. But this seemed to please Digby Stevens and he turned to Ibrahim Sokoto and asked, 'Is there anywhere in the

Gari where we could dance – or perhaps watch girls dancing?'

'I would not recommend it, sir. The dancing here is rough and low – very noisy. There are many of your soldiers who have drunk too much beer or palm wine.'

There was a constrained silence after this reply. But then Ibrahim Sokoto went on.

'I can however arrange for you to meet some nice girls if you would like that, sir.'

Jos again felt the tense conflict of excitement and panic which had assailed him in Soho. And he was fascinated and repelled by the pimp-like negotiations which now began to take place between Captain Stevens and their host. Stevens seemed to be in his element.

'Tonight?' he asked.

'Yes sir. That can be arranged.'

'Can we see them beforehand? And how much will it cost?'

Ibrahim Sokoto smiled and said he did not charge to introduce friends to each other. He rose and asked the three officers to accompany him.

They went back into the street, along past two or three windowless houses and then into another dark alleyway. This did not lead to a courtyard but to a door at which Ibrahim Sokoto knocked. Jos experienced feelings of shame and fear, but also of excited curiosity and the vague anticipation of pleasure.

Some high-pitched female voices were heard following Ibrahim's knock, and then the door was opened by a plump light-skinned Ibo girl. Jos thought that she shrank a little when she was confronted by Ibrahim. But he said in his soft, polite voice, 'I have brought some friends from the Officers' Mess who would like to meet you and the other girls Elizabeth.'

She opened the door, and they all filed into a small, stuffy room, smelling of spices and perfume and the kerosine lamp which hung from the ceiling and gave the room what light it had. Three other women were sitting on the two low beds which were all the furniture the room had. They all wore dresses of some thick cloth, unbecomingly fastened across the chest. On their heads were rather ugly voluminous turbans. They giggled slightly at the sight of Ibrahim and the three

176

Europeans.

'Well this is very nice,' said Digby Stevens, rising to the occasion, and taking his seat on one of the beds beside another buxom Ibo girl. The girl giggled and called something across in her high-pitched nasal tongue to Elizabeth, the girl who had opened the door to admit the men.

Dainton whispered nervously to Jos 'I don't like this set up at all. That Ibrahim bugger hasn't said yet how much this is going to cost: probably blackmail us for the rest of our lives.'

'I know. I don't like it either. But we can hardly pull out at this stage. We'd never hear the end of it from old Stevens – anyhow I think he probably knows what he is doing.'

Before Dainton could reply he was surprised by the first girl, Elizabeth, coming up to him, taking him by the arm and leading him to the other bed. The two other women now stood up. Ibrahim looked enquiringly at Jos. He felt the saliva drain from his mouth and wished he was back in the Mess playing darts or in his gidda reading *Middlemarch*. He looked at the women. One of them was a tall, statuesque girl with a broad face and a large well shaped body, the lines of which even the ugly dress could not disguise. The other girl seemed to be younger: a slight girl with a very black skin and the delicate, Arabic features of the Fulani. She looked as timid as Jos was feeling. He took her by the hand.

'Now, gentlemen,' said Ibrahim. 'I think it might be possible to rent a few rooms in which you and your new friends could get to know each other better. If you will entrust me with the necessary finance I think I can arrange it.'

'How much?' asked Stevens.

'Each room one pound.'

'Ten shillings,' Stevens countered quickly.

'No,' said Ibrahim silkily. 'I could not manage to arrange the necessary accommodation for as little as ten shillings. But if you like I will see if I can get rooms for twelve shillings each room. This may be possible – although the rooms may not be as spacious as those which I had in mind.'

Stevens handed over a pound note, a ten shilling note, and, after some token grumbling, six single shillings. In spite of their general unease, Jos and Dainton could not help admiring the hardheaded coolness with which Stevens had handled the deal.

As soon as he had the money, Ibrahim Sokoto motioned Jos and Dainton to follow him. The women they had paired off with and the statuesque one accompanied them as they left the room leaving Stevens and the girl he had sat down beside alone. They emerged into the street and then Ibrahim pointed down the next alleyway. Dainton and Elizabeth went down it. Ibrahim Sokoto then seemed to walk past several other alleyways before he nodded to Jos and the Fulani girl to turn down one. This led to a door which the girl opened. Inside was a scene identical to that in the room which they had left, except that instead of four girls there was one aged crone, who got up when they entered and shuffled off.

Jos and the girl looked awkwardly at each other.

'Do you speak English?' Jos asked.

She looked frightened and totally non-comprehending.

'Kana ji Hausa ko?' he asked (Do you speak Hausa) knowing that of course she could and that he barely did, but feeling that he must make some effort to establish communication between them. She indicated assent. Jos sat down on one of the low, mattress-like beds and held out his hand to her. She put her hand in his and he noticed that it was a beautiful slim hand. It felt cold and slightly rough to the touch. She sat down beside him, and as he looked into her large dark eyes she modestly lowered her head.

What in God's name am I doing here, Jos asked himself, as he looked at the slight alien creature sitting beside him. He noticed the delicate graceful lines of her neck, her cheek bones and chin. He felt out of place, bulky and ridiculous sitting there holding the girl's hand. She raised her eyes timidly and looked at him, and he returned her glance with a friendly smile.

'Mai-Gidda,' she said meekly – which in the circumstances he took to have the meaning of 'At your service, Sir.' And without further ado she began to unwind the elaborate headdress and the heavy cloth round her chest. She had soon got this sufficiently undone to reveal her small, pear shaped breasts. Jos was unsure what he wanted to happen and what was expected of him. He lay back on the bed, and the girl at once lay down beside him. He put his arms round her naked

178

back and they lay like that for several minutes. He stroked her slim arms and touched her long purplish black nipples. But all of this he seemed to be doing in a kind of slow motion as if he was not personally involved but seeing himself taking these actions. The girl was totally unresponsive, indeed she seemed almost inanimate except for a clumsy and perfunctory attempt to undo Jos's trouser buttons.

Although he had this curious sense of being outside himself, observing himself, Jos had felt some quickening of desire as his hands had touched the girl's smooth back and soft breasts but it was not strong enough to break through his strange sense of disbelief. And as he looked round the squalid little room he recoiled from what was happening. He felt pity for what seemed the clumsy innocence of the girl and disgust for himself and what he was doing. He drew away from the girl and leaning on his elbow took a long last look at her slim half naked body. Then he got up.

'Na Gode,' he said (Thank you). 'Na Gode diyawa.' (Thank you very much). The girl looked astonished and a little frightened. Jos wondered how Ibrahim treated girls who had failed to satisfy the customers.

'Here,' he said, lapsing into English. 'For you – kudi,' and he gave her a ten shilling note.

At this the girl looked terrified, no doubt wondering what extraordinary service she would be expected to perform in exchange. Jos pressed it into her hand and made for the door. Then on a sudden impulse he turned back and took her in his arms and kissed her hard on the lips. They felt leathery and did not respond in the slightest. He then kissed her gently on the cheek and on the forehead and withdrew. He stumbled down the little alleyway and out into the street. Then he turned towards the barracks and half walked, half ran back to his house. In the morning he would be able to exchange yarns with Dainton and Captain Stevens about how each had got on. But he wanted first of all to sort out his own confused emotions about what had and had not happened.

There was a good deal of excitement at breakfast next morning to discover how each of the three revellers had fared. Digby Stevens had a smug contented look on his face as he tucked his napkin under his chin.

'Well that was a very nice little bit of slap and tickle wasn't it chaps,' he asked as he sunk his spoon into a portion of paw paw.

'Slap and tickle!' Dainton scoffed. 'Didn't you go the whole hog then? I can tell you I bloody did. That Elizabeth should be renamed instant bloody seduction. Do you know she was stark naked in about ten seconds flat from getting into that little room? And she had me starkers and all in about another ten. Pass the sugar Billy will you? And what a smashing body she has I can tell you. You should have seen the boobs that were under that bloody dress. Absolutely luscious.'

Jos winced as he always did at the coarse forthrightness of Dainton's turn of phrase. Billy Rogers was clearly torn between prurient curiosity, outrage at the way Dainton's language kept letting the tone of the Mess down – and perhaps also an awful sense of missed opportunity. Jos was aware that all eyes were now turning to him.

'Well I suppose I had a bit more in Digby's slap and tickle line,' he said. 'The girl seemed a bit inexperienced.'

'The *girl* seemed inexperienced!' Dainton guffawed. 'I bet you someone was a bit inexperienced anyhow.'

Dainton was enjoying himself hugely as the only one who had really proved himself a red-blooded man. But just then George, the Quartermaster, who was breakfasting unusually early for him, no doubt to hear the gossip about the previous evening's adventure, opined gloomily

'Well I think you're three bloody Charlies, that's all. I've a good mind to report you to the CO. And if any of you really did go the whole hog I've no doubt he'll be reporting himself to the MO.'

'You're bloody cheerful this morning, George, and no mistake. Got up on the wrong side did you?' Dainton was still in high spirits, but a note of anxiety crept into his voice.

'No – George is right.' Billy Rogers chipped in, taking heart from the Quartermaster's intervention. 'I've sometimes thought of going up to the Gari myself – not that I'm really attracted to dark-skinned women – but it's the fear of the pox that has always held me back.'

180

'You're just a bloody snob and a racist and a pansy.' Dainton was becoming rattled. He and Billy exchanged some further abuse until called to order by the senior officer present, Captain Stevens.

Jos had almost – though not quite – forgotten about the risk of contracting a Venereal Disease in his high-minded and sentimental reflections on the Fulani girl, her youth, her delicate beauty, the trap in which her sex and economic circumstances had caught her and so forth. But now he had a sound, self-interested reason for being pleased that he had not had sexual intercourse – though he began to recall uneasily advice from the medical officer at cadet school never to "kiss a tart" on the lips. But he reckoned that he had probably taken fewer risks than either of the others. He could not believe that Stevens had stopped short at slap and tickle – but then he would probably know the ropes sufficiently to minimise the risk of infection. As for Dainton, he became a pitiable object. Instead of exulting in being the one thoroughly virile member of the trio, he acquired a distinctly hang dog and worried air; and muttered at times about people "welching on their commitments" – which seemed to Jos a curious way of putting things. In the first enthusiasm of his vivid and detailed account of the nubile charms of Elizabeth, he had indicated his intention to visit her again at the earliest opportunity. But instead he hung about the Mess every night, seemed anxious to be on good terms with everyone – a character trait not hitherto disclosed – and in particular with the boring little medical officer. No-one really liked Dixon, and Dainton had been one of those who took least trouble to conceal his feelings. But now he was forever laughing loudly at Dixon's ponderous jokes. He even took to accompanying Dixon on his weekend expeditions to the great boulder-like hills which were the only features to disturb the monotony of the seemingly endless Bush and which Dixon attacked with a neat little geologist's kit, painstakingly labelling the chippings of boulder and spreading them out – to the annoyance of his batman – all over the sitting room of his gidda. Dainton became an enthusiastic amateur geologist too.

Then one evening as Jos was returning from the company stores where he had been checking the equipment which he would require to take a platoon out to bush camp, he saw Dainton coming down the drive from the medical inspection room with, he thought, more of the old jaunty spring in his step.

'Jos,' he called. 'Thank Christ, Jos. I've been a bit worried about this pox scare you know. But old Fossil Dixon has just given me the complete all clear. What a weight off my mind. By God I'm never going back up to the Gari again though!'

'No I don't think I will go again either, Cliff.'

And by now Mrs Stevens had finally arrived. So there were no further trips to the Sabongari.

19

One result of Jos spending more time as a training officer was that he frequently found himself recalling his own time as a recruit, and marvelling at how similar British Army recruit training was here under a tropic sun to that which he had undergone in a Castle in cool and drizzly Scotland.

One day as he was walking through the company lines, after having checked the installation of a new hazard on the Assault Course, he came upon Sergeant Kalu's platoon standing at ease, each soldier with his left boot on and holding the right boot up for inspection to Sergeant Kalu, who was stalking round with a fierce and suspicious look on his face. As soon as the sergeant saw Jos, he roared words of command to bring the platoon to attention, and then took two or three swaggering steps towards Jos and saluted him with dramatic flourish. Jos returned the salute in the languid way which he had now come to affect.

'What on earth's going on, Sergeant Kalu?' he asked, pointing to the lopsided soldiery.

'Yes, sah,' Sergeant Kalu laughed. 'I go make dese boys show me de leather on dere boots. I know some of dem go burn on de polish, and I explain dem dey must not do dat. I tell em I go put em foh charge ifn dat dey do.'

'And if they don't get their boots up to a sufficient shine you put them on a charge anyway? As a matter of interest what do you charge them with if you find they've burned the polish on?'

'I go charge dem under section forty of de Queen's Regulations, sah. Conduct prejewdishal to good ordah and millterry displin.' Sergeant Kalu replied referring, without the batting of an eyelid, to the catch all section of Queen's Regulations. 'You see sah,' Sergeant Kalu went on in more serious vein 'Dey can get good shine foh dere boots ifn dat dey go use helbow grease.' He beamed at Jos obviously delighted at his use of this idiom.

'Oh well have it your own way, Sergeant Kalu. But I think you are calling "Heads I win. Tails you lose" to these poor devils.'

Sergeant Kalu took a moment to translate and grasp the point of the remark and then he roared with laughter at the witticism. Jos noted to himself once more how the most successful non-commissioned (and commissioned) officers in the army tended to be sycophantic bullshitters.

Jos took a last look at the platoon tilted awkwardly on its right hand side before walking on on his way to the Mess for lunch. As he did so there came vividly to mind the day of the foot inspection during his own basic training.

That was the day of poor Bob Finlay's discomfiture: Jos smiled as he recalled Bob's serious, fastidious face. Always when he thought of that countenance Jos was reminded of Erasmus who was said to have the appearance of one descended from a long line of maiden aunts. Bob had been a puzzle to NCOs and his fellow recruits alike. Perhaps it was only the officers who would have understood him, had they ever got close enough to the recruits. For Bob's public schoolboy life had made him in many ways a good deal tougher than the other lads in basic training – certainly a lot tougher than a bookish grammar-school boy and would-be intellectual like Jos. While the hard men in the Platoon from their ingrained wish to cheat authority (and while Jos for reasons of physical clumsiness and cowardice) were trying to dodge some part of an assault course, Bob would bash heroically on. But being rather clumsy and ill co-ordinated he would alarm the NCOs for his safety and thus get no thanks or credit from anyone for his endeavours. His family owned a chain of grocery shops – and Bob had a sharply defined sense of mine and thine which sometimes got in the way of what was known as the mucking in spirit. He had the courage to argue the point with the platoon bullies, protesting in his genteel outrage that no, the filthy, scorched, sweated socks he had found in his locker were not his and that he was sure the clean and wholesome pair in

MacGarrity's locker were. There was no doubt among the rest of the platoon as to who had lovingly invested funds in the NAAFI on packets of Persil and Lux and had spent his evenings tending his kit. Bob would gradually have won a measure of grudging respect from the rest of them despite his prim and slightly selfish ways had it not been for the occasion of the foot inspection.

The platoon had physical training three times a week. The element of training seemed to consist chiefly in practising how to get in and out of PT kit at breakneck speed. Once in the gym the recruits were given a certain amount of the knees bend sort of exercise and a little torment on the wall bar and on the horse, but most of the time seemed to be taken up by psychological torture by the two corporal physical training instructors: the PTIs. They wore black and red striped jerseys and black slacks, and walked with a curious muscly swagger. Jos winced ever afterwards when he thought of his first encounter with them. On that first day they were swaggering round the platoon getting everyone to identify himself. When they came to Jos and discovered how old he was – twenty-one whereas the others in the platoon were for the most part seventeen or eighteen – they must have decided to have some sport at his expense.

'Married?' asked the tall ferret faced one.

'No, Corporal.'

'Here's an old man and no' married yet,' said the smaller, pudgy faced one. Then suddenly, viciously he squared up to Jos. 'Whit's wrang wi' ye? Hae ye no' gote wan?'

He was looking pointedly, elaborately between Jos's legs, but Jos was too fresh from the sheltered world of school and university to believe that the gym instructor, the Teacher could really intend this coarse meaning. He must have misheard my reply, Jos concluded, and be asking again whether I am married or not.

'No, Corporal,' he repeated.

'Aw the puir wee bugger hisnae gote wan. I didnae think from the look of him that he had.'

Someone sniggered and had his name taken. And for the next ten weeks the PTIs referred to Jos with heavy sympathy as the puir bugger who hadnae gote wan.

One day after the Platoon had got down to the gym with their usual desperate struggle to get changed in time, the little pudgy faced wasp said, 'Come on then get fell in. Open order. Now will youse all take off your right gym shoe and sock.'

The Platoon did so, vaguely wondering what new torment was being planned. Jos thanked his stars that the night before he had at last had a bath. The recruits were allowed a bath once a week and were supposed to HAVE one once a week. But often there was so much work to be done cleaning weapons and kit, polishing boots and brasses, swabbing down tables and rifle racks, "bumping" i.e. polishing the barrack room floor, and so on that there was no time before the inexorable ten o'clock lights out to get to the bath. Bob, of course, was one of the keenest bathers and would forego the brief half hour at the NAAFI or letter writing in order to get his kit done and have a bath – often risking a conflict with authority by sneaking in a bath on an evening which was not his bath night.

It soon became apparent that this was a clean foot inspection. The platoon had been over its ankles in mud on the firing range the previous day so that there were a great many subjects for the PTIs' satire, including one poor devil whose feet were so dirty that he was made to strip further and finally marched off for a regimental scrubbing. Suddenly out of the corner of his eye, Jos saw that the heel of Bob's foot was extremely grimy: he was in the row in front of Jos and slightly to the right. Yes that was right, he had been meaning to fit in one of his extra baths the night before but had had difficulty in getting his boots up to what he considered a decent shine, and in the end had had to forego the bath.

The pudgy face PTI stopped in front of Bob and looked him slowly up and down.

'Corporal Arthur,' he called to his colleague. 'Would youse look at this?' and he pointed dramatically to poor Bob's foot. 'Did youse no' think, Corporal Arthur, that this was a clean decent like sort of lad?'

'Jesus Christ!' roared the ferret faced one, shoving his face to within an inch or two of Bob's. 'You dirty little beast. How long have you been going about like this?'

186

'I'm truly sorry, Corporal,' began Bob in his earnest genteel way. 'I was meaning to have a bath last night but there just wasn't time.'

'Oh there just wasn't time Corporal Todd. Dae ye hear that now? No time – whit a bloody shame. This is the kind o' potential fucking officer that leads good men into an ambush and then says he's truly sorry but there just isn't time to bloody well get them out again. Potential officer? Potential officer? I'll tell you what you are Finlay. You're a potential fucking shitehouse.'

Stung by this Bob, not unreasonably – but very unwisely – attempted to protest against the Catch twenty-two of having to be clean and not being allowed to bathe more than once a week.

'Well actually Corporal it wasn't my bath night,' he said.

'D'ye hear that Corporal Todd. First he tells us he was 'meaning to have a bath' and now he admits he wisnae entitled to one. This is more serious than it first looked. This recruit is not merely filthy he's fucking disobedient too.' The ferret faced one ceased addressing his pudgy faced colleague and closed in on Bob.

'Now look here you bolshie bugger I don't want to hear any more of your barrack room lawyer excuses. I know what you were doing with your precious time last night instead of getting yourself turned out clean and tidy. You was up at the NAAFI wasn't you rolling your lecherous little eyes at that bit of stuff behind the counter wasn't you?'

There was a smothered gasp from the entire platoon at the absurd injustice of this. Bob himself was too taken aback to speak.

'Oh dumb insolence we're getting now. I wonder if you can coax him to speak Corporal Todd.'

The pudgy faced one now took over again, feigning sorrow and surprise rather than anger. Suddenly to everyone's horror Bob began to blubber. Poor Bob, he cared too much, and from them on he was treated with contempt both by the NCOs and the recruits.

Jos thought kindly of poor Bob as he remembered the incident. He had reached the Mess totally absorbed in these reflections; and, as he unbuckled his Sam Browne and hung it and his slouch hat up, he resolved he must write to Bob and, if he was sent on the Signals course to Lagos, try to detour on the way south in order to call on him.

20

Jos enjoyed his work as a training officer. It got him away from the routine of office work and life at the Mess. Every third Monday he would take one of the platoons out trekking to do field exercises. They would return on the Thursday or the Friday. He used to like marching along the sandy paths which led through the light scrub, listening to his soldiers singing. He was amused and flattered by the scramble which always developed among them to see who would carry him shoulder high across the green muddy streams. He enjoyed meeting the occasional solitary traveller with stout staff and flowing robes and turban; and he relished the exchange of courtesies which took place. The Hausa traveller would begin them by raising his clenched fist and calling, 'Rana kai she Daidai!' (May the day go well with you).

To which Jos would reply, 'Sanu.' (Greetings).

'Sanuku.' (Greetings to you too). 'Ina gajiya?' (How are you – literally – where is your tiredness)?

'Ba gajiya.' (Fine – literally – I have no tiredness).

'Ina aiki?' (How is your work going)?

The correct reply to this "Na gode Allah" (I thank the Lord) was meant to assure the inquirer that the work was going fine. But at this point Jos would depart from the steps of the Minuet and point with exaggerated weariness to the soldiers behind him and sigh 'Aiki diyawa.' (Too much work).

This was always good for an easy laugh, both from the itinerant Hausaman and the platoon NCOs. The traveller would carry on his way in high good humour, calling back the greeting appropriate to a long farewell "Sai wata rana!" And the platoon would resume its march.

189

When Jos and the platoon sergeant had decided where to camp for the night the soldiers would take their axes, and in a very short space of time have cut enough of the bushes to build a little leaf and stick house for Jos, one for the NCOs and a larger shelter for themselves. Jos always selected one of the recruits to be his Batman for the period of the camp; and this recruit would be busy setting out his camp bed, canvas stool, washing basin etc., while Jos and the platoon sergeant made a recce of the surrounding country to plan the exercises for the following day. Then fires would be lit and the evening meal prepared. Sometimes they had difficulty finding water and had to live off their iron rations and the water in their water bottles. But usually any deficiencies in map reading by Jos would be made good by the platoon sergeant knowing the area, and making sure that they landed up near water – however doubtful-looking in quality.

After the meal the soldiers would begin drumming and dancing, working themselves up into frenzies of excitement as they writhed and leapt about in the firelight. Jos usually cut this short at about ten-thirty and sent them off to bed so that they didn't exhaust themselves in advance of the military manoeuvres to be performed the following day. Then he and the NCOs would sit lazily round the dying fire for another hour or so, drinking beer out of the bottles which the NCOs usually managed to carry no matter how heavily laden they were otherwise. They would reminisce about the villages or towns they came from, their families and their plans for the future. Jos would indulge in nostalgia for Scotland and tell tales about life there and in Europe, secure in the knowledge that there was very little chance of any of the things he said being subject to verification.

One night it happened that all the NCOs were northerners. This meant that Jos's beer-drinking was somewhat solitary, but it did not inhibit the feeling of camp camaraderie. And on this night they got on to talking about the future of Nigeria once the British had left – as they were scheduled to do in the next four or five years.

'Why you go sah? You no like it heah? You no like us?'

'I like it very much here. But it has been agreed that you

190

should run your own affairs, and it is time for the white man to hand the government over to you.'

'No sah. Is not true. We like foh you to stay. Why you no go come back as District Hapsa sah?'

'I'd like nothing better. But there is no future for the white man here.'

'Oh yes sah dere is heah in the North. It is de savvy boys from the coast who want you to go. But we like you to stay. We no want them.'

'Well that's what you say now, Ahmadu. But wait and see, as we get nearer to independence you will all be wanting to kick us out.'

'No, sah. And ifn de boys from de coast go come try to kick you out – Hey we get sword, we get horse. We go kill um one time.'

Jos thought that the prospect of a happy and united Federation was not being assisted by this conversation, and it was time they were all getting some sleep anyhow. So he got up and urging the NCOs to get themselves off soon and to make sure the fire was properly out before they did so, he made his way up to his leaf and stick hut, which had been built about fifty yards away from the others on a slight rise. As he strolled back to it he marvelled at how seductive he had found these words about British rule. The real me, he told himself, gets *The Manchester Guardian Weekly* and *The New Statesman*: it is not this budding blimp who is thrilled to hear of the arrest of progress by means of the sword and horse. Too much beer, he concluded, by way of excusing himself. He returned the salute of the two recruits who were doing their spell of guard duty round his hut. Then he pushed aside the branch which was suspended over the doorway of the hut and lit a match to guide him to the kerosine lamp. He was astonished to discover two pairs of eyes staring at him from the inmost part of the hut. The match went out.

'Jesus!' Jos exclaimed in alarm.

'Heah, sah,' whispered the soft voice of Usuman, the recruit he had selected to be his batman for this camp. Usuman shone a torch on the kerosine lamp and helped Jos to light it.

'What on earth are you doing here, Usuman? And who is

this?' Jos held the lamp in the direction of the other pair of eyes and saw a little girl with her eyes, lips and cheeks heavily made up. It was difficult to judge how old she was. Jos reckoned about ten. She smiled shyly and then looked modestly down at the ground.

'Usuman, what is this? Who is she?'

'Excuse me, sir. I think perhaps you like a woman for bush camp. This girl and her friends come watch the soldiers make camp. I go make your bed and get your table and chair. Then I think perhaps you like woman.'

Jos listened astounded, noting inconsequentially with one part of his mind the excellence of Usuman's pronunciation of the English language.

'That was very thoughtful, Usuman,' he said. 'But this is not a woman: this is a child.'

'You no like young woman, sir?' asked Usuman, displaying interest in this apparently unexpected sexual peccadillo.

'Not quite as young as this child thank you, Usuman.'

The girl was watching them both intently, her heavily made up eyes flicking from one to the other. Her gaze rested enquiringly on Usuman. He looked at her irritably and told her crisply in Hausa that the bature did not want her. Jos saw to his dismay that she looked disappointed and frightened.

'Wait a minute, Usuman. Where is she going to go? She can't get back to her village during the night. You are a bloody interfering idiot. Indeed how, without making me a laughing stock in the Unit, is she to get out of here? Or do the guards know that she's here? Jesus, Usuman: I could wring your neck. And what about you anyhow? How did you get out of bedding down with the rest of the Platoon?'

'Yes, sir. Everything is all right sir. I told Corporal Abdullai that you wanted me for extra work tonight – to go over the Hausa commands for platoon in the Attack. The corporal knows, sir, that you try hard for Hausa and that I speak English well. I waited here with the girl quietly before the guards were posted. They do not know about her.'

Jos recalled the sight of Corporal Abdullai's honest, stupid face and imagined Usuman pulling the wool over his eyes. It was an idiotic story. All commands were given in English as the lingua franca of the multi-lingual Army. But it was just the sort of mysterious "extra work" involving clever people like the Officer and this educated recruit which would impress Abdullai.

'You've got everything sewn up nicely haven't you, Usuman? Look: tell the girl she may stay here until it is morning when she can return to her village. You get back and get bedded down with the Platoon. And take that smile of your face, Usuman. I have no interest in the child. She will sleep there in the corner and I will sleep here in the camp bed. Tell her that. Tell her strange, strange bature.'

Usuman rattled off a quick explanation in Hausa. The girl looked puzzled, and then Jos heard her ask 'Akwai kudi ko?' (Is there money in it)?

'She is asking, sir . . . .'

'Yes I heard what she asked. Tell her that I will give her five shillings – and I've a good mind to stop it off your pay.'

The girl's face brightened when Usuman had translated this. He clicked his heels, bowed and withdrew with a knowing look on his face and the words – somehow suddenly pregnant with meaning 'Sai gobe, sir.' (Until tomorrow, sir).

The girl retreated to the corner of the hut which Usuman had indicated and sat there staring very frankly at Jos as he undressed. When he had got down to his underpants, he turned the lamp out and felt his away across to the bed. It was eerie lying in the darkness conscious of the child sitting on the ground in the corner. She was absolutely still: he thought he had made out Usuman saying in his head-butler way not to make a sound. What if she gets bitten by a snake, he mused. He began to feel caddish about having taken the bed and consigned the child to the ground. But then he reflected that she would never have experienced anything like the luxury of a camp bed before. Anyhow it would be impossibly complicated and open to misunderstanding if he were to suggest to her in his broken Hausa that they change places. And what if I got bitten by a snake, he thought. He lay intensely awake for another ten minutes. He tried and failed to hear her breathing. He sat up in bed and tried to pierce the darkness with his eyes. As he did so she said softly 'Ina zua, mai gidda.' (I am coming master).

And with that she came and stood by the bed. She was indeed just a child, very slight and thin. She was trembling. But in a way which was at once determined and resigned she made to climb into the bed. Jos edged as far as he could to one side in order to make room for her slight body. She lay on her back very still and tense, her legs slightly parted. Jos lay uncomfortably on his side and tried to explain to her in his halting and sketchy Hausa that he was going to sleep and that she should too – and that she would still get her five shillings. The message seemed to get across because she relaxed presently and quite soon she was in a deep sleep.

Jos lay awake cramped and uncomfortable from the strain of lying on the edge of the bed. He wondered nervously if the girl had lice or any unpleasant skin disease. He recalled the sight of lepers begging in the old city of Kebira – indeed there was a leper colony not far from the barracks. He remembered the make-up on the girl's face, and shuddered to think of her coming to hire her young – surely pre-pubescent – body to the soldiers. He heard the tread of the guards circling the little encampment. He thought of his last night with Jane and of all the other timid, self-controlled, frustrated goodnight necking sessions with girls at home. He recalled his sentimental inhibitions with the Fulani prostitute in the Sabongari. He wondered uneasily if perhaps he was a strange, strange bature. He too fell asleep.

When he awoke the light was streaming through the chinks in the leaves which made the hut walls. He was sprawled awkwardly across the ground, and Usuman was setting out his shaving things and a can of hot water on the little canvas table. Usuman was whistling softly to himself. The girl was still fast asleep, lying plump in the middle of the bed.

'Lafia sir?' inquired Usuman politely. Jos was sure that Usuman would normally have said 'Good morning, sir' but, with his tendency to sail as close to the wind of impertinence as he dared, had deliberately chosen the *double entendre* of the Hausa greeting of 'Feeling OK?' with its overtones of 'Get on all right?'

'No. I feel bloody awful. I know what you're thinking Usuman. But you're absolutely wrong. How are we going to

194

get her out of here now that it is daylight, without the whole unit knowing that she has spent the night with me?'

'Perhaps, sir, if you take the men away very soon and leave me behind? Then I can get her to go without anyone seeing.'

'You'll like that won't you Usuman? Loafing around here all day instead of taking part in platoon in the Attack.'

Usuman protested, explaining how keenly he had been looking forward to this particular field exercise. Jos was getting shaved and dressed while they were discussing what was to be done. The girl still slept. Usuman tidied away the washing and shaving kit and returned with a tray with eggs and coffee: tiny eggs bought from the village which the girl belonged to.

'What about breakfast for her?' Jos asked as, having finished the eggs, he tucked into some toast and marmalade which Usuman had somehow conjured up.

'I will give her some when you have gone, sir.'

Jos looked at him sharply.

'Well see that's all you give her Usuman; and see that she gets home safely. In my country you could be sent to jail for touching a child as young as that.'

Usuman clucked his tongue at the very thought of such a thing.

'Wait now Usuman. I am going to wake her, and I want you to explain what the drill is.'

The girl looked startled and frightened when Jos shook her, but a delighted smile spread over her face when he gave her the promised five shillings. Usuman explained in short rapid sentences that she was to remain out of sight until the soldiers had gone.

By the time Jos stepped out into the full glare of day, Sergeant Amadu Yola (the replacement for the disgraced Sergeant Yesufu Maiduguri) and the platoon corporals were bullying the men into three ranks for muster parade. Sergeant Yola marched smartly towards Jos and stamped to a halt in front of him. He gave a flashy salute and called, 'Number THREE platoon ready for your inspection, sah!'

'Thank you Sergeant. I think this morning we should get straight off to that little valley we spotted yesterday evening and get on with the Platoon in the Attack exercises. No-one sick? No defaulters?'

'No sah. But Private Usuman has not yet returned from yoh hut, sah.'

'Er, no Sergeant. I thought we ought to have someone looking after the kit. I've one or two quite valuable things with me which I don't want to take on exercises but I don't want to leave unguarded. I've asked Private Usuman to look after them.'

'Sah!' Sergeant Yola gave another dramatic salute, about-turned and marched back to the squad at which he began roaring various orders. Jos thought he had seen a flicker of incredulity in the Sergeant's eyes at the notion of Usuman being detailed to look after someone else's valuables, but he could not be sure whether the Sergeant's disbelief related solely to Usuman's trustworthiness or whether he thought there was something fishy about Jos's explanation.

That afternoon as Jos watched Corporal Abdullai's section crawling hundreds of yards on their bellies in the scorching heat to make a flanking attack on "the enemy", he thought of Usuman, lying somewhere in the shade – no doubt on his, Jos's, camp bed, or poking his nose into the stores they had brought with them, perhaps doing a bit of trade with the villagers, or chatting up the child prostitute or such of her friends as might have wandered over from the village. He made a mental note to the effect that Usuman's name should definitely be added to the list of potential officers.

They stayed at this camp for two and a half days, undertaking several other field exercises. (Jos told an increasingly sceptical Sergeant Yola that he had discovered that he could, after all, carry his valuables in his Bushjacket pockets and thus allow Private Usuman to take part in these exercises). On the third day, Thursday, they lunched late and then began the march back to the barracks at about half past three in the afternoon: 1530 hours as Jos called it when he remembered to do so. They kept up a good pace, but by half past six they were still six or seven miles from the barracks, the swift darkness would soon be upon them, and the paths were not very well defined. Sergeant Yola said that there was a small Fulani village about half a mile off where they could get water and buy eggs and perhaps hens to cook for the evening meal. Jos decided to make for this and to camp near by it, completing the remaining six miles early the next morning.

The villagers were most co-operative in selling them all they required: Jos hoped he could square the expense all right with his superior officers back at the unit. He was brooding over this problem as they completed their meal and as he walked across the village to pay his respects to the Headman. He turned out to be a frail old thing with several sons and grandsons who grouped themselves round him while he and Jos exchanged greetings. Jos always fantasized about being Stanley or Livingstone as he entered into such dialogues. But in truth they quickly palled.

'Sanu!'

'Sanu!'

'Sanuku!'

'Yawa Sanu!'

There would then be an awkward pause before the Chief sneaked in a quick "Sanu mai-Gidda", taking Jos off guard and making him gabble out a clumsy Anglo-Saxon 'Sanoo' instead of the clipped nasal grunt that it should have been. Jos reflected after a few moments of this interchange that the situation was taking on the infinitely tedious quality of squabbles in his Scottish childhood – " 'Tis not . . . . 'Tis sot . . . . 'Tis not . . . ." Suddenly one of the many awkward pauses was shattered by a female voice calling out with great warmth and vehemence 'Mai-Gidda!'

Jos looked across to where the sound came from and saw Gude standing at the doorway of one of the thatch houses.

Gude was the Fulani woman who brought milk, carried on a great gourd on her head, for the cats and other pets of various Europeans in and around the barracks. The owners of the pets lived on dried or tinned milk themselves, but they gave their pets milk from the local cattle. She reached Jos's house each day at about three o'clock – near the end of her round – just before Jos settled for his siesta. He would watch her walking gracefully down the path to his house, her hips swaying slightly as part of the art of balancing the gourd but in a way which Jos always found disturbing. When she reached the compound she

197

would set the gourd of milk down and engage in an elaborate exchange of courtesies and formal greetings with Okoko. These never varied even in the months when Okoko's wife was away and Gude disappeared into Okoko's little round hut for half an hour some afternoons. When, as was usually the case, Okoko's wife was at home, Gude would withdraw, after the exchange of courtesies, and rest for about half an hour under the shade of a large tree. But invariably, whether her immediate destination was the shade of the large tree or Okoko's bed, she would conclude her greetings by calling out to Jos. He used to listen for her raising her voice so that it became even more sharply nasal and firing many Mai-Giddas Mai-Dokis or Babbanbatures in the direction of his house. Then Jos would come to the window and greet her and, within the severe limitations of his Hausa vocabulary and with the help of sign language, he would tease her about the amount or quality of milk she gave the cats or about her visits to Okoko. Gude would grow angry and spit out what was clearly abuse in any language at the suggestion of short measure for the cats, but she would laugh and shrug her shoulders about Okoko.

Jos felt the pleasure of coming unexpectedly on a long lost friend at the sight of Gude in these strange surroundings.

'Sanu, Gude,' he called.

Gude clearly reciprocated the emotion: her face was alive with pleasure and she bowed and called out 'Marhaba! Barka da zuwa' (the calls of welcome for those one has not seen for a very long time – though in truth she and Jos had been having one of their disputes about the level of milk poured into the cats' dish only the previous week).

The old Chief observed all this with interest, and in a statesmanlike way struggled to his feet and discreetly withdrew shooing his sons and grandsons before him. Gude went into her house and brought out some rush matting which she spread on the ground before the doorway and bade Jos to sit on. She sat down beside him and offered him a kola nut from a small brass dish. Jos disliked the bitter taste very much but there could be no question of refusing it. Indeed Jos realized he had to nibble at it with apparent enjoyment.

The village was bathed in cool moonlight; away on all sides

stretched the endless bush and scrub. Jos sat for a time silent, hearing the rhythmic beating of the drums from somewhere in the centre of the village and the occasional, inimitable shout of African laughter. Gude sat decorously beside him, biting her kola nut and sometimes smiling benignly upon him. After a while Jos attempted in his usual combination of sketchy Hausa and sign language to try to express how amazed he was to discover that Gude walked about twelve miles every day, six of them with a heavy load of milk on her head. But she dismissed it all with a shrug of her slim shoulders and a contemptuous spit of kola nut.

'Kai Bature!' she said (Pah, you white man).

Jos was vaguely aware that, among the many confused emotions which he was experiencing as he sat beside Gude, sexual desire was present. But the circumstances were impossible. He must disengage with dignity and as much speed as was consistent with not offending her in her role as hostess. And if possible without having to get through another kola nut. So with many references to Gobe (tomorrow) and Aiki (work) he began to excuse himself and to say goodnight. Gude returned his farewell greetings graciously, but, it seemed to him, in a curiously bright-eyed way, as if to imply that this was not the end of the story. Jos walked thoughtfully back to the new leaf and stick hut which the soldiers had put for him and fell quickly asleep.

Next morning as Jos trudged the last dusty, thirsty miles to the barracks he thought of Gude's slight, shapely figure with the great gourd on her head, of how cool and poised she always seemed, and of the easy tireless swagger of her walk. When he was getting ready for his siesta that afternoon, he asked Okoko if he knew how far Gude walked each day. Okoko looked at him with a queer grin on his face.

'Oh sah,' he said. 'Dat Gude she get power sah. European no get dis power – at all!'

21

On the first Monday of each month a Mess Night was held, and for this occasion all the officers, married or single, who were on the station at the time, were required to attend, dressed in their regimental blues or a tropical equivalent of the same. All the officers had to assemble in the ante-room before the arrival of the commanding officer, and none could leave until he did. Mess nights were, on the whole, events of great tedium.

Although Jos had not spent money on buying a set of regimental blues, relying instead on the suit of cheap white cloth and crimson cummerbund which he had bought from Sunday Mbula, there were some trappings of his parent regiment which he grafted on to this tropical mess kit, for example the buttons bore the stag's head crest of his Scottish regiment; and he wore his tam o'shanter bonnet instead of his African regiment's slouch hat. (The purchase of this smart, officer's style, tailored tam o'shanter had been one of the few sartorial extravagances in which he had indulged on being commissioned, and he always felt complacent pleasure as he donned it, contrasting its neat cut with the cow-pat appearance of the headgear which had been issued to him as private soldier).

On the first Mess Night after the encounter with the child prostitute and with Gude the milkwoman at bush camp, Jos discovered that it was his turn to be vice president of the Mess committee for the evening. This was a purely formal role: it involved sitting at the foot of the table opposite to the officer of field rank (in effect one of the majors) who was president. At the end of the meal, once the decanters of port were in place and each officer's glass charged – but before the port had been passed or cigars and cigarettes lit, the president of the Mess committee would get to his feet and, looking down the length of the table to the subaltern at the other end, would raise his glass and propose the Toast "Mr Vice, Our Colonel in Chief." Whereupon the subaltern would get up in turn and respond with the words "Gentlemen, The Queen." All the officers would then rise muttering the words "The Queen" – with those who had reached the rank of Major adding a fatherly "God Bless Her".

Jos had been surprised to realize how much he enjoyed this little piece of mumbo jumbo. He experienced a mild thrill when, as on this evening, he was the subaltern who had to utter the words "Gentlemen, The Queen." He supposed it was something to do with all the Mess Nights held in the British Army over the centuries and in all parts of the world at which this solemn toasting of the Sovereign had taken place and, for that matter, would take place in the future.

And for the period during which the port was circulated round the table, a Mess Night continued to hold some attraction: it was a fine art getting one's glass empty quickly enough to secure a complete refill as the decanter was next passing by, but not too quickly to leave one empty-glassed as various subordinate toasts were proposed. But, oh dear, the boredom of the Mess Night once the meal was over and the entire complement of officers settled down in the ante-room. The knowledge that they could not get back to their quarters and into bed until the Colonel had withdrawn acted as a kind of group sleeping tablet on the subalterns. And of course the skilful and rapid consumption of port – in which all of the subalterns had been strenuously engaged – added to the soporific atmosphere which enveloped them once the meal was over.

The Colonel, by contrast, always seemed stimulated by Mess Nights. He had recently added a feature to them of which he seemed inordinately proud: the fifes and drums of the unit were required to parade, once the dinner was over in order to play – in the garden outside the Mess – the regimental marches of each of the officers who were present at the dinner. To his embarrassment, Jos found himself moved, tears in his eyes, as the little band (my tin whistle band, as the Colonel was jocosely wont to refer to it) squeaked out an uncertain rendering of *The Cock of the North*. In his mind's ear Jos could hear the beat of the drums and skirl of the Highland Bagpipes thundering out the tune on the windswept parade ground by the North Sea.

It took quite a long time for the band to honour all the officers in this way, and so it was already late – ten-thirty or so – by the time they all returned to the ante-room and began to order brandies and further cigars and coffee. For the married officers this was a convivial men's evening at their Club. They were all of an age to have been in the Second World War, and their exchanges of anecdotes became more hilarious and far fetched as the brandy was consumed and the hands of the clock stretched past midnight. The subalterns had each other's company every evening and by this time were in a state of great boredom and sleepiness. They kept sneaking glances at their watches and willing the Colonel to leave. But it was into the small hours before the Colonel got to his feet and went pottering off to his house. The other senior officers then started looking fussily at their watches and exclaiming with astonishment how late it had got and that they would have to be careful not to disturb the good lady and so forth. And so they went off leaving the Mess to the subalterns and George, the Quartermaster. George had become very drunk in the course of the evening and had to be escorted, protesting, back to his house by Jos, Billy Rogers and Dave Lawson.

Jos then made thankfully for his own gidda, thinking of the blessed dark, green oblivion to be found under the mosquito net. So intently was he concentrating on this desideratum that he did not at first realize that someone was following him. Once he became aware of the sound of footsteps behind him, he stepped quickly into a gap in the bush hoping that his pursuer would carry on past him and that he would thus discover who it was. The figure who hurried by was a young recruit in Jos's company: Jos recognized him at once as an articulate and intelligent boy. He remembered thinking that it was young people of this calibre who would be needed to run the new independent Nigeria which was soon to come into being. He found it odd and disappointing that this boy should be out of the bounds of his barracks in the middle of the night.

Jos resumed the walk down to his gidda, and soon could make out the figure of the nightwatchman dozing by his doorway. The nightwatchman contrived a clumsy salute as Jos approached.

'Did you see a young recruit hurrying past?' Jos asked.

The nightwatchman was, like most of his kind, a former soldier. They were posted, on a very generous ratio, of one for every two or three houses. Jos was never clear what their precise function was. He supposed that they constituted a kind of human burglar alarm in the evening if the inhabitants of the houses were away from home, but he could not fathom what purpose they served during the night dozing on the doorsteps of houses which were occupied. However, no-one enquired too closely: appointment as a nightwatchman was a much-prized perquisite among retired soldiers which helped to eke out their small pensions.

This nightwatchman was – or seemed to Jos to be – elderly: he was probably aged about fifty-three. He had not quite followed Jos's question.

'Sah?' he enquired.

'Did you see soja run?' articulated Jos slowly.

'Na yes, sah. 'E de go foh dere,' and the nightwatchman pointed to the path which ran from Okoko's house to the Barracks.

Jos looked in that direction, and as he did so he was taken aback to see the young recruit emerge from the side of the house, and come walking briskly towards him. The boy stopped a few feet away and saluted smartly.

The nightwatchman seemed to feel that some action on his part was called for and made as if to seize the recruit. Jos motioned him to stand aside and said sharply to the recruit, 'What are you doing here in the middle of the night? You know you're not allowed to leave the barrack area after Lights Out.'

'Yes sah,' the recruit replied. 'But I must see you sah. I must tell you.'

'You'll see me all right. You'll be on company commander's

orders tomorrow and I'll give you three days confined to barracks.'

'Yes sah,' said the recruit politely and resignedly. 'But I must see you sah, I must speak. I must tell you.'

'If a recruit has something he wants to report, he must see his platoon Sergeant first,' said Jos primly. However his curiosity was getting the better of him and there was a suppressed desperation in the recruit's eyes which he found upsetting. He went on. 'But since you'll have to pay the penalty for this breach of lights out you may as well say what you have to. What is it that you want to tell me?'

'Is Company-Saji Major, sah.'

'CSM Musa? What about him?'

'No sah is British Company Saji-Major. Is Mister Roberts.'

'Well?'

'Sah, he be bad man proppa. He make young recruits go with him.'

'Go where?' Jos asked, feeling unease. He did not care for Roberts and he could quite believe that he was "bad man proppa" in all sorts of ways. But he could see at once that it was "not on" for an African other rank to be complaining to a British commissioned officer about a British warrant officer. The bonds of convention and trust which held the hierarchical society of a colonial regiment together could not stand strains of this sort.

'Go to his bed sah,' the recruit blurted out, compounding and intensifying Jos's unease. He was stunned and felt slightly sick. To an inexperienced heterosexual just beginning to realize the astonishing physical intimacies involved in sexual intercourse between a man and a woman, the notion of homosexuality was all but incomprehensible; and in so far as he had any understanding of what presumably took place in homosexual intercourse, he was filled with revulsion. Roberts? That racist initiating acts of physical intimacy with young African soldiers?

The nightwatchman broke the silence.

'You want me go arrest dis boy?' he enquired, looking at Jos's troubled expression.

'No, leave him.'

Jos turned to his recruit. 'What is your name?' he asked.

'Private Robert Samali, sah.'

'How did you manage to avoid lights out?'

'I go foh my bed with de udder sojas. But when dat dey all asleep I get dressed and come wait foh you, sah. I hope go catch you when you come from Hapsas Mess foh you house.'

Poor devil, Jos thought to have chosen a Mess Night and had to wait so long.

'Well get back to your barrack room now. I will send for you to my office tomorrow.'

'Yes, sah. Tank you sah.' And with that Private Robert Samali saluted again smartly and marched off towards the barracks.

Jos glanced at the nightwatchman. He doubted if that puzzled-looking veteran had understood much of what had been said or grasped its implications. Jos bade him goodnight and unlocked his way into his gidda. There he quickly undressed and slipped into bed. He needed time to think. He was dumbfounded by the recruit's allegation; and he was not at all sure what he should do. If it was true that Roberts had been engaging in homosexual relations with recruits he would presumably face a courtmartial. And if he had been forcing his attentions on them unwillingly the punishment would be severe, probably prison sentence and loss of pension rights. God, what a mess. What a disaster for smart, swaggering, bullying, bull-shitting Roberts, so careful not to put a foot wrong in the everyday minefield of Army rules, regulations and conventions.

In telling the recruit that he would send for him, Jos had remembered that Major Hamilton and Captain Stevens would be away for the day on a TEWT (tactical exercise without troops) with some company commanders from other battalions in the brigade. But it could be awkward if CSM Roberts himself was hanging about the company office when he sent for Private Samali. Jos was therefore relieved when the Sergeant-Major said to him as they were returning from Company Muster Parade, 'Weapon training is a bit dodgy, sir. The platoon sergeants are all right dressed up to the nines and bawling out commands on the Parade Ground, but they leave weapon training to the corporals, and, quite honestly sir, some of them don't know their arse from their elbow when it comes to stripping a weapon down.'

Roberts's choice of language seemed suddenly unfortunate.

'So I think I'll do the rounds this morning, sir, and make sure that the recruits in each platoon are at least getting the basics right on the rifle, the bren and the sten.'

'Good idea, Sergeant-Major.' Jos said. 'I'll take company commander's orders at 1000 hours, and I've got quite a bit of paper work to do in the office.'

The CSM saluted as they reached the company office and then set off briskly to where the various platoons were assembling for the morning's activities.

Jos watched the CSM's retreating figure, wholly unable to credit the implications of what had been alleged against him. Was he making too much of what the recruit had said? – "bad man proppa" "make recruits go with him to his bed". Jos shuddered as he turned away and walked up the wooden steps to the office and went into the room which was shared by CSM Musa and Lance-Corporal Michael. He looked warily at them. Did they know about Roberts's behaviour? So often he had discovered that some matter of the utmost confidentiality spoken of in coded whispers and communicated in sealed envelopes by the Europeans was common knowledge among the Africans.

'Anyone for company commander's orders today?' he asked as CSM Musa leapt to his feet, his hand rigidly pointing to his forehead in salute.

'Yes, sah.' CSM Musa barked out. 'One recruit from No. 1 Platoon foh talking on parade and one from No. 3 Platoon foh dirty web belt, sah.'

'OK Sergeant-Major: I can deal with these – company commander's orders at 1000 hours as usual. But see if you can get Private Robert Samali from No. 3 Platoon to report here straightaway.'

'Yes, sah!' CSM Musa replied briskly, glad as always to have something specific to do.

Jos went into his office and started looking through the various papers which Lance-Corporal Michael had put in his

206

in-tray. He found he was able to dispose of most of them himself: those which would require the company commander's authority or which Major Hamilton should at least see he put together in a separate pile and took through to the company commander's desk. As he was returning to his own room, he saw the company runner and Private Samali marching at the double across the parade ground. Jos sat at his desk and awaited Private Samali's arrival. After a few moments he heard some scuffling and whispering outside his office door. Then there was a sharp knock on the door and CSM Musa opened it, stepped in and saluted smartly.

'Private Robert Samali de heah, sah!'

'OK. Send him in.'

The CSM about-turned and roared out, 'Private Samali, attenSHUN! Left right, left right, left right, HALT!'

The recruit was brought crashing to this halt about one foot away from Jos's desk and stood there, somewhat pop-eyed, his limbs tensely at attention.

'Thank you, Sergeant-Major,' said Jos. 'I want to talk to this recruit in private.'

'Sah!' roared the Sergeant-Major in acknowledgement, and then turning to the recruit, he commanded, his voice at full throttle in the tiny room, 'Stand at ease! Stand EASY!' Swivelling to face Jos, he saluted, about-turned and marched out of the office, closing the door with elaborate care behind him.

Jos looked intently at the recruit. 'All right then, Private Samali, what exactly is it that you want to tell me?'

'De European Saji-Major, sah. He make some of de boys take off dere cloth and go play with him.'

'Where does this happen?'

'Foh his house, sah.'

'That can't be right. That could never happen with Mrs Roberts there.'

'But she no de, sah. She de go foh England last month because dat her mudder she no well and Mrs Roberts must go help her.'

Jos had forgotten, but now he recalled the laborious joking among the European NCOs about Roberts being a grass-widower: would he be sober at any stage before he and his old dutch were reunited? Would he turn Moslem and acquire one or two supplementary wives? And so on.

'So what you are telling me started only after Mrs Roberts left for Britain?'

'No sah. De Saji-Major always like touching boys before dat. But is only now he get dem to take off their cloth and go to his bed.'

'How do you know this? Are you one of the boys?'

'De Saji-Major want me to. But I no gree foh dat. Den de Saji-Major go make it bad foh me.'

'What about the other recruits? Would any of them tell what has happened if they were asked?'

'I tink so sah. Dey no like it with de Saji-Major, but dey have fear foh him.'

'How many boys are there?'

'Dere are tree boys who de Saji-Major make go to bed with him, sah.'

'Do the platoon sajis know about this? Does CSM Musa?'

'I tink so sah. But dey no say. Dat is why I tell you.'

Jos could follow Private Samali's line of reasoning. If the African NCOs had decided to turn a blind eye on Roberts's behaviour, the recruits would be chary of reporting the matter to a British NCO, reckoning that they would be unlikely to listen to complaints against one of their number. Thus they would really have no means of redress – unless to go over the heads of all the NCOs and appeal to an officer.

'In what way exactly does the CSM make it bad for you?'

'Ebery inspection he say my boots dirty, my belt dirty. He make me parade and parade in field service marching order ebery night. He say I no fast enough on de assault course and he make me go over de wall and de water jump again and again.'

'Well maybe your boots were dirty. Maybe you were too slow. I can't waste my time because a recruit can't take the discipline here or isn't turning out a good soldier.'

'No sah!' Private Samali almost shouted in his indignation. 'I good soldier. I know dat. Is because Saji-Major angry with me. Dat is all.'

'OK, Samali. You have made a most serious accusation. I hope for your sake that you can produce proof of it. First of all give me the names of the three recruits whom you say the sergeant-major is forcing his attentions on.'

'Sah?' Private Samali queried, confused by the delicacy of Jos's turn of phrase.

'Who are the three boys the Saji-Major make go to bed with him?'

'Hassan Dikwa, Ali Zaria and Johnston Owerri.'

'If they do not give evidence against the sergeant-major have you any other way of proving what you say is true?'

Private Samali thought for a few moments and then muttered, crestfallen, 'No sah.'

'All right, Samali. I'll have to think about what I should do. You can go now. Don't tell anyone about this until you hear from me.'

Private Samali came smartly to attention, saluted and withdrew.

Jos felt an uneasy weight of responsibility descend on him. He did not really doubt that Private Samali had been speaking the truth, and he knew that he must do all he could to see that justice was done and that the young soldiers were released from the unwelcome practices which he assumed Roberts was forcing on them. (It did not occur to him for a moment that any of the boys might be willing partners). But Roberts was a wily and dangerous adversary. Jos was sure that he would have been careful to cover his tracks; and he would be ingenious and aggressive in wriggling out of accusations which were not fully substantiated. And Major Hamilton would approach matters with a strong bias in Roberts's favour and would no doubt tend to dismiss the recruit's tales as incredible and vicious – unless supported by cast iron proof. The other British NCOs would almost certainly rally round Roberts: they might dislike him and would perhaps be disgusted by the thought of such goings on. But they would not want to see one of their number publicly disgraced. The more Jos thought about it, the less certain he was that even the testimony of all four recruits would go for much. He could imagine Roberts putting up a scathing defence on the lines of four thoroughly bad, malcontent soldiers conspiring to blacken his character; and Jos could not see much chance of the boys standing up to hostile cross-examination in a language which was not their own. Jos realized that if he were to make any sort of report now, he would be cast in the role of the gullible tell-tale, quick to believe ill of an NCO whom he did not like. For a moment Jos was tempted to forget that Private Samali had ever spoken to him. But only for a moment. He thought of the hurt anxious young eyes of the recruit, so desperate to break out of the wall of indifference and deafness; and he saw the small, crafty, knowing eyes of the sergeant-major, secure in his knowledge of the ropes of army life. He remembered the racism which seemed to influence every deed and word of the sergeant-major and he felt anger at the thought of how the cards were stacked in Roberts's favour, and the unfair way in which so many of the British officers and NCOs derided and took advantage of the Africans.

Jos sighed wearily: he began to conclude that the only way in which he could help the young soldiers and justify Private Samali's trust in him would be if he could set a trap for the Sergeant-Major and then himself give evidence against him. He felt a prickle of excitement and nervousness as he thought of the irregularity of what he was contemplating, and indeed of the risks he would be running. He had no very clear plan as to what might be done. Presumably he would have to hide near Roberts's house until he had seen the recruits enter it and then burst in catching Roberts *flagrante delicto*. The more he thought of such a plan the more clearly he saw ways in which it could go ridiculously or horribly wrong. How could he possibly explain his presence to the nightwatchman, for example. The Roberts's house was quite near the RSM's house: he would have to ensure that he was concealed from the RSM's house as well. And as he thought of this he again wondered if it was really credible that Roberts could be holding the alleged sex orgies more or less in the middle of the British NCOs' married quarters. No, the idea of him, a British commissioned officer, skulking in the bushes beside the house of a warrant officer waiting to surprise the sergeant-major in bed with young soldiers was too ludicrous to contemplate.

He was aroused from his brooding by the arrival of the

defaulters for company commander's orders. Each recruit was bustled in before him to the accompaniment of the usual hectoring words of command from CSM Musa, who then solemnly recited the offences for which the boys were being arraigned. Jos regarded them benignly. How much easier it was to deal with this sort of thing than to decide what to do about Private Samali's accusation. He lectured them in turn about the importance of silence on parade and spotlessness of uniform, and then dismissed each with an admonishment.

It was while he was going on about the virtues of a smartly blanco-ed web belt that he thought of one possible source of help and advice over the Roberts problem. George, the Quartermaster, himself an ex-ranker, seemed to have a marked contempt for the Unit's British NCOs. He got on well enough with the RQMS with whom, of course, he worked very closely: indeed at times it seemed that the two of them were in league against the rest of the world, certainly against the other members of the Unit whose greed, say, for a pair of socks or boots had to be restrained and contained at all costs. But the RSM, the CSMs, colour sergeants and sergeants were all clearly regarded by George as a feeble, second-rate bunch to whom he would have given a hard time in the days when he was a regimental sergeant major. And Jos had noticed that George seemed to have a particular dislike of and contempt for Roberts. Jos had never quite been able to fathom the reason for George's attitude to the NCOs. He supposed it was partly a decision by George to distance himself from his past as an 'other rank' and partly envy for the much jollier and livelier life in the sergeants' mess. There was always an atmosphere of the local pub there: by contrast the officers' mess resembled a stuffy, sleepy club. It was a dull and lack-lustre place with virtually no form of organized entertainment. Jos resolved to confide in George.

211

22

Accordingly, that evening Jos set off rather earlier than usual for pre-dinner drinks in the ante-room. There, as expected, he found George on his own downing his first litre of Carlsberg and throwing his head back to catch in his mouth the roasted peanuts which he was tossing up into the air. He looked abashed when he saw Jos observing this.

'You're early,' he said accusingly.

'Yes,' Jos replied. 'I'm glad I've caught you on your own. I want your advice about something.'

George's suspicious little eyes looked warily out from his large red face.

'Oh yes,' he said. 'And how can I be of assistance?'

Jos found it difficult to know how to begin. George grew restive during this silence.

'Not been up to the Gari again have you, Jos? If that's the problem it's the MO you should be seeing, not the Quartermaster.'

'No, George. It's really, well, a sort of company matter, nothing to do with me personally.'

'Well your company commander should be your father confessor then.' George declared, pleased as always to have found a home to which a buck could be passed. 'Another litre of Carlsberg,' he bawled at the young Mess Boy who was waiting on them, resplendent in a gleaming white suit and smart red fez. 'And bring this master a litre too.'

'No I'd rather not discuss with Major Hamilton yet, George. I need your advice first. It's about an accusation made against one of the British NCOs, and I thought you might know how to handle it.'

George bridled slightly at this. He always resented any implication that as an ex-RSM he knew the mind of the NCO or was an expert at dealing with them.

But Jos could see that he was curious to know which NCO was accused of what.

'One of those bastards been nicking equipment have they?' he asked.

'No it's – well one of the British NCOs seems to be a homo and been interfering with the recruits.'

'What!' roared George, his curiosity now in full command. 'You mean been coming the Vicar or the Scoutmaster?'

Jos was at first slightly flummoxed by this reference, but the occasional prurient glance which he had given to *The News of the World* now came to his aid.

'Yes,' he confirmed.

'Jesus Christ!' George sighed heavily. 'Whose made the accusation? And which of them is accused?'

'One of the recruits in my company, and it's against CSM Roberts.'

'Oh dear, oh dear, oh dear!' George said. 'Jesus!' he added thoughtfully. He took the two Carlsbergs from the tray the Mess Boy had brought in, and signalled to the boy to withdraw. Then he looked sharply at Jos.

'Never liked Roberts, did you Jos?'

'No, not much. But that's got nothing to do with it.'

'But you believe the accusations don't you?'

'Yes. I do,' Jos replied.

There was a long silence at the end of which George drank deeply from his glass of beer. Then he plonked it down on the side table, and turning to Jos he looked him full in the face and said, 'So do I. I've always thought that Roberts a bad 'un. This doesn't really surprise me. Tell me about it.'

Jos then related to George what the recruit had told him, explaining the desperate way in which Robert Samali had contrived to make contact with him. George was clearly disappointed by the absence of specific physical details.

'No but I mean, Jos, didn't this Salami bloke tell you what exactly went on. I mean who was pulling whose pud and that sort of thing. Three of them! Phew! What a greedy bugger! –

213

Bugger! Ha! that's a good one eh?'

Jos shivered with distaste, and his obvious revulsion seemed to dampen down George's curiosity. George looked at his watch.

'Ten past seven. The others will be over for their beer and peanuts any minute. You'd better come over to my gidda after dinner and we can have a think about how to deal with this.'

Jos was relieved that the Quartermaster had reacted so positively, and after they had finished dinner he accompanied him back to his gidda. George settled himself down in his armchair and brought out a bottle of whisky and two glasses from a drawer in the desk which was part of the standard furnishing of a single officer's accommodation.

'Well, Jos,' he began. 'I've been thinking about this nasty business while getting through my nosh. I reckon the only way forward is for me to sound out the RQMS.'

Jos's heart sank: he had never encountered such a negative, grudging man in his life as Regimental Quartermaster Sergeant Blackett. And he was sure he would be anti-African, anti-Officer, and pro-fellow non commissioned officer if approached about an accusation of this sort.

His dismay must have shown because George immediately said, 'Oh I know what you're thinking, young fellow me lad: that the RQMS is a prejudiced old sod who'll stand up for his mucker against slander by one of the niggers – or by a greenhorn young subaltern for that matter. But Blackett and I have worked for a long time together you know, and he won't refuse a request from me.'

'What will you ask him, then?'

'I'll ask him first if he has any suspicions about Roberts's behaviour, and then I'll ask him to keep an eye on Roberts – all informal like at this stage. And I won't mention your name or young Salami's.'

'Samali.'

'Well whatever he's called. Anyhow didn't I just say I wasn't going to mention it? I'll just say that rumours have come to my ears, and that for the good name of the unit in general and the sergeants' mess in particular I want to be satisfied there's nothing to them.'

'So there's nothing for me to do at this stage?'

'No. But if Mr Blackett does discover something, you'll have to inform your Company Commander about the complaint from the recruit and so forth. And no doubt you'll find yourself with a star role in a courtmartial.'

Jos began to feel wretched at the train of events in which he was now caught up. He had a clear vision for a moment of Mrs Roberts who had always seemed a sad, wistful woman. He had sometimes wondered how she had ever come to marry Roberts, and he now thought uneasily of the unhappiness being prepared for her. He gave vent to his feelings by sighing and letting a soft "Oh Bugger!" escape from his lips.

George snorted with laughter. 'Now, now that's what there's been too much of from what you tell me. We don't want any more of that.' George was now in high good humour, and he marked this by pouring another generous measure of whisky for each of them.

But when he had downed that, Jos resisted the invitation to stay and "help demolish the bottle" and managed to get off to bed at a reasonably early hour and still fairly sober.

It was some days before anything further was said between him and George about their discussion that evening. Indeed so studiously was the subject avoided between them that Jos at times began to wonder if George had changed his mind and decided to do nothing about it. Nor was there any further communication between him and Private Samali. Jos tried to avoid encountering the boy as he was sure that there was an increasingly desperate and accusatory look in his eyes. Roberts on the other hand was uncharacteristically jovial and friendly. He seemed to have abated his points-scoring style of general conversation, and no longer condescended to Jos as a wet behind the ears subaltern: indeed to be treating Jos as if he had earned the respect which was formally due to him by virtue of his higher rank in the military pecking order. Also his gratuitously insulting behaviour towards the Africans was no longer so much in evidence. One day he astonished Jos by strolling into the company office and saying, 'You know sir, it's bloody marvellous isn't it? Here we are running this country and this army by what we're accustomed to and think right and in our language, and we lose our temper if the poor black sods don't immediately savvy what we want. I wonder how we'd fare, sir, if we was recruits in the army of some Hause Emir or, for Chrissake, one of them Chief Owolowolows in the South. Makes you think sir, doesn't it? I expect they'd be calling us a bunch of stupid white bastards – eh? I could never bloody parley-vous-francais let alone one of these Godforsaken tribal lingos.'

Jos was completely taken aback: he had for some time now been rehearsing a speech very much on these lines to deliver the next time Roberts came out with some sneering racialist remark, emphasizing how unfair and absurd it was to attribute stupidity or lack of enthusiasm to people who were having to struggle with alien ways and in an alien tongue, posing just these questions of how would you, Roberts, get on if you were being bullied round the barracks and shouted at in Hausa or Ibo.

'Yes. I've often thought that,' he said, wondering uneasily how far Roberts' apparent change of heart resulted from the intimacies in which he was allegedly indulging with some of the recruits. 'I know that judged by our conventions and background the Africans sometimes seem thick and comical, but when you think of the tremendous adjustment they are having to make – because we are too lazy and stupid to make any effort to understand them or their languages – it amazes me that things run as well as they do and that we are able to have such good personal relationships with so many of them.'

As soon as he had said these last words Jos felt himself blushing and wished them unsaid, but Roberts did not seem to take them amiss and merely nodded in a kind of vague, general agreement, which might have implied that he did not want to go too far in any high-falutin praise of the wogs.

It was late that afternoon that George knocked on the door of Jos's gidda and said, 'We've got the bastard. The RQMS was bloody stubborn about helping. Denied there were any rumours about Roberts – but I could tell he was covering up. Anyhow he agreed to have Roberts' house watched, and last night there was a bloody orgy apparently. Roberts left the sergeants' mess about nine o'clock, and the RQMS had

216

arranged for two of the junior sergeants to follow him. He'd no sooner got into his house than the three recruits emerged from the bushes and were let in. The sergeants waited about twenty minutes and then went up to the shutters and peered in through cracks. There was Roberts absolutely starkers and the three boys too and all manner of how's your father going on.'

Jos wondered what exactly was meant by this, but he was both shy of asking and felt slightly sick when he thought of what the answer might be. So he simply asked, 'Did the sergeants confront Roberts?'

No. They waited for the boys to come out and took their names, numbers, platoon etc. – they were out of bounds after lights out for a start. And the boys started to spill the beans about what had been going on without being asked. The RQMS has reported all this to me and he thought he'd better cover himself also by telling the RSM. We must now inform Hamilton as Roberts's – and the recruits' – company commander and then the adjutant. Then I expect the military police will be brought in.'

Again Jos felt revulsion and sadness at what lay in store now for Roberts and his unfortunate wife. He wished Roberts hadn't made that decent little speech earlier in the day. But then he thought of the strained look in Private Samali's eyes, and that thought sustained him.

'Major Hamilton will take this very badly,' he said. 'He's always held Roberts to be a model NCO.'

'I know,' said George maliciously. 'That's always bloody annoyed me. I knew straightaway that Roberts was just a load of wind and piss. Bullshitter.'

As always Jos found himself momentarily distracted by the imagery conjured up by the barrack room language. He was for ever fretting over the imprecision and overkill of the metaphors. He realized that George was looking at him questioningly.

'I suppose I'd better be the one to inform Hamilton?' Jos said.

'Too bloody right. The man's in your company; so are the recruits; and Hamilton is your and their company commander. In fact you'll have to be a bit diplomatic about not having come to him sooner. Then it will really be up to Hammy how he proceeds with the Adjutant, the CO, Provost Marshall and all the rest of it. But proceed he will damned well have to now that the RQMS has reported to me and the RSM has been involved.'

'I suppose I'll have to mention all this stuff about the sergeants watching what was going on,' said Jos, now foreseeing the possibility of an explosion of outraged picque from Hamilton because all this suspicion of and spying on his company sergeant-major had gone on without a word to him.

'Of course you will.' George replied snappishly. 'That's the bloody *evidence*. You'd better say you simply couldn't believe the tales about Roberts and were anxious to clear his name without troubling the company commander over some malicious gossip. And now dear, oh dear, oh dear, it looks as if it all turns out to be true.'

Jos took that general line with Major Hamilton the next morning who nonetheless became very angry and indignant when he heard of the accusation and the "spying methods" used to test it, and was all for sending immediately for Roberts to "let him have a chance to give the lie to all this foul-mouthed nonsense." Jos had half-expected this reaction, and had waited until CSM Roberts was inaccessible on the rifle range before speaking to the company commander. The quartermaster's office on the other hand was only a few yards away and, denied the chance to confront Roberts, Major Hamilton stalked off to quiz and browbeat the Quartermaster. He came back in half an hour, having spoken to both the Quartermaster and the RQMS, a sadder and a wiser man. He slumped into his chair at his desk, looking drawn and miserable and called out for Jos to come in. He looked up as Jos entered the office.

'This is absolutely awful,' he said. 'Just incredible and awful. I would have trusted that man with my life, my wife, my family, everything. I feel as if the world has been turned upside down.'

Jos made what he hoped was a suitably sympathetic and astonished facial grimace. He felt a momentary stab of guilt when he recalled that it was him, Jos, and not poor Roberts whom Hamilton's wife had once passionately embraced.

218

But Hamilton went on, 'My God to think I invited him to come over and help fix up the boys' model railways the last time they were out here for their school holidays! Ugh!' And Hamilton shivered with distaste.

'Roberts should be back from the rifle range in two or three hours, sir. Do you want him to report to you?'

Major Hamilton looked aghast at the thought. 'No, no,' he said. 'This has gone too far to be treated as a company matter. I must see the CO and the Adjutant rightaway. I want nothing further to do with Roberts. I couldn't bear to have the man in the same room as myself. We'll get the provost people to put him under arrest until he's courtmartialled.'

Jos was surprised that Major Hamilton should have abandoned Roberts so quickly and completely: it was only half an hour ago after all that he had expressed disbelief in the accusations and was wanting to give Roberts a chance to clear his name. Jos concluded that the Quartermaster and the RQMS must have been graphic and brutal in relating Roberts's acts of depravity. Jos was left in charge of the company office while Major Hamilton went off to battalion headquarters to inform the Colonel and the Adjutant of the accusations and the evidence in their support.

The Colonel took a more relaxed view of Roberts' alleged misconduct than Major Hamilton did, and would not hear of calling in the military police at this stage.

'No, no, not at all,' he protested. 'Innocent until proved guilty. Corner stone of English law. Isn't that so Tony? We'll have this Roberts chappie confined to his house until a courtmartial can be held, but we don't want any of those red-capped fellas strutting around here at this stage. And we'll have to see that he gets a decent defence lawyer. See if the poor devil's pension rights can be salvaged. Which one is Roberts, anyhow? I always get mixed up with the British CSMs. Is he the Royal Berks one, middle height, a bit toothy – slimey really?'

Before either Major Hamilton or the Adjutant could attempt to answer this not entirely straightforward question, the Colonel was off on another tack.

'I suppose the sentence will depend largely on how far the

man forced himself on the recruits and how far they fancied that sort of thing themselves. Fiendishly difficult business really. Need a Solomon to sit in judgement. Solomon in all his glory . . . .' The Colonel's voice trailed off and he looked out the window of the office across the parade ground. But there were no lilies to be contemplated on that sterile field, and after a moment or two the Colonel settled back in his seat and looked up at Hamilton and the Adjutant. He stared at them blankly for a little and then said with a heavy sigh ''Strordinary creatures human beings, What? Gad, what a business!'

The Colonel picked a file out of his in-tray to indicate that the discussion was over and began to unscrew the top of his fountain pen, preparatory to inscribing the marginalia with which he liked to enliven what he regarded as the dull reports, notes of meetings etc. which came his way.

Once he was back in his own office the Adjutant sent for the RSM and arranged that he should go with an escort of soldiers to meet Roberts on his return from the rifle range, charge him and put him under house arrest. The RSM – and others when they were told about it – were surprised that Roberts, when charged, made no attempt to bluster or scheme his way out of the accusations against him. He seemed almost to welcome the arrest. And he "assisted with the enquiries" so extensively and thoroughly that the courtmartial (which was quickly arranged) turned out to be a speedy and largely formal affair. Furthermore Roberts seemed to bear no ill will either towards the young soldiers who testified against him or towards Jos as the officer who had initiated the investigations which had led to his downfall. However despite his helpful and co-operative attitude, the sentence was a harsh one. He got two years imprisonment and was dismissed from the Army with loss of pension rights. On appeal, the last element in the punishment – loss of pension rights – was overturned by the General-Officer-Commanding.

The night before Roberts was due to be sent back to Britain to begin his prison sentence, he asked to see one or two of his friends in the British sergeants mess, and also (to Jos's surprise and slight alarm) to see Jos. The guardroom at the Kebira barracks was an austere place: dark cells in which young recruits spent two or three days and nights as punishment for a variety of on and off duty misdemeanours. It had not been designed with any thought that one of the British soldiers might be imprisoned there for any length of time. The Colonel had accordingly overridden the Provost Marshall and decreed that Roberts should simply be confined to his house, closely guarded.

Jos walked up the path to the front door of Roberts's house, observing the neatly laid out garden which Mrs Roberts had lovingly tended until her sudden recall home and which the CSM's Boy had looked after carefully throughout all the upsets of the past weeks. The Guard at the door was expecting Jos, and unlocked it for him. Behind this – the front – door were stationed another two guards, one of whom now inserted a key into a lock newly fitted on the living room door. He opened the door and motioned to Jos to go in.

As Jos stepped into the room, Roberts came forward to greet him.

'Thank you for coming, sir.'

'I'm glad to see you Sergeant-Major,' said Jos.

Roberts smiled ruefully. 'Mustn't call me 'Sergeant-Major' any more, sir: just plain 'Roberts' now, sir.'

'Well it's difficult to break the habit,' Jos replied, trying to keep the tone as light as possible.

'That was the trouble, sir,' Roberts said. 'I got so addicted I couldn't stop myself even though I knew it was madness and was bound to end in disaster. It was just like being hooked on a drug. And when Maisie went home I felt I had to have as much of it as I could while the coast was clear: that I'd never have such an opportunity again and would regret it all my life if I didn't make the most of it. And in my greed I was careless about the boys I approached and the way I approached them.'

Jos could scarcely recognize in this calm, sorrowful man the bigoted know-all who had been such a bane of his life. He wanted to say something of comfort which would show compassion and understanding. But the words would not come. Roberts did not appear to mind the silence however. Jos looked at him carefully: his entire physical appearance had changed. The pert, slightly bustling style and swagger, the barely

221

concealed sneer, all seemed to have fallen away. He looked humble and somehow collapsed in on himself. Roberts broke the silence.

'I wanted to see you, sir, because I feel bad about the way I made things difficult for you when you first came out here.'

'Oh gosh, that's all right, Sergeant – er Mister . . . .'

'No, sir. I know I came the old soldier something 'orrible with you. There was something about you that brought the worst out in me. I got on not too bad with the ladeda boys, and had no difficulty "yes sir, no sir, three bags full sir" with them. But you wasn't ladeda. You was really just like me, only you'd got an education and that was what meant you became an officer. And all I'd got was army bullshit. I twigged that the way to get at you was by treating the Africans like dirt and speaking about them as if they wasn't really human. And that wasn't hard. Because that's how I felt about them. And I could see you choking with all the things you wanted to say but couldn't get out before I changed the subject or buggered off.'

Jos remembered what Roberts had said to him in the Company Office the day before he was arrested.

'Do you still feel like that?' he asked.

'I've had a lot of time to think about things these past few weeks – since I was arrested, but before that, really since poor Maisie went home. No, I don't feel like that any more. Maybe I never did. We all as kids just assumed the Blacks were dirty and stupid. And if I was to keep my place in the pecking order out here I had to believe it. But it's like I said that day in the company office: they're really just the same as us – well better really when you think it is them that has to make the effort to understand us, because we don't move a bloody muscle to understand them.'

There was a pause, and then Roberts, speaking more crisply as if to indicate that he now thought the meeting was at an end, said 'Anyhow, sir, I wanted to say I was sorry for being such a proper bastard so far as you was concerned. And I wish you all the best, sir, for the rest of your national service – not so long now – and in whatever job you go in for in Civvy Street.'

'Well thank you. But, honestly, there's no need to apologize to me. I shouldn't have been so bloody spineless when you were baiting me about the Africans. I'm always making the mistake of not wanting to have unpleasantness with anyone.' As he said these words, Jos realized that he had uncovered and confessed a character flaw of which he had previously been only dimly aware.

'Ah well, sir but you can't re-live what's happened. I wish to God I could.'

Jos saw how beaten and close to tears Roberts was. Again he sought for words of comfort, but could find none which seemed to carry conviction. He didn't even know if Mrs Roberts was going to "stand by" her husband.

'God I know this is a hellish low point, and it's difficult to think of it ever getting better. But it will. For one thing *you've* changed a lot. You must keep thinking about making a fresh start once you're free again. The length of the sentence will be cut for good conduct, parole and all that.'

Jos was hazy in the extreme about the grounds if any for these words of reassurance and comfort, but they served to close the meeting on a hopeful note. As he said them, he seized Roberts's hand and shook it warmly in farewell. Then he was out into the hallway and to the garden, the Guards locking each door behind him.

23

The months were passing. Jos had now seen two fasts of Ramadan. The second rainy season had come, and at home it would be summer. In less than four months he would leave Africa and the army. In the first few weeks and months of national service, during basic training and at Cadet School, the thought of demobilization had filled Jos with unspeakable longing: it had seemed so far off that it was best not to think about it. Before he had left Scotland for Africa, Jos had gone for long walks, trying to imprint on his mind the greens and browns of trees and grass and fields, the purplish tint of the hills, the clear water of burns running over pebbles. At first the shimmering heat and the harsh, garish colours of Africa had made him think nostalgically of the subdued tones of Scotland. But now that he was to leave Africa – and probably for ever – Jos realized he was experiencing a strange sadness and nostalgia in prospect. He would walk through the Sabongari, happily dazzled by the bright colours, fascinated by the abandoned wrangling and arguing of the market place, captivated by the sudden gaiety of African laughter.

He would look now almost with affection at the vultures which frequented the meat market, hobbling about with their awkward, graceless walk and the greedy, jabbing movement of their ugly heads. When he had first encountered them in what was essentially the local, open-air butcher's shop, he had been filled with incredulous horror that these hideous creatures should be given the run of the place. But now he regarded them complacently, with a sense of familiarity – and with some understanding of the sanitary job they were in fact accomplishing in disposing of scraps of fly infested meat. He remembered the exotic feeling which had swept over him the first time he had come across a traveller mounted on a camel; and he treasured now the occasional sighting of one of these beasts, moving with its curious, carpet-slippered shuffle across the sandy scrub. He found that after he had been out visiting or wandering round the Gari he would return to his gidda, hoping that Okoko would be in it, ironing his uniform or engaged in some other household chore so that he could talk to him and watch his pleasant, expressive face. He would look wistfully at Ernest as the little dog padded happily at his heels, and hope that the new young manager of the Bank of British West Africa had meant what he said about taking Ernest over and giving him a good home.

But, apart from all these sentimental causes for regret at the thought of leaving, there was one harsh, practical consideration which nagged at Jos increasingly as the weeks passed: the car. The car had broken down more or less permanently about three months after he had bought it. Festus had been consulted but seemed to have lost interest in the vehicle, and kept pleading other commitments, so that Jos eventually got tired of trailing up to the Gari to badger him. Months passed and the little car, parked beside Jos's house, became a fixed part of the scene. Okoko would sometimes wash the dust off it and polish it, muttering that 'dis ting go chop my mitre's money too much'. Then one day just before lunch Jos got a message to report to the Colonel.

Jos went in to the Adjutant's office intrigued to know what the Colonel wanted him for and slightly apprehensive. He looked enquiringly at the Adjutant before knocking on the door of the Colonel's office.

'I'm not sure, Jos,' Tony replied to the unspoken question. 'He said something about it being really a personal matter.'

This did nothing to reassure Jos who began to cast his mind anxiously over lapses in his private life which might have come to the Colonel's attention. Had he heard belatedly about the trip to the Sabongari with Stevens and Dainton? Had the business about the child prostitute at bush camp come to light? He knocked, entered and saluted.

'Ah yes Maclean, come in,' said the Colonel. 'Now I'm going

to come straight to the point: no beating about the bush. The thing is we've got to keep the place tidy: a place for everything and everything in its place. D'ye follow my drift? I've been meaning to have a little chat with you for quite some time. The point is that car of yours. It's damned unsightly you know. Lets the tone of the entire place down. What you might call a blot on the landscape. No offence intended, none taken, I trust, but it's really just scrap iron isn't it?'

'Well it hasn't been running too well of late, sir.'

'Hasn't been running at all in fact. Must learn to call a spade a spade, Maclean. Absolute folly to pull the wool over your own eyes. Camouflage to deceive the enemy yes, but don't fall for it yourself. Didn't they teach you that at Cadet School? Now in the present case what are the facts? – Fact One: the car is U S. Fact Two: the car is an eyesore. Fact three: the car must be removed. "Motor Caro est delenda" as the Romans might have said.'

This last flight of fancy and the adaptation of the relic from his schoolboy Latin seemed to put the Colonel in high good humour. He beamed kindly at Jos and said as if offering a major concession, 'Now what I suggest you do is this: get rid of the car – right out of the barracks. And don't hesitate to get the MT boys to help you tow it away. No problem can't be solved by sitting down round the table and talking it through. Jolly good, Maclean. Jolly good.'

Jos, who had not in fact been sitting down round a table or anything else but standing more or less at attention for the short period of this harangue, saluted and withdrew. He was feeling profoundly depressed. Where was he supposed to tow the car away to? Would Festus or some of his cronies give him anything for spare parts? Oh God! it really had been a daft waste of money for the rare occasions when he had managed to get any benefit out of owning the car. And even these few occasions had been wracked by worry that the wretched little vehicle would let him down at the point of maximum inconvenience and or public humiliation. Bugger! What an idiot he had been.

The Colonel had not set a deadline by which the car must be removed but Jos knew he would have to act quickly. One could

226

not in fact see his house (or the car) from the Mess or the Colonel's house and certainly not from the parade ground or Unit offices. Thus it was really absurd to describe it as a blot on the landscape, letting the tone of the Unit down. But there was nothing to be gained – and a good deal to be lost – by arguing or disobeying. His target must be to have the car removed by the next time the Colonel happened to take one of his waddling little walkabouts round the single officers' lines. That probably gave him two or three weeks. Jos was brooding in this way as he cycled down from the company office to the Mess for lunch, and indeed so deep was he in thought that he almost bumped into a pleasant-looking young man who appeared unexpectedly on the driveway leading up to the Mess. Jos got off his bike and apologized.

'Not at all,' said the young man. 'I wasn't looking where I was going. I was admiring your Mess.'

'Yes: it is rather fine, isn't it. It's basically just a very large mud hut with a great thatch roof. But it is the building for the climate: amazingly cool compared with the modern buildings.' Jos, in saying this, had been managing to place the newcomer. It wasn't difficult: he had a white-kneed, fresh out from Europe look about him, two pips on his shoulders and the letters RADC – standing for Royal Army Dental Corps – as shoulder tabs.

'You must be the new Dental Officer. My name's Jos Maclean. I'm getting within sight of the end of penal servitude here.'

'Mine's Robin Williams, and my sentence has just begun,' the young man replied. They shook hands and walked up to the Mess together, Jos wheeling his bicycle.

The Dental Officer was stationed at Kaduna, and bad cases of toothache were sent through to him from Kebira. But he came out for a week or two at a time to visit the other battalions in the brigade and give routine dental checks. Lieutenant Robin Williams had just taken over the post. He had been in Africa for only two weeks; and he was clearly captivated by the exotic new world he was experiencing. Jos and he struck up an immediate friendship, and Jos enjoyed showing him around, and telling him what he knew about the country and the people. "Shooting the shit", as Dainton put it, after listening to Jos over dinner one night describing how the women braided each others' hair into elaborate styles. Jos and Robin went riding together and swimming. They wandered through the Sabongari and the old city, Robin indulging his hobby of taking photographs.

The day before Robin was due to return to Kaduna, Jos invited him to have afternoon tea in his gidda. The water was always so heavily chlorinated that tea and coffee each tasted rather peculiar, but particularly tea. For that reason Jos usually had coffee in the afternoons as well as at breakfast and after dinner. But the notion of having a congenial guest to take afternoon tea with him was appealing. Okoko opened the shutters and woke him from his afternoon siesta at about a quarter to four.

'I no bring you coffee like you say, sah?'

'No, that's right, Okoko. I am expecting that Dental Hapsa to come, and when he does I want you to go up to the Mess and get a pot of tea and cups and saucers and a tin of milk – but put the milk in a jug – oh and get some sugar in a bowl and tea spoons – and bring it all down on a tray. And see if Corporal Samuel will give you some biscuits.'

Jos was fussing around in his little sitting room, arranging chairs and scraps of carpet to best advantage when he heard a light knock at the door, and Robin Williams appeared.

'Oh good, Robin. You woke up in time then. Take a pew. My boy will bring us some tea in a few minutes. Hurry up now Okoko.'

'This is a super little house you've got here, Jos,' said Robin stretching his long legs as he settled into the wooden framed arm chair. 'And it's such a lovely walk down from the Mess with those bushes on either side of the path.'

'I'm glad you like it. I was warned it had a bad Ju-ju when I took it over. But honestly I've had a pretty good time here. As a matter of fact I'm going to be very sorry in some ways to leave.'

'I well believe it,' said Robin. 'By the way whose car is that at the side of the house?'

'Oh that! That's mine, Robin. I got it ages ago because I was finding it so difficult getting transport to go anywhere. But

228

. . . .'

'Yours? Gosh. I envy you. That's just what I need: a little bus like that to get around in.'

'Well, as you know I'm off home in another few months, and I'd sell you that like a shot if you were really interested.'

'Would you really?'

'Yes. But the snag is that it hasn't really been all that satisfactory a car. As a matter of fact it has been laid up for quite a while.' Jos was aware that conflicting emotions were confusing him. Seen in one light, Robin was the classic sucker delivered into his hands: seen in another he was a most agreeable chum to be protected from the kind of anguish which the Sergeant-Major's car was sure to bring. The result was a very soft sell indeed. But the softer he sold, the more diffident he was about the car and any possible transaction, the more greedily Robin Williams took the bait.

'No honestly, Jos, I think these little Morrises are basically super cars. My mother has one, and it has been very reliable. I could get the RASC boys at HQ in Kaduna to fix it up, I'm sure.'

'Well, Robin, it would be a great weight off my mind to get the car sold before I start packing up ready for home, but I couldn't honestly say this one has been reliable. In fact to tell you the truth . . . .'

Just at this point Okoko who had been laying out the tea things with elaborate fussiness straightened his back and directing a dazzling smile at Lieutenant Williams exclaimed, 'Hey dat mato he be fine, fine mato too much, sah. Dat mato belong Regimental Saji Major before my mitre go buy um, and he be fine fine mato.'

Jos could scarcely believe his ears. From the moment the car had entered their lives Okoko had adopted a consistently sullen and reproachful air about it. His periodic washing of it was always done with venomous vigour as if working out his annoyance on it.

But Robin Williams was clearly besotted by the idea of acquiring the car. He clutched at Okoko's intervention.

'Your Boy seems to think it's OK,' he said. 'Look, I don't see how I could go wrong by giving you fifty quid for it.'

Jos gasped: the base emotion drove out the finer feelings.

'Well if you're absolutely sure, Robin, and are confident about your RASC chums . . . .'

'Done,' said Robin Williams. 'It's a bargain.'

Well, yes, thought Jos, for someone. But the feeling of relief overwhelmed him. He even began to share Robin Williams' confidence that the car could be made to go satisfactorily again. Okoko looked ecstatic and expressed his feelings of triumph by an absurd eulogy of the car.

'Hey dis mato go take you from here to Kaduna one time sah. Dis be proppa British car – not like dose cars foh Roads Engineers and Tobacco mitres!'

Indeed not, thought Jos guiltily, recalling the powerful Peugeots and Buicks driven by most of the European civilians.

The deal was concluded the following day before Robin Williams left for Kaduna, but the car could not actually accompany him back to HQ since the motor remained stubbornly inert. However within a week of his departure a large RASC truck with a tow rope appeared and removed the little Morris. Jos watched the car go, with a feeling of enormous relief. Okoko laughed with abandon as it disappeared from sight, bending forward and striking his thighs with joy.

After one or two weeks had passed, word came back to the Mess that the efforts of the RASC mechanics to mend the car had been neither successful nor well received by the General commanding the Brigade. Lieutenant Williams seemed to be caught in the trap of his superiors being unwilling to allow the Army mechanics to fix the car but also critical of the stationary little heap of metal as an offence against the neatness and good order for which the Military Hospital was renowned. Jos felt great sympathy for poor Robin Williams – and a good deal of guilt – on hearing this news. He was astonished at the reaction of the Colonel who got his driver to stop his car one day as he was passing Jos and called out cheerily from the back seat.

'I hear you managed to pass the parcel before the music stopped, Maclean. Jolly good, jolly good. All's fair in love and war. Drive on, driver!'

What an old sod, thought Jos. But of course, he loathes the brigadier and will be rejoicing that the headache has been

transferred to him. What shocked Jos most, however, was
Okoko's reaction. He came in one afternoon with Jos's post-
siesta cup of coffee, giggling to himself. He had just heard a
graphic account (via the Batman network) of the Brigadier's
irritation about the perpetual presence of the immobile little
car in the single officers' lines.

'Oh, sah,' he said, mastering the giggles for a moment. 'You
remember how I go tell that Dental Hapsa dat de Saji Major's
car be fine fine mato? Kai! He still no go, sah! And Babbanbature foh Kaduna HQ no 'gree foh dis at all, sah – at all! Hey!'
Okoko had to pause again to wipe the tears of mirth which
were running down his cheeks.

Jos was sipping his coffee and looked uneasily at Okoko.

'You are a dreadful fellow, Okoko,' he said. 'And have
undoubtedly perjured your immortal soul.'

This brought a further burst of hilarity.

'True, sah, na he be true.' Okoko assented joyously.

Jos bit thoughtfully on the rather hard biscuits which Okoko
had got from the NAAFI. What a couple of rotters Okoko and
the Colonel are, he was musing, as he crunched further into the
biscuit. And as he was chewing, and turning these lofty
sentiments over in his mind, he became aware that a large
filling had disengaged from a troublesome tooth, and that
already a shaft of pain had come from contact with the hot
coffee.

'Christ!' he exclaimed.

'Sah?' inquired Okoko, at once all concern.

Jos got up and withdrew to the baian gidda and spat out the
filling.

'Sah?' inquired Okoko again, displaying his magnificent
teeth, teeth with which he was said to have opened beer bottles.

'A large filling has come out of one of my teeth. I'll be in for a
bout of toothache now.'

'Kai!' muttered Okoko sympathetically. 'I go fetch whisky
and aspirin from de Hapsas Mess and make it all daidai.'

'Well it's not as bad as that yet,' said Jos as he felt gingerly
with his tongue round the cavity. 'I'll get the MO to fix up an
appointment with . . . .'

Jos's voice trailed off in mid-sentence.

231

'With de Dental Hapsa in Kaduna, sah,' Okoko completed the sentence cheerfully. And then the implications of what he had said struck him also. 'Oh, sah!' he exclaimed, aghast.

'Precisely!' Jos retorted. 'You and your fine fine mato too much!'

By the next day it had become clear that Jos was in for a bout of miserable toothache: a chronic throbbing and a sharp, wincing pain if he accidentally put pressure on the tooth. He glanced at the map of West Africa on the wall of his office: to the north the Sahara Desert; to the west and east the sparsely populated scrub; to the south more of the scrub and then the jungle. He focussed his attention on the nearest centre of Western Civilization, the town of Kaduna, and saw there in his mind's eye the dental surgery at the Military Hospital and Robin Williams, white coated, bending over the chair holding one of the many instruments of torture available to him. However there was nothing for it but to seek an appointment: his cheek was already beginning to swell, and at the earliest it would be as long as three months before he was on the journey home and anywhere near an alternative dentist. He took a sheet of paper out of the desk drawer and wrote

Dear Robin

I gather you have been having some trouble with the little Morris. I am sure you are right in your conviction that it is basically a sound little car, but I cannot help feeling some responsibility for your present difficulties. I am therefore enclosing with this letter a "rebate" on the price you paid me for it. Here is a cheque for £20.

Yours aye, Jos.

Now the thing is, he thought, to get this off as soon as possible and then get the MO to fix up an appointment for me. He stepped across to the company clerk's office.

'Corporal Michael, do you know if there is any transport going through to Kaduna today?'

'One moment, sah,' replied Lance-Corporal Michael flicking through some papers with his long, beautifully shaped, light brown fingers. 'Yes, sah. De Second-in-Command is going for a conference about the Army in aid of the civil power.'

'Good. Get a company runner, to take this note to the orderly office and see that it goes with the Second-in-Command's Driver to Kaduna and is given to Lieutenant Williams.'

Lance-Corporal Michael permitted himself a slight smirk – 'You get sore tooth, sah?'

'Yes,' Jos replied curtly.

'You sell Lieutenant Williams dat Saji-Major's car, sah?'

'Yes.'

'Eeeeh!' Michael let his breath out in a long, slow hiss and rolled his large eyes expressively.

As always Jos felt discomfited and put down by Michael's silent observation of and implied commentary on his behaviour.

The next day he called on the MO, Bert Dixon. Bert was his usual irritatingly condescending self.

'Come in, Jos,' he said. 'What can I do you for? No more naughty trips to the Gari I hope?'

'All I want, Bert, is an appointment with the dentist. I've got toothache.'

'Let's have a dekko then,' said Dixon, peering into Jos's mouth in a way which Jos felt to be both amateurish and unnecessary.

'Uh-huh!' Dixon grunted with significant stress on the huh. 'Quite a bit of swelling and inflammation there. Look, I'm sending some recruits through tomorrow morning to have various ailments checked and treated at the Hospital in Kaduna. I'm sure Robin Williams will be happy to deal with you then.'

Jos contemplated with mixed feelings the Dental Officer's assumed felicity in being given the opportunity to deal with him, but he gratefully agreed to the arrangement. At 0800 hours next morning he was sitting in the passenger seat of a three Ton Truck with a miscellany of young soldiers crowded into the back. The driver was a taciturn Hausaman, and this suited Jos's mood as the truck bumped the fifty miles along the laterite road.

When they reached the military hospital, the Lance Corporal in charge of the Recruits marched them over to the main

233

reception area. Three of them stayed behind with Jos as they, too, were to go for dental treatment. Jos's tooth was already beginning to feel much better as he contemplated the session in prospect with the man to whom he had sold a used car.

'You go first,' he said to the recruits as they were approaching the dental surgery. They looked at him in disbelief. Two of the recruits were Southerners and fairly fluent in English. The third was a very large, gawky and silent young man, from his features obviously a Northerner. Jos noted that he seemed particularly ill at ease and confused. He must have come in from the latest recruiting tour in the Lake Chad area, Jos reckoned, and still be very disoriented by this new life.

Jos reported their arrival to the orderly at the reception desk and motioned the three young soldiers into the waiting room. He wandered off by himself, going over again the best way of handling the forthcoming encounter with Robin Williams. He did not for a moment think that Robin would abuse his professional trust and ill treat him. But it was just so bloody embarrassing to find himself literally at the mercy of someone about whom he had been getting a guilty conscience. He finally decided that a tone of rueful sorrow would be the best line to take: a suggestion that he had always made it clear that the sale had been somewhat against his better judgement and finer feelings and that the twenty pounds rebate should simply be viewed as a recognition of these feelings now that the car was indeed proving so unsatisfactory. Thus resolved Jos hurried back to the Surgery, anxious to get it over.

The two Southerners had already been dealt with and were just about to report back to the main party. The gawky Northerner, looking even more frightened and confused, was shuffling into the Dentist's Room. Jos sat down on one of the hard wooden chairs and picked up one of the ancient *Punches* which were laid out for the entertainment of patients. He wondered what on earth the African Recruits made of this sort of reading material. These speculations were interrupted by a confused noise from the surgery and then the door opening and the soldier and Robin Williams stumbling out together, the soldier tripping over his shorts which were half way down his legs.

234

'Jos!' cried Robin Williams. 'Thank God you're here. Try to find out what's wrong with this chappie. Every time I get him to sit in the dental chair, he starts pulling his trousers down and pointing to his private parts.'

Jos, with his smattering of Hausa, began to question the boy and at length discovered that there had been an idiotic muddle over the case. The unfortunate soldier seemed to be suffering from Venereal Disease and had been sent to the military hospital for an investigation of his genito-urinary system. However as a result of his limited grasp of English and of incompetence either in the MO's Office or the Orderly Office at Kebira, he had somehow been grouped with the soldiers going for dental treatment.

Once he had been re-routed to the main hospital block, Robin Williams turned gratefully to Jos.

'You were splendid,' he said. 'I must really get down to swotting up some Hausa.'

Jos felt that things could not have got off to a better start. He sat down in the dentist's chair and explained how the filling had come out. Robin worked quickly and quietly at the problem. Jos was particularly grateful for the silence. He recalled civilian dentists who had rammed their views on the Korean War or private enterprise versus nationalization down his gagged throat. However as he got up to go he felt some reference to the motor car was necessary.

'You got my letter all right then, Robin?'

'Yes,' said Robin, blushing. 'I don't quite know what to do about it. It's not your fault that there turns out to be such difficulty in getting the car fixed. I bought it with my eyes open, and, having done so, I must take the consequences.'

Jos began to feel home and dry: tooth fixed and apparently no ill feeling on the part of this nice young man. His only concern now was to get rid of his own nagging feelings of guilt, and he now saw how he could do that.

'Not at all. I think we've both been had by that car to some extent. Sending you back twenty pounds was the least I could do. You must take it.'

'Well it's very good of you, Jos. I have spent a good deal on parts and repairs so this will come in very handy.' He looked at his watch. 'When are you going back to Kebira?'

'Oh mid-afternoon, I suppose: once the last recruit has been attended to.'

'Excellent,' said Robin. 'Let's go over to the Mess now and have a drink, and then lunch there.'

And as Jos downed his litre of Carlsberg and subsequently munched his way through minced bushcow, he felt a great wave of relief and contentment engulf him: within sight at last of going home; car off his hands; Colonel off his back; net increase of thirty pounds in his bank account; congenial glow of friendship between him and Robin restored; and, perhaps best of all, the whole of this satisfactory conclusion of the car saga to be reported to Okoko.

Lunch in fact took an agreeably long time, and it was nearly five o'clock before Jos and the soldiers set off on the return journey. It was dark before they reached Kebira, and it was the headlights of the truck which picked out Okoko's figure waiting by the soyer stove which was burning in one corner of the little compound round Jos's house. His friendly face lit up into a dazzling smile as Jos stepped down from the truck.

'I get Ruwan Safi (hot water) one time foh yoh baff, sah,' he said pointing to the stove under which a wood fire was blazing briskly. 'And yoh close foh ebening aw ready, sah.'

Jos was intensely aware of how much he liked Okoko, and he was suffused by a general sense of well being.

'Yoh tooth be daidai now, sah?' Okoko inquired solicitously as Jos sat down in one of the armchairs and Okoko began to unwind his puttees.

'Yes, thank you, Okoko.'

'And dat Dental Hapsa he no do you bad foh de mato?'

'No, Okoko. Everything is daidai.'

'Kai!' said Okoko as he got up, straightening his back, and breathing out a sigh of satisfaction which was the very essence of all things brought to a happy ending.

24

And now suddenly events seemed to move very quickly. The long awaited moment of going home and leaving behind what was surely just a strange interlude in his life all at once came rushing at Jos. The thick wodge of immovable months which had seemed to lie between him and return to normal life had broken up; and the time remaining could be measured in summer holiday periods of three weeks, a fortnight . . . .

Certainly there was an undertow of exaltation as he thought that, yes, he had got through what had seemed such a long exile. But the vague sadness and nostalgia in prospect for the daily sights and sounds and smells which were presently about him grew stronger and stronger. And it was not merely the pull of Africa which was affecting him. He realized to his horror that he was becoming wistful about the thought of leaving the little community of the Unit at Kebira. He found to his embarrassment a lump in his throat as the Second-in-Command confided to him over a beery lunch that he had always regarded him as an outstanding young officer and would greatly miss him.

Jos went moodily down to his house upbraiding himself vigorously under his breath. You sentimental fool. This is all rubbish. You hate the army. You are a rotten soldier. Most of your fellow officers are second-rate soaks who are out here because it is the only way they can get a reasonably paid job and life style above their means and capacities. The whole place is riddled with snobbery and racism. You have been having a nice time because you have a white skin and a commission and have been prepared to toady and conform. But get out of it. Do not repine. Get back to the society you

237

understand and feel at home in, and live there by a set of honest and decent values which you do not have to betray in order to "get on" and feel comfortable in polite society.

His thoughts turned at this point to his "affair" with the Resident's niece. At first after going home Jane had written frequently, her letters full of fond memories of their time together and eager anticipation of their meeting again. And Jos had replied in similar vein: it had, after all, greatly lightened and enlived his early days in Kebira to have dates with this pretty girl to look forward to and to enjoy. But the longer Jane was absent the more clearly he realized how little in common they had and that the letters were working to death the shared reminiscences of an abnormal period in each of their lives. Then Jane's letters had become fewer and further between and began to be dotted with references to a "super chap", Derek, son of a new neighbour of Daddy's, "awfully good at tennis" – indeed awfully good at bloody well everything else as far as Jos could see. And although Jane in a doggedly loyal – or perhaps simply possessive – fashion kept sending love and kisses to Jos and saying how much she was looking forward to seeing him again, Jos would have had to be very blinded by love (which he was not) if he had not been able to read between the lines. Jane's last letter, received that morning, had said in referring to his imminent homecoming that she was looking forward to Jos and Derek meeting and that she was sure they would get on well together. Jos had surprised himself by giving vent to a bitter laugh out loud as he had read these words. And I am sure, he said to himself as he scrumpled the letter up into a tight, bad-tempered ball, that we would hate each other's guts. He knew that his heart was intact and had not really been much involved in the relationship with Jane, but he was surprised to find how much his vanity seemed to be affected by the manifest waning and then switching of her affections. This recollection added zest to his exhortations to forget about Kebira society.

Ernest, padding along at his heels, looked anxious as Jos swiped savagely from time to time at the long grass with his swagger stick. By the time he had reached his gidda the self-reproach and exhortation had reached such an intensity that it was no longer wholly under his breath. He stumped into his bedroom where Okoko was laying out his afternoon civilian clothes. Okoko looked up and surveyed Jos's peevish expression and moving lips with concern, 'You get belly palaver, sah?' he enquired sympathetically.

Jos looked at Okoko's friendly, anxious-looking face and felt his ill-humour dissipate.

'No Okoko: just too much beer at lunch. I'll be OK after my sleep. Bring me coffee at four-thirty.'

Okoko picked up Jos's jacket, shorts and belt as he discarded them, and took them off for washing, polishing etc. as appropriate, and then returned to close the shutters. Jos lay down on the bed and looked up at the heavy thatch roof. He noted a large, black spider engaged on some intricate web weaving in the area just above the bed, and thought wryly to himself that there was no longer much point in him undertaking the enquiries he had been meaning – and failing – to make for all these months to discover how to identify the Black Widow and whether it or any noxious relatives were to be found in West Africa. If only he had not been so lazy and incurious how much more rewarding this year and a half in Africa would have been. And now there was so little time left. He thought of Bob Finlay and how he would probably have arranged for the West African counterpart of Rentokil to deal with the spider population – or of Robin Williams who would perhaps have written some scholarly paper by now on the subject of tropical spiders. He hadn't even managed to get on that signals course which might have given him the chance to call on Bob Finlay; and of course despite his good intentions he hadn't got down to writing to Bob. This brooding sharpened his sense of loss at the thought of leaving Kebira. And the really hard part of going away, he realized, was going to be taking leave of Okoko. He wondered if Okoko would be at all affected or if his thoughts would be confined to whether or not he was likely to get an agreeable successor to batman to. Well he has certainly shown no signs of grief so far, Jos thought to himself, as he heard Okoko chatting and laughing with some passer-by outside. Jos drifted off into sleep.

He was wakened as usual by the strong shaft of sunlight

which pierced the room as Okoko opened the shutters before setting down the cup of coffee. Jos took the cup and swallowed a mouthful or two of the strong, bitter, chlorinated liquid.

'Have the joiners made up that wooden trunk for shipping my heavy baggage home yet, Okoko?'

'Yes, sah,' said Okoko joyously clapping his hands together. 'He be bery fine box. He de come dis morning with de white writing foh top.'

'You mean my name is written in white paint on top of the box?'

'Yes sah. I tink so sah.' A note of uncertainty entered into Okoko's joyous tones as it always did when he was asked a question which touched on his illiteracy.

Again Jos felt a curious lurch of affection for his servant. He remembered afternoons and evenings in the rainy season when he had been reading or writing at the desk in his sitting room and when Okoko used to find some pretext for coming in, so that he could witness the miracle of someone understanding the tiny black marks on the page, and the astonishing feat of making such marks so quickly that soon a page was covered with them. On one of these afternoons he had startled Jos by saying in a quiet, sorrowful way, very unlike his usual matter of fact or laughing style. 'Sah when dat I go see you with de books and paper I know dat I am a BLIND man.' Jos remembered this as he detected the note of uncertainty in Okoko's voice, and he felt himself again in danger of sinking into a soggy state of sentimental throat-lumpiness.

'For Christ's sake, Okoko. Surely you know what my name looks like by now.'

'Yes sah. I tink it be bery like dat sign outside yoh house.' Okoko was here referring to the white board nailed to a wooden post outside each officer's house on which his name and rank were neatly painted.

'What do you mean "bery like"?' Jos asked roughly. 'Oh God I'd better have a look at it myself. Where is the trunk any how? We'll have to get a move on packing it.'

''E de foh heah, outside,' said Okoko opening the back door which led on to the verandah, shaded by the steep slope of the thatched roof. Jos felt a mixture of triumph and sorrow as he looked at the black trunk with his name painted in white lettering and below his name his home address. He had really ceased to think of his father's house as home. The sight of all this made him feel that the time remaining to him in Africa was slipping away out of control.

Okoko was studying Jos's face anxiously. 'De writing daidai, sah?'

'Yes, Okoko. Now look: we must sort out this evening all the heavy stuff – like my books and ornaments, and my wireless – and that dreadful khaki drill that was no use, and get it all packed into the trunk.'

Okoko's eyes lit up. This was the sort of valeting job which he enjoyed and was very good at. He laughed with pleasure. Jos looked at him a little bitterly. So much for me getting all soppy about leaving him. He seems to be looking forward to it.

Just then a bicycle bell rang loudly, and looking up, Jos saw one of the Hausa traders, Mohammed Kano, braking and slithering to a halt. It always astonished Jos how the traders managed to get around on their bicycles with their voluminous robes and beneath them panniers and parcels attached to the sturdy BSA and Raleigh frames.

Jos, who had just pulled his shorts on in order to inspect the trunk, did not feel properly attired to engage in the elaborate exchange of greetings which was now bound to ensue. However Mohammed Kano himself seemed anxious to cut this short after a few obligatory "Mai-Giddas" and "Yawa Sanus". He was looking suspiciously at the trunk.

'You go home soon, sah?' he asked.

'Yes, Mohammed, in a week or two. And, Mohammed,' Jos went on, seeking to avoid an exhausting and timewasting bout of haggling 'you have already sold me enough junk to fill this box at least once. I have no room, no time and no money for any more.'

Mohammed laughed wheezily revealing several gold-filled teeth in his fleshy, handsome face.

'Kai, sah. I no try to sell you tings like ifn you were a new Hapsa from England,' he said. 'I know you be Africa man proppa now. I have no power to beat you foh price sah.'

Jos marvelled at the bare-faced flattery even as he felt

himself falling for it.

'Why did you come round then, Mohammed?' he asked. 'I can't believe you had not heard that I was due to go home.'

'I be looking foh dat Master Langley, but 'e no de foh house. I wonder ifn you know where 'e de?'

'He's out with a platoon at bush camp this week. What do you want with him?'

Jos knew that Peter Langley, a very young and somehow gullible subaltern, who had been in Kebira for less than six months, had saddled himself in that time with a vast array of carpets, carvings and musical-instruments-which-did-not-play. And Jos also knew that these ill-considered purchases had been financed by a sort of never-never invented by the traders and implying a horrific rate of interest. Jos regarded Mohammed coldly.

'Oh is not foh me,' protested Mohammed, reacting to the hostility in Jos's look.

'But tell him, sah, "Remain one month foh Garba".'

For a second Jos was at a loss. Then he remembered. Langley's crowning folly had been the purchase of a really expensive, large carpet from the most unscrupulous of all the traders, one called Garba. This had been very much on the never-never. And the instalments were so steep and frequent that poor Langley seemed forever plagued by the ringing of Garba's bicycle bell, and his meagre pay was clearly being swallowed up by the repayment of his debts. And then some two months ago had come a wonderful deliverance. Garba had been convicted of some piece of villainy and jailed for six months. A great cloud lifted from Langley. He began to stand his hand again in the Mess and at the Club. He got a crush on the daughter of one of the lecturers in the Technical College and took to hiring Recreational Transport to go out to dinner at her house, a bottle of wine coyly produced from behind his back on greeting the girl's mother. From time to time Jos had vaguely wondered how long the stay of execution occasioned by Garba's timely incarceration would last. But it was not really his worry, and after a while it did not seem to worry Langley either.

Remain one month for Garba, he mused, and poor old

242

Langley won't be out of the country for another year at least. Presumably that rogue Garba has had some sort of remission for good conduct in prison, or perhaps just an automatic parole.

'OK, Mohammed. I'll tell Mr Langley.'

'Tank you, sah, tank you,' said Mohammed in his courteous way. Then he breathed deeply and lugubriously and said, 'I sorry you go sah. Why you no come back as District Hapsa sah?'

'Well thank you very much, Mohammed. I will be very sorry to leave.' Here Jos stole a glance at Okoko to see if any trace of sorrow could be detected on his face. Not at all. Okoko was beaming with the complacent pride which always seemed to come over him whenever Jos was engaged in conversation or an exchange of courtesies with someone of dignity or importance.

'Hey!' sighed Mohammed wearily gathering his robes together for the mounting of his bicycle, managing to convey by that monosyllable his sadness over Jos's departure and his own resigned acceptance of his hard and heavy lot as an itinerant pedlar of knick-knacks and minor luxuries. Jos felt his wariness relax a little in sympathy and in appreciation of Mohammed's kind and flattering words. Mohammed seized the handlebars and turned his head for a last farewell. Jos knew it would be the farewell uttered when it was unlikely that those involved would meet again – or at any rate not for an uncertain and long time. 'Sai wata rana': this could be translated simply as 'until another day'. But the Mallam who had given Jos some Hausa lessons when he first arrived in Kebira had rendered it as 'Until some other moon', and in the case of a really final farewell Jos thought of it in these romantic terms. He stood poised ready to hear Mohammed say the moving words. But Mohammed did no such thing. The expression on his face all of a sudden changed, and he took his foot off the pedal again.

'Sah!' he exclaimed as one who had just remembered an important commitment. 'I de forget to give you dis.' And here he took from one of the panniers a wood carving: these were very much part of his stock in trade.

'But Mohammed, you have already sold me half a dozen

carvings like that.'

'Oh no, sah: not like dis one. I get dis one specially when dat I know some Babbanbature go foh home.'

Okoko literally clapped his hands at this point. 'Is true!' he said. 'Dat my mitre he be Babbanbature!'

Jos made an attempt to stem the tide of flattery. 'You know that's not true,' he said. 'I am just bature – it is only the Resident and the Brigadier – and maybe the Colonel who are Babbanbature.'

'No sah,' wheezed Mohammed solemnly. 'Some of de other Hapsas are Babbanbature. And foh dem I get dis black wood before dat dey go foh home.'

Jos took the carving in his hand. It was very heavy, and it did seem a particularly fine piece of wood: the wood looked to be ebony. The head was that of a Fulani girl, a type of African beauty for which Jos had a distinct weakness. He thought for a moment of the strange visit to the young Fulani prostitute in the Sabongari – and of Gude, the milkwoman, and his encounter with her in her village in the moonlight. He handed the carving back to Mohammed and then, incredulous, he heard himself asking, 'How much do you want for it?'

'Oh sah, I like to give you dis ting foh free. But,' and here he sighed deeply, 'Is so much money foh cloth and dis bicycle and foh my wives . . . . Hey . . . . But I give it you foh small small price . . . . And den I be happy. I know dat you have dis ting from me from Africa.'

'How much?'

'I give you dis foh just one pound sah.' Mohammed uttered these words with an air of great magnanimity, and leaning the bicycle against the verandah wall he stepped forward proffering the carving with a graceful flourish.

'I'll give you five shillings for it and I must be mad to clutter myself up with it.' Jos replied.

Mohammed laughed in his wheezy way until the tears came from his eyes. 'Five shillings!' he repeated when he had got his breath back. 'Oh sah! You be hard master proppa. Hey Okoko dis master of yours he be business man!'

Thus addressed, Okoko looked puzzled and uncomfortable and did not reply.

'No sah,' said Mohammed changing his tactic. 'I no like foh you to have dis ting foh Africa ifn dat you no like it.' And he began to repack the carving into the bicycle pannier. His air was now one of huffiness and offended dignity. Okoko looked even more puzzled and decidedly miserable. Oh to hell with it, thought Jos. He's not such a bad old stick Mohammed, and it really is rather a nice carving.

'All right, Mohammed,' he said. 'You win. I'll give you seven and six for it.'

Mohammed went on with the fastening of the pannier straps in a slow and meticulous fashion. 'I sorry foh dis,' he said. 'I tink you go like dis ting foh Africa. I no want you to have something you no tink good.'

'Ten shillings then, and that is my absolute limit.'

'Kai sah you be hard man too much. But I gree foh you. So heah I give you dis ting foh ten shillings.'

There then followed a ceremonious handing over of the wooden head in exchange for a crumpled ten shilling note which, Jos noted, was quickly tucked into a bulging wallet in one of the undergarments concealed by the flowing robes. Then with a flurry of good wishes and 'Sai wata ranas' Mohammed cycled off. Jos watched the colourful figure toil up the pathway from his house to the road which ran from the barracks to the Sabongari. Then he looked down sheepishly at the heavy lump of wood in his hand.

'That cunning old devil Mohammed Kano,' he muttered to himself. 'The one thing I swore to myself when I saw him here just now was that I wouldn't buy any more junk off him. And now just look at this.'

'You no like um?' Okoko enquired, still clearly very puzzled by the whole transaction.

'Yes I 'like 'um' all right. We can wrap this up in something when we do the packing of the heavy gear tonight.'

Okoko's face cleared. 'Yes sah. I know how to go pack tings like dis one.'

25

It was on the Thursday afternoon of that week – just before Jos
was due to have his siesta – that he was in the bedroom with
Okoko discussing the arrangements which would have to be
made to ensure that the traders continued to bring firewood so
that his successor in the gidda would have a supply to feed the
stove which heated the water. Outside the afternoon had
assumed that drowsy quality which came in the wake of the
hottest part of the day. Suddenly that drowsy silence was
pierced by a strident, high-pitched and somehow imperious
call –

'Mai Gidda!'

Jos and Okoko exchanged looks.

'That's your girl friend, Okoko. But you'd better get rid of
her quickly hadn't you? I think your wife's at home?'

Okoko laughed, 'Gude no come foh me today, sah. She come
foh you.'

'What do you mean?'

'When dat a young Hapsa go foh home dat Gude like she
come to say goodbye and let him go play with her.'

'Mai Gidda!' The loud, almost raucous call came again, and
then before Okoko could be told to usher her in or send her
about her business, Jos heard the leathery slap of her bare feet
walking across his living room floor. He felt a queer mixture of
nervousness and excitement. He turned to Okoko for advice
and support only to see that discreet Jeeves slipping out
through the bathroom and back door, shooing Ernest out
before him. Gude was standing now at the door between the
bedroom and the living room. Jos was again impressed, as he
had been when he saw her in her home village, by how slight a

246

creature she was, minus the tall and heavy loads which she usually had on her head. She was looking at him with a ludicrously wanton and seductive expression, partly the result of the heavy make up which she habitually wore round her eyes, and which she seemed to have applied in double measure today.

She advanced towards Jos in her graceful, sensuous style, and stood very close to him, pressing the full length of her body to him. She looked up at him and smiled. Then she stretched out her slim arms and took his hands firmly in her henna-stained palms. She pressed herself to him. Jos was thoroughly discomfited. He liked Gude and he was anxious not to offend her, but this leave-taking seemed to be entering unknown and potentially absurd territory. An off-putting feature of Gude's curious semi-embrace was that she still had her elaborate headdress on: presumably she did not want to undo this, the platform for her stock-in-trade. Jos edged slightly backwards, and as he did so Gude let go of his hands and began to unwind her clothing. Very quickly she had wriggled out of it, and stood a slight but voluptuous figure before him. She gave another of her wanton smiles and said 'Mai Gidda!'

And then she put her arms round Jos and pressed herself hard against him. Jos was uneasily conscious of the incongruous headdress, but he was rapidly more aware of the soft contours of the body touching his. He was wearing only a pair of shorts, so that the tactile impact was considerable. His hands moved over Gude's smooth-skinned back: then he took her hand and led her to the bed. Gude looked at him with an approving smile, and they lay down together. Gude's hands began to caress his chest and back. And as her hands touched Jos, the incongruous headdress did not matter any more: soon he was feeling waves of excitement mount in him. Gude's hands were now slipping under his shorts; and all too soon he realized that he was going out of control: his own hands were now clutching at Gude, every part of her. But Gude's strong, deft fingers and his desperate, pent-up sexual frustration brought matters to their conclusion long before he wanted it. He lay in disbelief at what had taken place, with his head on Gude's shoulder, "all passion" all too quickly "spent". Gude

247

hoisted herself up and looked benignly down at him for a few moments. And then it seemed to be over. Gude got up briskly and began to get into her clothes again. Jos likewise did up his shorts and put on the civilian shirt which Okoko had laid out for him to wear after his siesta. His feelings, he realized, were extremely confused: it had been a kind of consummation, at any rate a release of the vaguely lustful feelings which, he supposed, Gude had always awakened in him. And yet how terrible, how squalid, what an unsatisfactory half measure. Premature ejaculation and masturbation rolled into one at the hand of his Batman's bit on the side. And how strange that not a word – even of broken Hausa – had been spoken.

Gude was now fully clothed and was looking at him intently still with a benign smile on her face. Oh of course, Jos realized, I'd better give her some money. He went to the drawer in his desk where he kept his cash, and then turned to Gude with the money in his hand. Gude's expression changed: the smile vanished and a furious scowl came over her pretty, painted features.

'Ba kudi!' (no money)! She snapped and flounced out of the room. Jos heard her shouting angrily at Okoko, and in a few minutes Okoko came in looking rather crestfallen and embarrassed.

'Sah, dat Gude angry sah when dat you go try to give her money.'

'Well, yes so I'd gathered.'

'What she do, sa, is she say goodbye, and she no want money foh dat ting.'

'What should I do now then Okoko?'

'You must give me small-small money, sah, which I go then give to Gude some other time, and for now you must go say sorry to Gude. I go fetch her and you say sorry about de money.'

But Gude was already in the room again, and smiling again. That's another astonishing thing about this unbelievable afternoon, Jos thought to himself. In all this time I've been here, almost a year and a half now, Gude has never crossed my threshold – and now here she is popping in and out uninvited.

'Tell her I am very sorry, Okoko, and that I greatly valued

248

her 'goodbye'.' Gude beamed after Okoko had rendered something on these lines into his somewhat shaky Hausa; and there then followed the kind of exchange of greetings which she had obviously expected and desired: many thank yous and enquiries about health and tiredness and work and hopes of meeting again at the waxing or waning of some future moon. And then Gude picked up the tall gourd, set it on her head, and went with her swinging graceful stride up the path and out of Jos's life.

'Gude give you good jig-jig?' asked Okoko conversationally as they watched the slender female form swaying sensuously out of sight.

'Sort of,' muttered Jos still scarcely believing what had happened. 'Okoko, does Gude really give "jig-jig" as you put it to all the officers before they go?' Okoko laughed.

'Oh no sah. Only she tell me dat some of de young hapsas look her like dey want to touch her, and if she gree foh dem she, let em before dey go. She no gree foh old hapsas or foh married hapsas. But she sorry foh de young hapsas.'

Jos felt more and more confused. How could it be that in a country where the native inhabitants lived just on the breadline, where the first question in any transaction was 'Akwai kudi ko?' (Is there money in it or not)? this desperately poor and handsome, youngish woman could disdain to cash in on an asset for which there would clearly have been a steady and lucrative demand – and yet choose to dispense her favours as her fancy and compassion took her? Other questions formed in his mind, but remembering that Okoko was one of Gude's regular partners, he decided that it would be too indiscreet to ask them. He doubted if there was anything in Queen's Regulations about sharing mistresses with one's batman but only, he supposed, because the drafter of the Regulations had failed to contemplate such an enormity. But Okoko himself was not so inhibited.

'Is good, sah. Is good foh you. I de worry dat de young hapsas no have ooman all dis time.'

'Well maybe so, Okoko. Very nice of you to worry about it. But I'm going off for a swim after my sleep, so wake me at about quarter to four. and then we'll start sorting out the packing of the stuff for the trunk before I have my bath.'

For the rest of the day, as he cycled down to the pool, as he lay in the sun, trying to improve his tan ready for going home, as he and Okoko squabbled over the gear to be put into the trunk, through dinner, and finally as he crawled into the haven of the dark green mosquito net, Jos kept thinking of the encounter with Gude, not so much in itself but wondering if he had perhaps wasted all those months during this, his young manhood, womanless – or virtually so. Indeed had the entire period of his manhood to date not been one of frustrated sexual desire, sublimated in grinding study and hearty sporting activities. It rankled with him to think that his longing must have been so evident to Gude – and, damn it, to Okoko that they had pitied him, and that Gude had felt such confidence in her ability to break through all the barriers of rank and race and wealth in order to give him such swift, perfunctory comfort. And yet he was glad that Gude had broken through those barriers. He was glad that the strange events of the afternoon had happened. And he resolved that he would not tell any of the Europeans about it. Not Dainton, not George the Quartermaster – he shuddered to think of the ribald talk they would indulge in. Not Langley who would be so flabber-gasted . . . . Ah Langley: now there's someone who is going to have something to worry about. I must see him tomorrow when he gets back from bush camp. And with that he slipped into sleep.

26

Next morning Jos was at his desk in the company office trying to reconcile a discrepancy between the "shorts jungle green, soldiers for the use of" which had been – or were said to have been – issued from the Quartermaster's stores to No. 3 Platoon and the number of pairs of underpants which the platoon sergeant could account for. His arithmetic and his suspicion as to the honesty of the Quartermaster's staff and or the platoon sergeant were disturbed by the sound of marching feet, and looking out the window he beheld Second Lieutenant Langley striding in grand style at the head of his platoon, on the way back from their week's field exercises at Bush Camp.

Peter Langley was a gawkily enthusiastic youth who, for all the years spent in his school's officer training corps and the months doing national service so far, continued to look a most unmilitary creature. His boyish, rather pop-eyed face appeared over shoulders which, already at age eighteen, had a scholarly stoop and were part of a figure which could at best be described as ramshackle. He was enjoying himself at the moment hugely, every now and then bawling out 'Left, wight, left, wight . . .' and then as he reached B Company Lines he brought the Platoon to a rather ragged halt before handing over to his platoon sergeant.

Typical, thought Jos. Why on earth didn't he hand over to the sergeant as they were passing the officers' mess and get himself a cup of coffee and a change of clothing? But even as Jos posed the question he could see the answer in the Walter Mitty-like fantasy being enacted by Langley as he strode, flatfooted, across to his company office, tapping his swagger stick against the side of his shorts. There he goes the brave young officer back from patrolling the outposts of Empire, proud of the honest muck on his sweat-stained uniform. I'll bet he made those poor recruits of his do alternate marching and marching at the double. Jos looked forward meanly to seeing Langley's *Boys' Own Paper* perception of himself disintegrate at the mention of the return of Garba the trader.

As Jos addressed himself again to the problem of the missing underpants, he was aware that he himself had been under scrutiny – from Lance-Corporal Michael, who was hastily returning his glance to the papers on his desk.

'Can you think what No. 3 Platoon have done with all these missing underpants, Michael?' he asked.

'Yes, sah. Is simple. Saji Yola signed foh too many. More dan de Quartermaster give um.'

'But that's crazy. Sergeant Yola couldn't have been tricked like that. And anyhow what possible use could anyone in the Quartermaster's office have for these ghastly pants?'

'Sah. I no say why it happen. I just say how it happen.'

As so often in his dealings with Lance-Corporal Michael, Jos was aware of a touch of insolence in the tone. But, as usual, there was nothing tangible to fasten on and take exception to. If Michael is right, Jos thought to himself – and he probably is –, then my last week in Kebira will probably be spent in hateful argument with that arch "old soldier" RQMS Blackett and repeated interrogations of the touchy and excitable Sergeant Yola. He decided that the best course for him would be to draft a humble note to the quartermaster, copy to the company commander, reporting the unaccountable loss and requesting a supplementary issue of underpants to make good the deficit, but to arrange with Michael that the typing and despatch of this was delayed until the point when any further involvement of himself would be impossible. He scribbled away at a suitably servile draft and then handed this complacently to Michael with instructions that it should not reach the desks of the recipients until the day he was due to leave. By the time he had done this and taken a squad for a spell of shooting on the indoor rifle range, it was time for lunch, and he cycled down to the Mess looking forward to a glass of beer. As he hung up his belt and hat, he heard a babble of conversation and laughter, and on entering the ante-room he discovered Peter Langley in full flow recounting the thrills and hardships of the week at Bush Camp.

'Dwinks are on me, Jos,' he called out. 'I'm so thankful to get back to semi-civilization. Well I mean at least we've got cold running water here. Not to mention the company of one's brother officers – even if you are the most fwightful shower.'

Jos looked round warily when he heard this playful jest. It was just the sort of thing that some of the more pompous Majors might take exception to as "rank bad form" and impertinence on the part of a junior officer. Fortunately none of them was present: only subalterns, the Medical Officer, the Quartermaster and the Education Officer. But young Langley is clearly getting a bit tight and could do with sobering up.

'Thanks, Peter.' Jos replied. 'My usual litre of Carlsberg please.'

While the beer was being brought and served, Langley kept up an excited narrative about the exercises he had made his soldiers do and the villages and villagers they had encountered. Jos felt he was making altogether too much of a few days in The Bush.

'I heard news of an old acquaintance of yours, earlier in the week, Peter,' he said, as soon as there was a gap in Langley's flow of anecdotes. 'I gather he's going to be out soon.'

'Weally!' cried Langley, agog with interest. 'I wonder who that could be? Not Smythe: he's been posted to his Wegiment, I gather – the Gween Howahds – lucky sod. I wonder if Fothehwingay-Thomas might be coming. He did his basic twaining with the Welsh Guards – but of course he'd never get a posting to the Wegiment.'

Langley had attended a minor public school, and tended to pepper his conversation with references to Cwookston Minor and Digthorne Major and so forth.

'Well, as a matter of fact, no – someone nearer to home. It's Garba, the trader. Mohammed Kano told me to warn you that he would be out of jail in a month, and would be looking for his money then.'

The gaiety died all over Langley's face. His lips which had been relaxed in a complacent smile – the result partly of contemplation of his thrilling adventures at Bush Camp and partly at the prospect of some public school chum coming out to join him – parted now in an incredulous gasp.

'Gawaba?' he gulped 'Oh Chwist.'

'You've got his money all ready for him though haven't you?' asked Dainton maliciously. Dainton was far and away the most careful of the Subalterns, genuinely shocked at how most of his fellow officers frittered away their pay on drink and horseriding and gewgaws purchased from the traders. Just then there was a commotion at the door of the ante-room, and the loud and genial voice of the Colonel could be heard. He was accompanied by Major Hamilton.

'G'morning, g'morning' the Colonel beamed. 'I thought I'd just pop in for a noggin before lunch. See how the other half lives y'know. Oh thank you very much Hammy. I'd like a pink gin. Now, all fit and well are we?' He surveyed the assembled company benignly. And as he did so his eyes lit, in a startled double take, on Langley. That normally keen-as-mustard-particularly-in-the-presence-of-senior-officers young man had only just managed to get his features together into a ghastly simper. The Colonel's eyes travelled down from the simper to the mucky uniform and back up again to the not very clean face.

'You feeling' all right, Langdale?' he enquired solicitously.

'Oh yes sir,' Langley managed to squeak with some vestige of his customary enthusiasm, but slightly slurring his 's' es as a result of the drinks which he had been imbibing. The Colonel's bushy eyebrows went up a good half inch. He took the pink gin from the tray presented by the mess waiter, and sipped at it thoughtfully. Jos looked at him with the sinking feeling that they were in for one of the Colonel's peptalks. Sure enough, the Colonel ambled over to one of the armchairs and settled himself comfortably in it. He waved one of his rather podgy arms and said 'Gather round, chaps.'

The chaps duly gathered round, settling themselves in whatever seats were available.

'Now you know I'm not one for pie-jaws,' began the Colonel. 'But a Commanding Officer cannot but feel responsible for all of his men all of the time – and perhaps particularly,' and here the CO looked pointedly at the luckless Langley, 'for the younger officers. The claw of the lion is a potent force.' This obscure statement was incomprehensible to the Colonel's audience, but it seemed to please him greatly because he repeated it slowly to himself with obvious relish. The chaps shuffled doubtfully in their chairs. The Colonel looked up sharply as at a class of inattentive dim wits. 'What I mean to say is that Africa is a big country, far away from home.' The Colonel warmed to his theme 'A country which fascinates and can change and destroy the people who come to live in her.' He regarded his audience hopefully to see if his eloquence was making any impact on their glassy stares. He ploughed on. 'And it's a hot country.' Here he dabbed at his forehead with a large blue handkerchief before going on to conclude, 'It is therefore only natural that some chaps will go off the rails.' And at this point the Colonel looked hard at the wretched Langley whose colouring now oscillated between sickly green and bright red. The Colonel refreshed himself with an appreciative sip of pink gin. He went on 'It is my duty as your Commanding Officer to look for danger signals and to nip 'em in the bud. Now what are these danger signals? Well they might be if a young officer were to go to pigs and whistles as regards the state of his uniform.' Another glance at Langley. 'Or you might find a young officer drinking too much. These might be the signals. What is the danger they might be alerting us to? Loneliness perhaps? A sweetheart back home who is not being true?'

Good heavens, thought Jos, I had no idea the old man had so much poetry in him. The litany of possible problems went on, the Colonel clearly enjoying each fanciful speculation very much.

'Money problems perhaps: not being able to live within one's pay?' Langley's face managed to look green and crimson at the same time, 'Or perhaps just the damned heat!' This last suggestion was made with fervour, as the Colonel looked crossly at the rather slow, inefficient fan which laboured round the ceiling of the Mess: Jos knew that the Colonel had a much better one in his house. 'Anyhow,' said the Colonel drawing matters to a close, 'I'm glad we've had this little chat. Quite informal y'understand. No names no pack drill. But I know you'll see the sense in what I've said, and I look forward to you pulling your socks up and mending your fences wherever that should be necessary.' The Colonel fixed his eyes unsubtly on poor Langley for a moment or two before getting up and wandering off to his favourite chair by the window where he and Major Hamilton downed another two pink gins before strolling off to their respective married quarters for lunch.

'You're really up the creek now, my lad,' commented the Quartermaster as he surveyed the retreating backs of the Colonel and the Major. His temper was always soured by any reminder of the marital bliss and comforts being enjoyed by those officers whose wives had come out with them. 'What is it? – in Queer Street with one of those rascal traders?'

'Yes,' blurted Langley miserably.

'How much do you owe him?'

'Thirty pounds,' whispered Langley.

'Jesus Christ!' exploded the Quartermaster. 'What did you buy – two of his wives?'

'A vewy good carpet, actually,' said Langley, trying to recover some of his dignity. 'Weal Persian.'

'Real absolute bloody rubbish you mean. Cor blimey! He saw you coming a mile off. And I suppose you been giving him payments on the never never? How much?'

'Quite a lot actually,' said Langley, stiffly, torn between a desire to protect himself from being held up to ridicule as a sucker, and the glimmer of hope that this hard and worldly old Quartermaster might be able to get him out of his financial nightmare.

'You'd better leave this to me, sonny boy. I know how to handle these rogues. He's in prison at the moment do I gather? Well I think I can get him to understand that he'd better give up swindling you over this real bloody Persian rubbish if he doesn't want to stay there.' The Quartermaster was beginning to enjoy himself. All at once there was an opportunity for hardnosed action, for haggling and wheeling and dealing of the kind he most enjoyed – and at the same time the chance to patronize a crass young puppy of an officer, while at the end of the day perhaps earning the gratitude of the CO. But he had

256

reckoned without Langley's stiffnecked, public school boy sense of honour and spirit of fair play.

'But look here, George,' Langley protested. 'I contwacted this debt with the twader. I am bound to honour it.'

'Whaaat?!' roared the Quartermaster, scarcely able to believe his ears. 'Why you stupid young git. All right then stew in your own bloody juice.'

'Peter, don't be daft.' Jos intervened. 'These traders screw us for every cent they can get. You were just particularly unlucky in falling into the clutches of that devil Garba so early on in your time out here. It would be absolutely right if George could undo some of the damage now.'

'Do you weally think so Jos?' asked Langley, hopefully.

'Only if Mr Ladeda wants to be helped of course,' said the Quartermaster spitefully. But it was obvious that he was itching to sort things out.

'Of course he does, George – don't you, Peter?'

'Well yes. It would be super if George could help.'

And so it was settled. The Quartermaster visited Garba in prison, having first assembled from police records and from rumour in the Kebira underworld a variety of felonies in which Garba was suspected of taking part. He managed to deceive Garba into thinking that charges were just about to be brought in several of these cases; and in gratitude for his assurance that he would do what he could to prevent this, Garba agreed to limit his demands on Langley to an outstanding debt of ten pounds to be paid over the next two months.

Langley was mightily relieved by this outcome and was observed shortly afterwards by the Colonel, striding out with a happy face and shining eyes, his boots and belt gleaming and his uniform immaculate. The Colonel turned away from the window of his office and addressed the Adjutant, who was standing by the CO's desk with a pile of bulky and complicated-looking documents on which he required decisions or at any rate a signature.

'Tell you what, Tony,' said the Colonel, regarding the pile of papers with distaste. 'I think we should organize some form of counselling for the younger officers. Or perhaps I could do a series of lectures or seminars, somethin' of that sort. Just seen a bit of fatherly advice pay enormous dividends.'

'Yes sir. If you could just sign these orders where I've put the pencil crosses we could get our reports to Brigade this afternoon . . . .'

27

Jos was due to leave on the first stage of his journey home on the Friday. By the Wednesday evening all the major packing had been done and various handing over duties performed. Thursday was to be a day of leave-taking: of his fellow officers and their wives and of the NCOs and soldiers in his company.

On the Thursday morning Jos was already awake when he heard the scrabbling at the door which meant that Okoko was using the key on the padlock on the outside of the door to come in and waken him. He heard the door open and Okoko padding softly into the room and undoing the shutters: Jos pretended to be asleep. He felt the firm and gentle touch of Okoko's hand on his shoulder.

'Mitre, sah, it be time to wake up. I go bring you yoh coffee one time.'

And as soon as Okoko was sure that Jos was awake, he walked quickly away to get the cup of coffee. Jos was sitting up on the edge of the bed when Okoko returned. The cup of coffee was placed carefully on the little bedside table.

'Thanks, Okoko.' Jos was suddenly aware of a miasma of misery surrounding Okoko: he looked up at his batman's kind and pleasant face and saw that it was quite twisted with gloom.

'What's wrong, Okoko?' he asked. 'Aren't you well? Are the piccin OK?'

'Yes, sah. I no well sah. I sorry too much dat you go. I never gree foh any udder mitre like I gree foh you.'

'That's very nice of you to say so, Okoko. I wouldn't have had any other Boy but you – even if you did let Ernest on parade.' But this reminder of what had become an affectionate tease between them did not assuage Okoko's grief: in fact it intensified it.

'Poor Henrest,' said Okoko. 'He sad too much as well.'

And indeed the little dog, aware that something was afoot and no doubt affected by Okoko's air of gloom, was looking very pathetic, with his large ears flopping down over his worried-looking face. Jos felt a spasm of misery as he looked at the dog and reflected that he would have to hand him over that day to his new owner.

'Come on Okoko,' he said with a heartiness he was far from feeling, 'this will never do. Bring in my shaving water: I've a lot of things to attend to and cheerios to say this morning, and I'd better be up sharp to the Mess for breakfast even though I'm not required for Muster Parade.'

'Yes, sah I go work hard foh you today. But tomorrow sah I no work at all. I want one day to be sad foh you.'

'But Lieutenant Jenkins will want you to begin looking after him,' said Jos, referring to his replacement who was to inherit Okoko as his Batman.

'Not tomorrow, sah,' said Okoko with the downcast eyes which always accompanied absolute stubbornness. 'Tomorrow I need foh myself to go be sad foh you.'

'You're a strange bloke, Okoko. You haven't shown the slightest sign of grief up until now that I am going.' Here Jos stopped as Okoko raised his head and looked at him with a face of abject misery and with tears in his eyes.

'All right. You win as usual. I'll fix it with the House Member and Lieutenant Jenkins that you are left undisturbed tomorrow.'

'Tank you, sah. Tank you.'

That was the part of that leave-taking day which Jos was to remember long after all the other firm grippings of hands and exchanges of UK addresses and enthusiastic kissings and huggings of Officers' wives had been forgotten. And when at six o'clock next morning the landrover which was to take Jos to Kaduna pulled up at his gidda, Okoko and Jos looked at each other for the last time with mutual feelings of love and deep sorrow at parting. There were no words to be said, and neither party would have been confident to uttering them without breaking down. Just before getting into the landrover, Jos

260

turned and held out his arms to Okoko, and for a few seconds the two men embraced: and then Jos turned and put his foot on the step of the truck and climbed up into it, while Okoko went running off, with the tears now streaming down his face.

Jos sat tensely upright in the passenger seat of the landrover. He noted, with a curious feeling of the wheel coming full circle, that the driver was Corporal Francis, the soldier who had fetched him from Kano Airport some eighteen months ago. Corporal Francis was doing his best to look suitably solemn and subdued. Jos was doing his best not to disgrace himself by blubbering all down his smart "going home" uniform. For a while they proceeded in silence. When Jos felt sufficiently in control of his voice, he ventured, 'An early start for you today, Corporal Francis.'

'Oh yes, sah. But I no mind sah. I get time in lieu foh dis.'

They reverted to silence for a few miles. Then from Corporal Francis

'You gree foh dat Private Okoko sah? He be berry good Boy I tink sah? Turn you out smart-smart?'

'Yes,' squeaked Jos, feeling the tear ducts threaten.

Corporal Francis realized he had blundered, and was silent again for a while. But his naturally jolly and talkative nature was not to be suppressed.

'Hey,' he said, stealing a glance at Jos's strained and unhappy-looking face. 'But dis be de best day foh you sah. Dis be the day you go foh home to yoh mudder and yoh brudder.'

'That's right, Corporal Francis,' said Jos, rallying a little, and thinking it was odd that his soldiers were always referring to his mother and his brother, relatives whom as it happened he did not have, his mother being dead and his only sibling a sister. 'It will be grand to get away from all you rogues out here with your infinite capacity for getting hold of the wrong end of every conceivable stick.'

Corporal Francis grinned broadly recognizing affectionate abuse in Jos's voice even if not wholly understanding what he had said.

'You like go come back sometime, sah?' he asked.

'Well yes I'd like to return someday. But I'll have to earn my living first, and I don't think I'll be doing it here.'

261

Jos waited for the usual flattering assurance that no-one could be more welcome than a young former British Army officer in the new independent Nigeria which was shortly to come into being. Corporal Francis drove on thoughtfully.

'Na he be true, sah,' he said. 'I tink is best foh you to work in yoh own country and den come visit. We must do the work ourselves foh heah in Nigeria sah.'

Jos felt a sudden picque that this cheerful young Ibo Corporal was agreeing with the political stance which he, Jos, was always adopting in public. He realized that he preferred having to advance it against the flattering denials of the conservative Northerners.

'Want to get rid of us do you Francis?'

'Hey I no say dat!' exclaimed Corporal Francis roaring with laughter and – as he was wont to do – expressing his emotion of the moment with jerky acceleration and extravagant movement of the steering wheel. 'You be berry welcome always heah in Nigeria. But we must try sah. Is no good if you do de work for us.' Corporal Francis decelerated as he made this cautious political point. And Jos reflected that it was right that on this his last day in Nigeria the conversation should be taking this turn.

There was no time for much in the way of leavetaking of Corporal Francis once they reached the airport, as all was bustle, getting cases weighed and checked into the hold of the aircraft, and Jos himself checked ready for boarding the plane. Indeed there was only time for a wave as the little landrover was driven sedately away by Corporal Francis.

The flight home was not the long dull haul over the Sahara but south to the coast and then hopping along to the Gold Coast, Sierra Leone, The Gambia, then north to Gibraltar and over Spain to the west of France. Jos's fellow passengers were young national service second lieutenants like himself returning home, and also some Regular Army officers and NCOs with their wives and children returning from a West African posting or going home on long leave. They were accommodated at good hotels, with – in Jos's case – the almost forgotten luxury of bathrooms with hot and cold running water. The airports at which they touched down – the small plane in which they were flying required frequent refuelling – had the impersonal identity of airports everywhere but, such as it was, that identity was lost in the vivid sights and sounds of Africa: the strong sunlight, the glistening black and brown skins, the brightly coloured robes and skull caps, as passengers arrived and departed and mingled with those greeting them or seeing them off. Jos found that he was eagerly drinking in these impressions of Africa, rather as if he was having a final binge before embarking on a life of total abstinence.

The bleakness of such a life of abstinence came upon him as the plane landed at a drab military airfield in the south of England at about five o'clock on the Monday morning. As he sat in the bus which was taking the passengers to London, Jos rubbed a clear space on the window with his hand and looked out at the green, damp fields and hedges. He turned round to survey his fellow passengers with their pale faces, the men with greyish complexions, here and there the pink skin of a bald head, the women tanned yellowish or flushed with the strain and bother of the long journey. He was overcome with longing for the strong, bright, garish colours of Africa, for the heat of the African day, the sound of African voices, high pitched and quarrelsome then suddenly changing into loud abandoned laughter. He looked again at the inhibited, dull coloured faces of his fellow countrymen and felt a great sadness and sense of loss: because he knew that there was no future for him as a 'District Hapsa' in a continent which was becoming a patchwork of independent nation states. And indeed he knew that to some extent he was romanticizing and idealizing the charms of Africa just because he was about to lose them. Nevertheless the attraction was a strong one, and he sensed that he must shake it off now at the outset of his career. He tried to convince himself that, even if he could have put the clock back fifty years and if there had been an assured period of British colonial rule ahead, he would not have wanted to spend his working years, his best years, in one country and environment and then come home to live out the rest of his life an exile in what had become an alien country.

It was getting lighter as the bus got closer to London. Jos rubbed the window pane again and peered out. The wet

263

looking green fields had given way to rows of shops and houses. The bus stopped at traffic lights, and he saw some pedestrians cross – two labourers with small haversacks over their shoulders, presumably containing their sandwiches, and a middle aged woman in a plastic raincoat with a shopping bag. It was drizzling. Jos closed his eyes tight and brought to mind for a second the smell of the sandy earth at Kebira as the morning sun began to heat it up, of the bright colours, the black and brown limbs of the people as they walked with easy, graceful stride in the sunlight, calling greetings to each other . . . .

He felt a nudge in his ribs. Jimmy, one of the fellow subalterns from another battalion, grinned at him.

'We've made it then, Jos,' he said. 'As soon as we get off this bus I'm just going to "stand on the corner watching all the girls go by".' He attempted to sing the last few words to the tune of a then popular song of that name. He looked more closely at Jos.

'You feeling OK?' he asked. 'You look distinctly off colour, not to say down in the mouth.'

'No. I feel great. I will join you on the corner watching all the girls go by – and prevent you singing that refrain or they'll go by so damned fast we won't have the chance to observe them properly.'

But, Jos thought to himself, what I have been feeling my cliché-ridden commanding officer at Kebira would undoubtedly diagnose as a slight scratch from the claw of the lion. Fortunately it is only a slight scratch, and if I don't rub it or dwell on it, it will soon heal. He looked again, more charitably, at his fellow passengers, and again out of the window at the great city. He thought of his national service, now all but completed, his short exile now over, and of all the things he was now free to do with his life. It was, after all, good to be home.